FANBOYS™
VS. ZOMBIES

VOLUME FIVE

4 STORIES OF THE APOCALYPSE

BOOM! STUDIOS

ROSS RICHIE CEO & Founder • JACK CUMMINS President • MARK SMYLIE Founder of Archaia • MATT GAGNON Editor-in-Chief • FILIP SABLIK VP of Publishing & Marketing • STEPHEN CHRISTY VP of Development
LANCE KREITER VP of Licensing & Merchandising • PHIL BARBARO VP of Finance • BRYCE CARLSON Managing Editor • MEL CAYLO Marketing Manager • SCOTT NEWMAN Production Design Manager • IRENE BRADISH Operations Manager
DAFNA PLEBAN Editor • SHANNON WATTERS Editor • ERIC HARBURN Editor • REBECCA TAYLOR Editor • IAN BRILL Editor • CHRIS ROSA Assistant Editor • ALEX GALER Assistant Editor • WHITNEY LEOPARD Assistant Editor
JASMINE AMIRI Assistant Editor • CAMERON CHITTOCK Assistant Editor • HANNAH NANCE PARTLOW Production Designer • KELSEY DIETERICH Production Designer • EMI YONEMURA BROWN Production Designer
DEVIN FUNCHES E-Commerce & Inventory Coordinator • ANDY LIEGL Event Coordinator • BRIANNA HART Executive Assistant • AARON FERRARA Operations Assistant • JOSÉ MEZA Sales Assistant • ELIZABETH LOUGHRIDGE Accounting Assistant

FANBOYS VS. ZOMBIES Volume Five, July 2014. Published by BOOM! Studios, a division of Boom Entertainment, Inc. Fanboys vs. Zombies is ™ & © 2014 Boom Entertainment, Inc. and Electus LLC. Originally published in single magazine form as FANBOYS VS. ZOMBIES No. 17-20. ™ & © 2013 Boom Entertainment, Inc. and Electus LLC. All rights reserved. BOOM! Studios™ and the BOOM! Studios logo are trademarks of Boom Entertainment, Inc., registered in various countries and categories. All characters, events, and institutions depicted herein are fictional. Any similarity between any of the names, characters, persons, events, and/or institutions in this publication to actual names, characters, and persons, whether living or dead, events, and/or institutions is unintended and purely coincidental. BOOM! Studios does not read or accept unsolicited submissions of ideas, stories, or artwork.

A catalog record of this book is available from OCLC and from the BOOM! Studios website, www.boom-studios.com, on the Librarians Page.

BOOM! Studios, 5670 Wilshire Boulevard, Suite 450, Los Angeles, CA 90036-5679. Printed in China. First Printing.
ISBN: 978-1-60886-395-2, eISBN: 978-1-61398-249-5

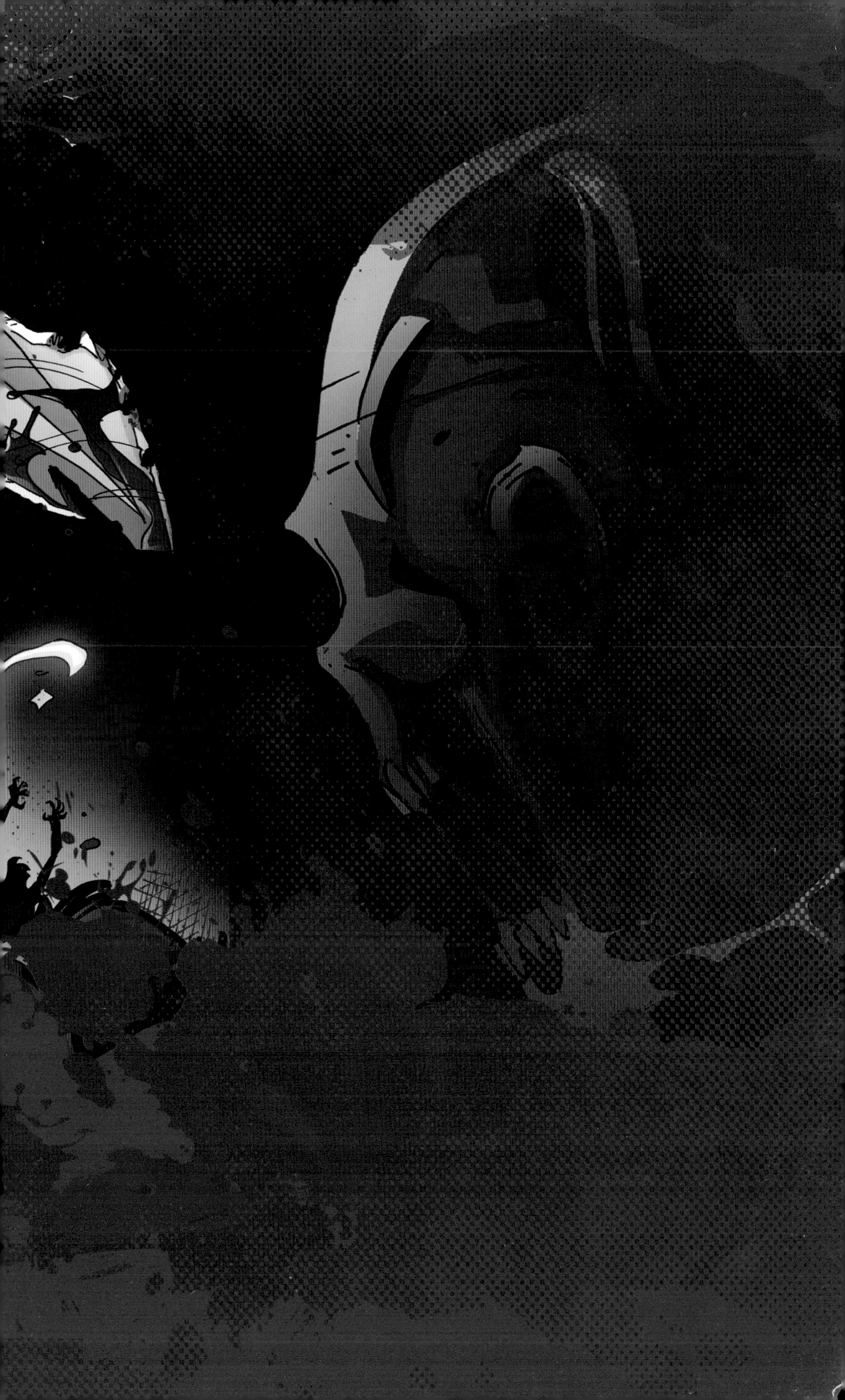

WRITTEN BY
SHANE HOUGHTON

ART BY
JERRY GAYLORD
BRYAN TURNER

INK ASSISTS BY
PENELOPE GAYLORD

LETTERS BY
ED DUKESHIRE

COLORS BY
MIRKA ANDOLFO
WITH
ANDREA DOTTA

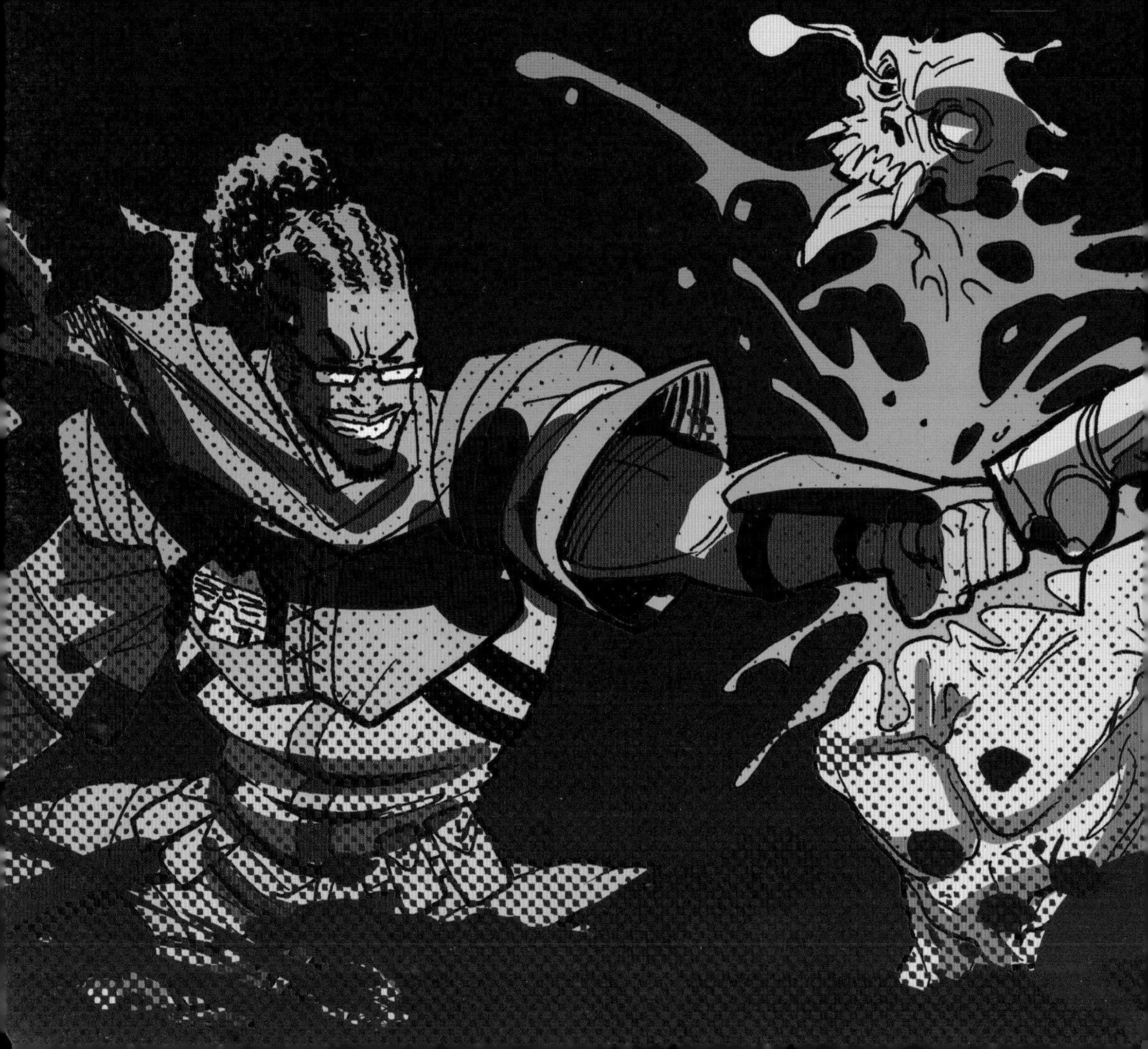

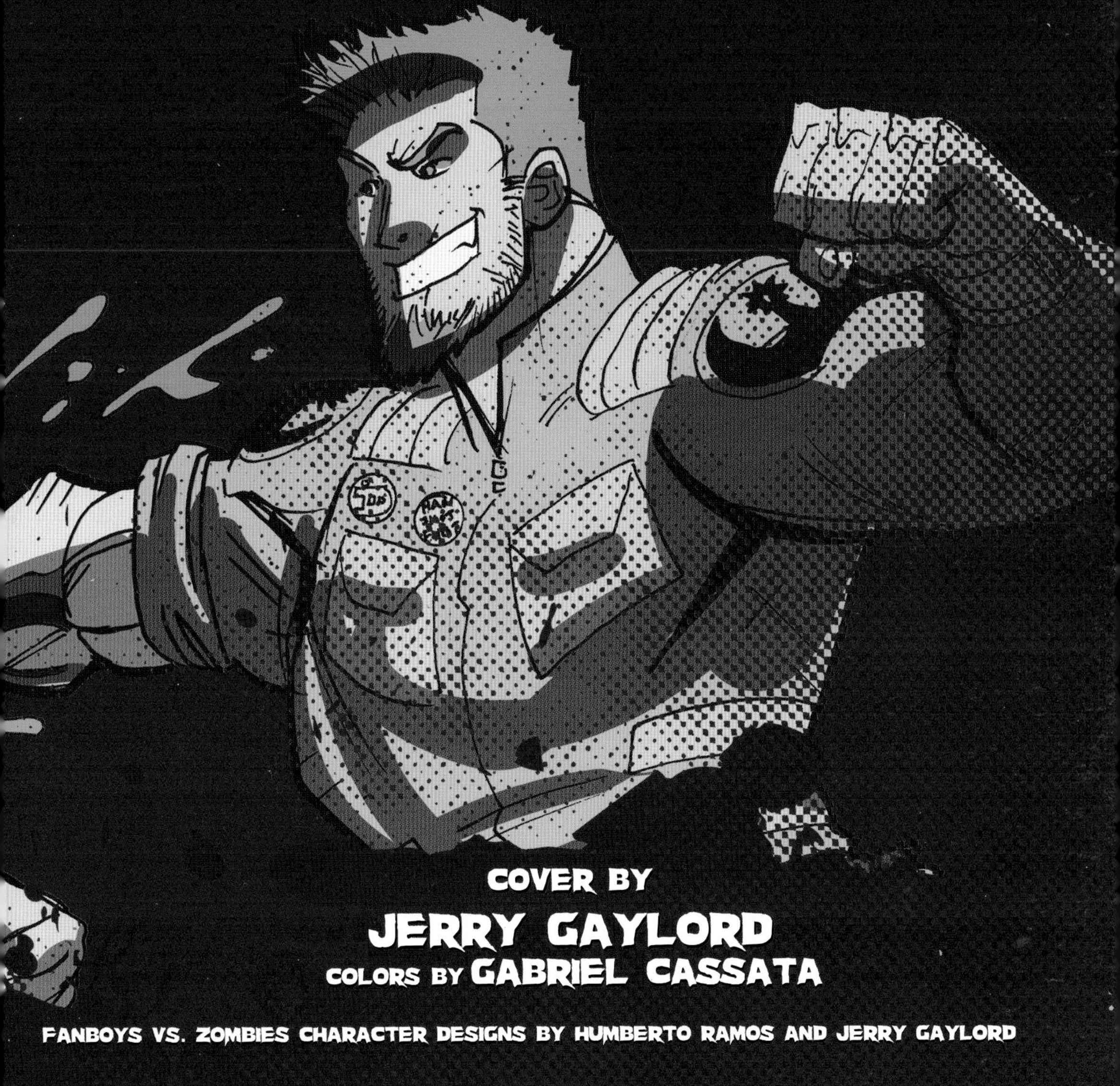

COVER BY
JERRY GAYLORD
COLORS BY **GABRIEL CASSATA**

FANBOYS VS. ZOMBIES CHARACTER DESIGNS BY HUMBERTO RAMOS AND JERRY GAYLORD

EDITOR
ERIC HARBURN

MANAGING EDITOR
BRYCE CARLSON

DESIGNER
EMI YONEMURA BROWN

FANBOYS VS. ZOMBIES CREATED BY BEN SILVERMAN AND JIMMY FOX

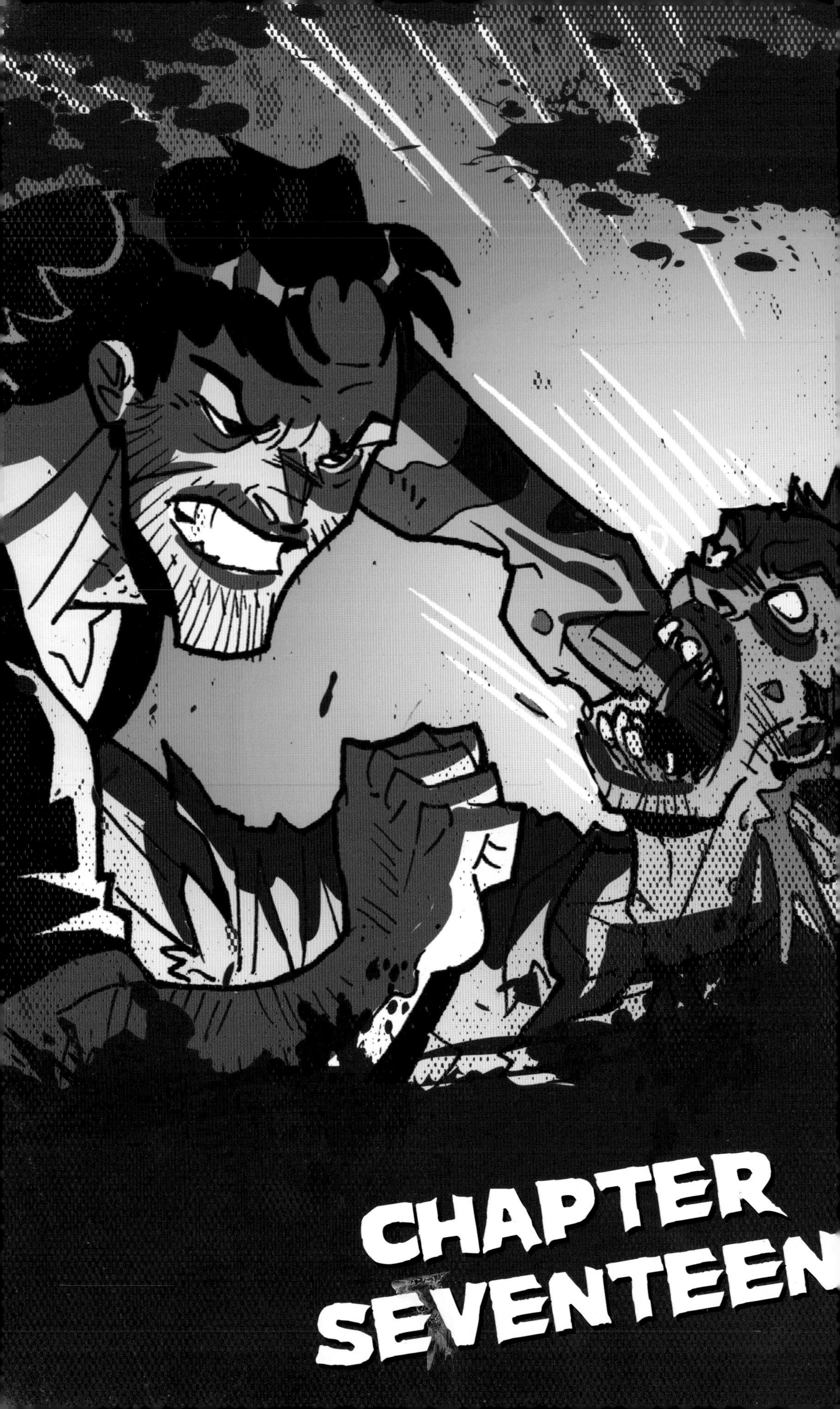

CHAPTER SEVENTEEN

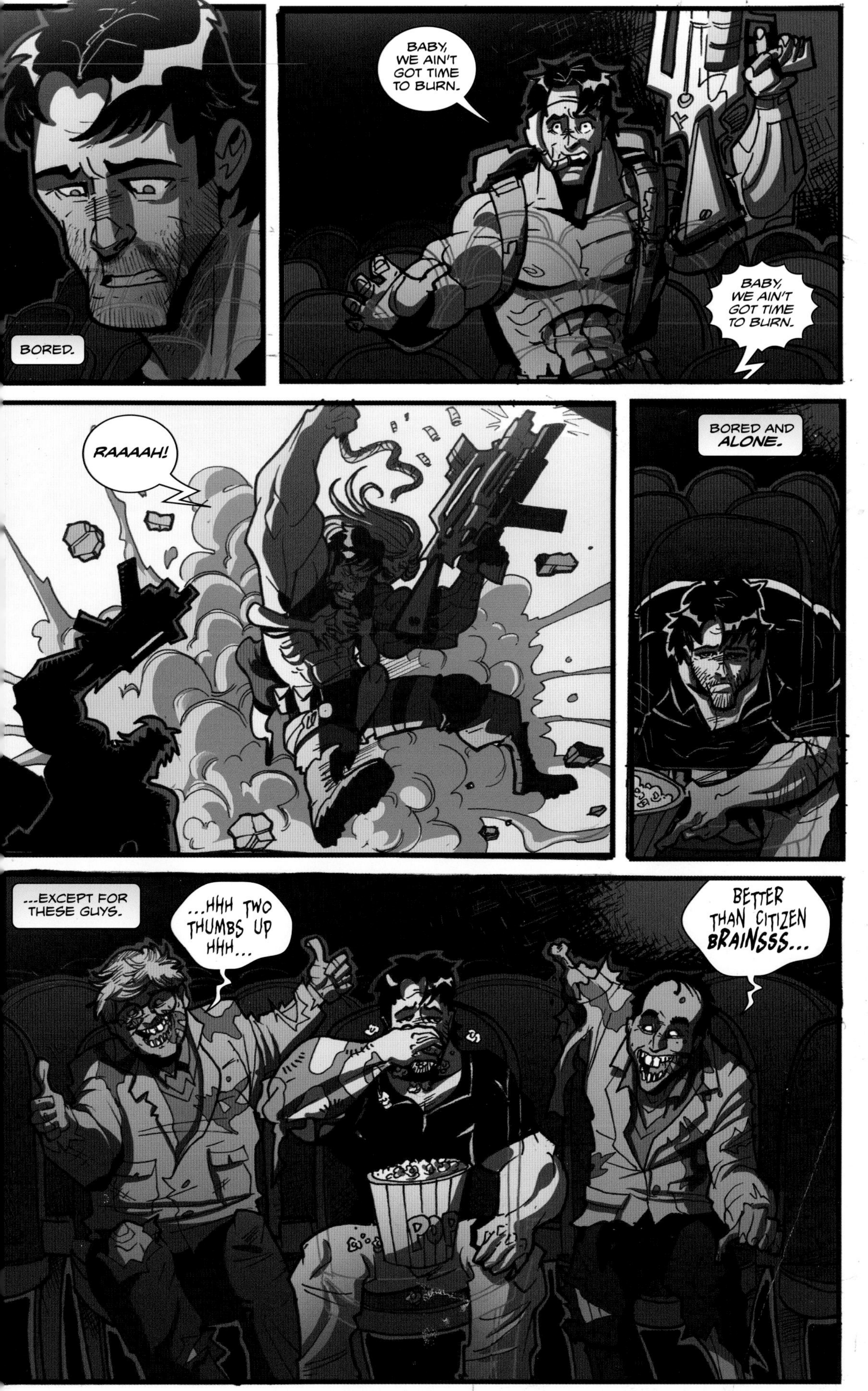
BORED.
BABY, WE AIN'T GOT TIME TO BURN.
BABY, WE AIN'T GOT TIME TO BURN.
RAAAAH!
BORED AND ALONE.
...EXCEPT FOR THESE GUYS.
...HHH TWO THUMBS UP HHH...
BETTER THAN CITIZEN BRAINSSS...
POP

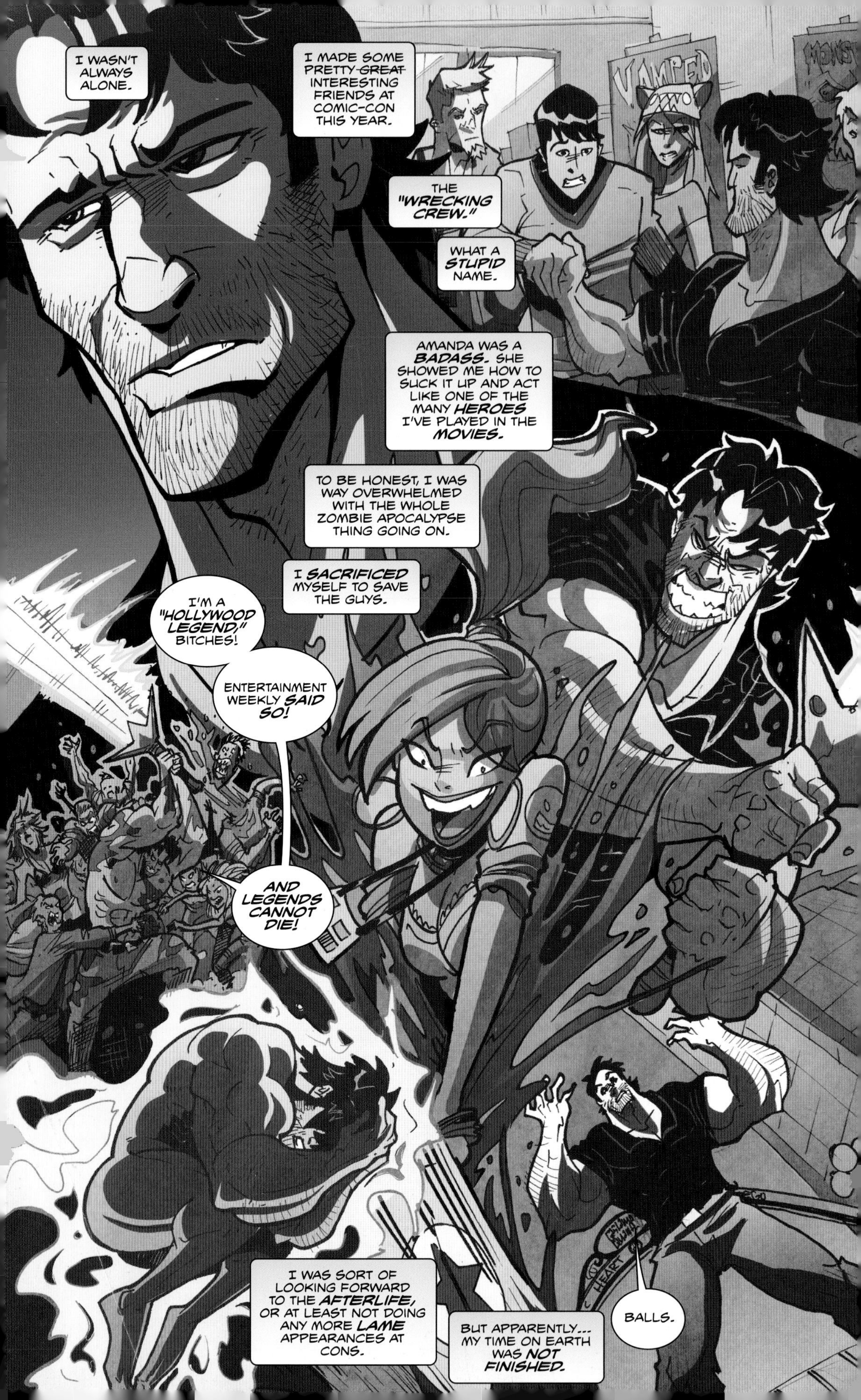

I WASN'T ALWAYS ALONE.
I MADE SOME PRETTY ~~GREAT~~ INTERESTING FRIENDS AT COMIC-CON THIS YEAR.
VAMPED
THE "*WRECKING CREW*."
WHAT A *STUPID* NAME.
AMANDA WAS A *BADASS*. SHE SHOWED ME HOW TO SUCK IT UP AND ACT LIKE ONE OF THE MANY *HEROES* I'VE PLAYED IN THE *MOVIES*.
TO BE HONEST, I WAS WAY OVERWHELMED WITH THE WHOLE ZOMBIE APOCALYPSE THING GOING ON.
I *SACRIFICED* MYSELF TO SAVE THE GUYS.
I'M A "*HOLLYWOOD LEGEND*," BITCHES!
ENTERTAINMENT WEEKLY *SAID SO!*
AND LEGENDS CANNOT DIE!
I WAS SORT OF LOOKING FORWARD TO THE *AFTERLIFE*, OR AT LEAST NOT DOING ANY MORE *LAME* APPEARANCES AT CONS.
BUT APPARENTLY... MY TIME ON EARTH WAS *NOT FINISHED*.
BALLS.

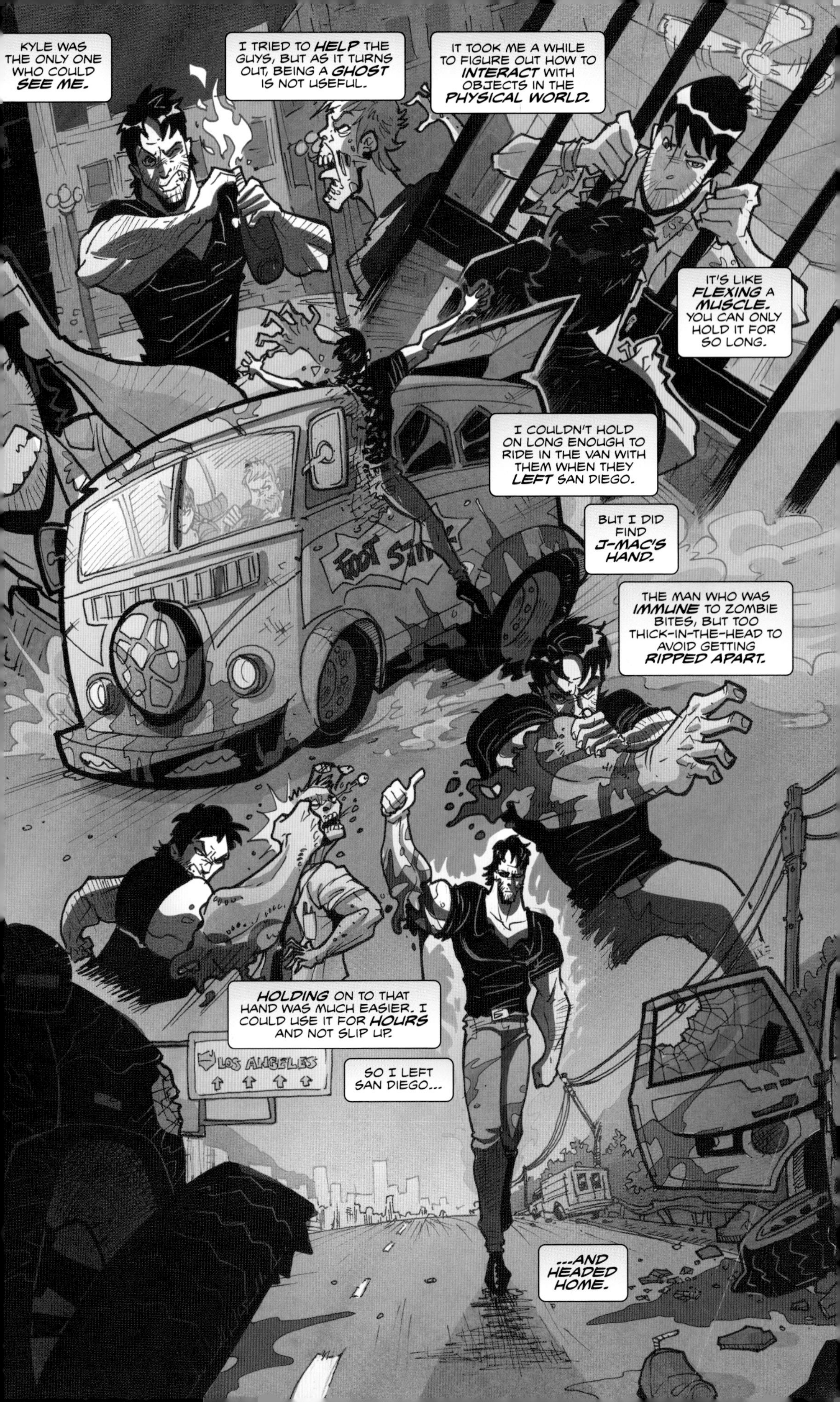
KYLE WAS THE ONLY ONE WHO COULD SEE ME.
I TRIED TO HELP THE GUYS, BUT AS IT TURNS OUT, BEING A GHOST IS NOT USEFUL.
IT TOOK ME A WHILE TO FIGURE OUT HOW TO INTERACT WITH OBJECTS IN THE PHYSICAL WORLD.
IT'S LIKE FLEXING A MUSCLE. YOU CAN ONLY HOLD IT FOR SO LONG.
I COULDN'T HOLD ON LONG ENOUGH TO RIDE IN THE VAN WITH THEM WHEN THEY LEFT SAN DIEGO.
BUT I DID FIND J-MAC'S HAND.
THE MAN WHO WAS IMMUNE TO ZOMBIE BITES, BUT TOO THICK-IN-THE-HEAD TO AVOID GETTING RIPPED APART.
HOLDING ON TO THAT HAND WAS MUCH EASIER. I COULD USE IT FOR HOURS AND NOT SLIP UP.
LOS ANGELES
SO I LEFT SAN DIEGO...
...AND HEADED HOME.

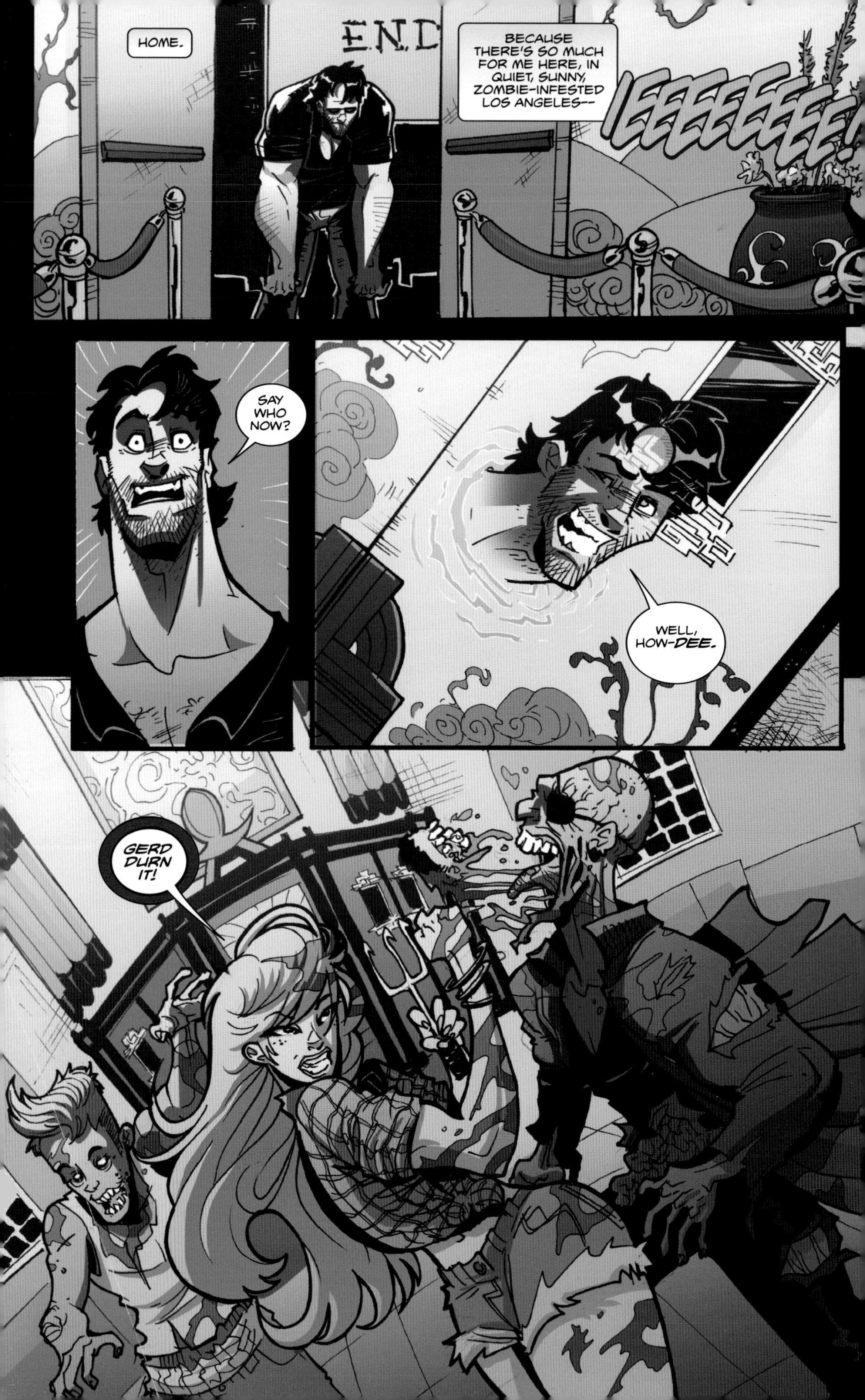

HOME.
E.N.D.
BECAUSE THERE'S SO MUCH FOR ME HERE, IN QUIET, SUNNY, ZOMBIE-INFESTED LOS ANGELES--
IEEEEEEEEE!
SAY WHO NOW?
WELL, HOW-DEE.
GERD DURN IT!

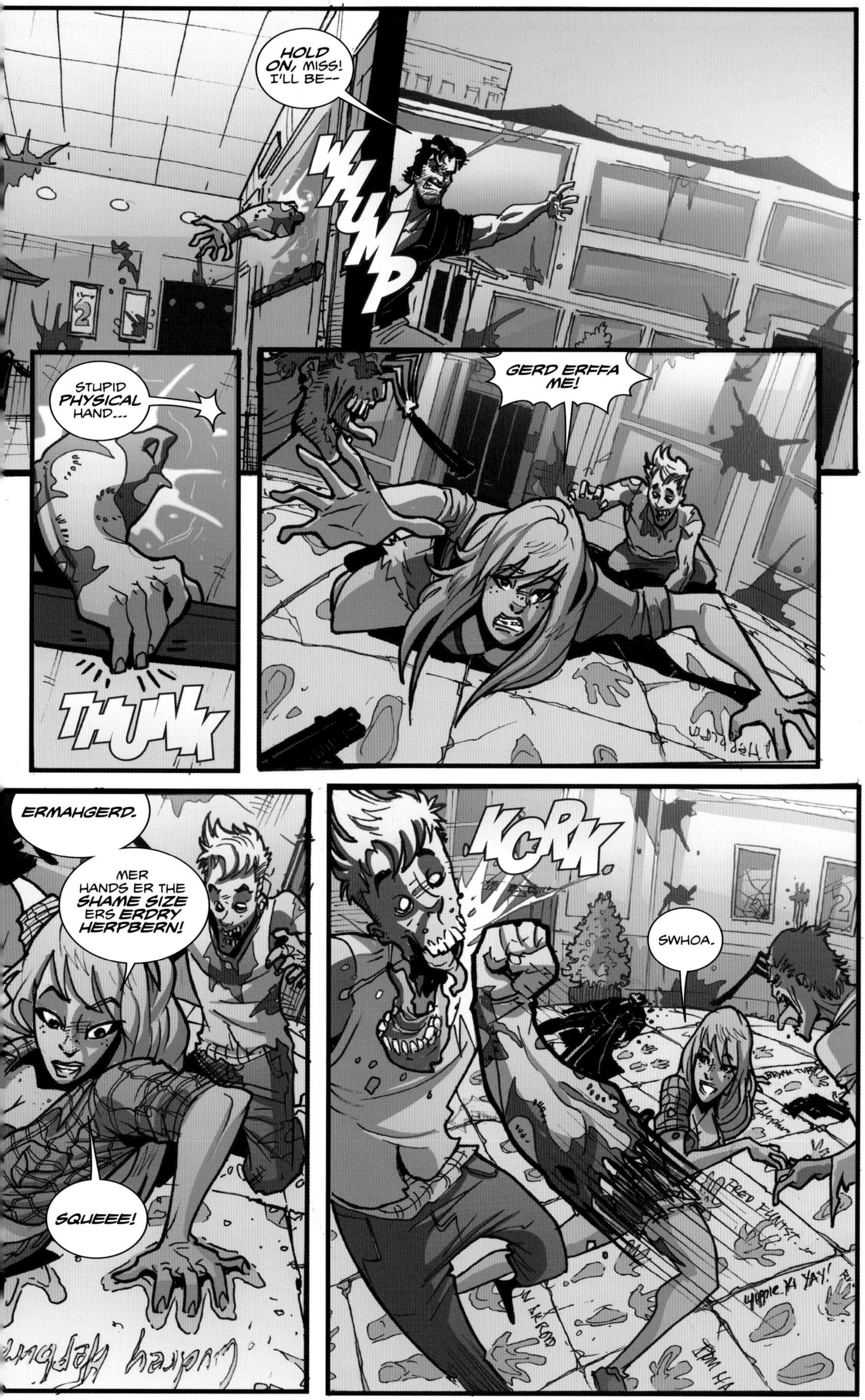
HOLD ON, MISS! I'LL BE--
WHUMP
STUPID PHYSICAL HAND...
THUNK
GERD ERFFA ME!
ERMAHGERD.
MER HANDS ER THE SHAME SIZE ERS ERDRY HERPBERN!
SQUEEE!
KORK
SWHOA.

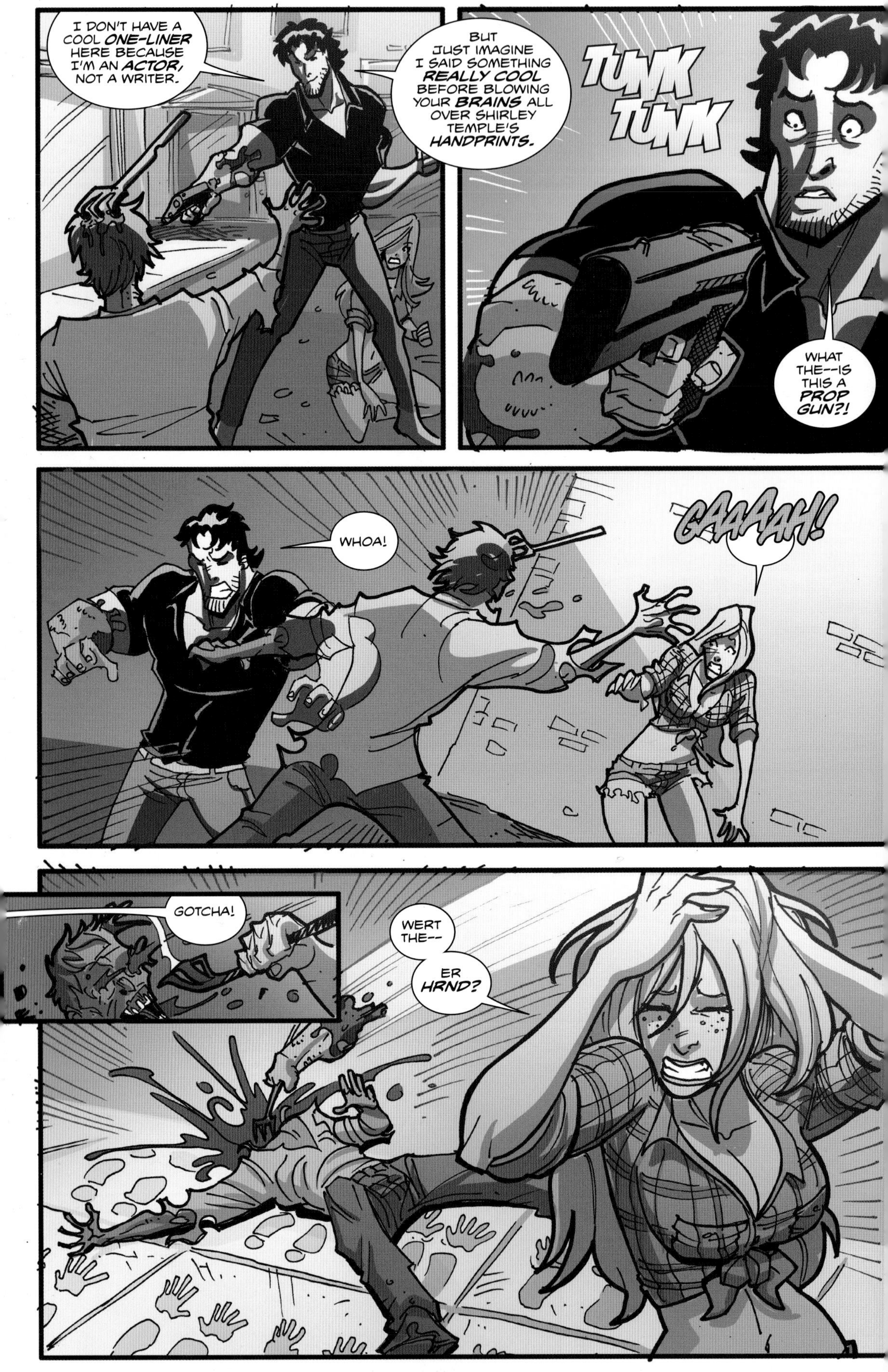

I DON'T HAVE A COOL ONE-LINER HERE BECAUSE I'M AN ACTOR, NOT A WRITER.
BUT JUST IMAGINE I SAID SOMETHING REALLY COOL BEFORE BLOWING YOUR BRAINS ALL OVER SHIRLEY TEMPLE'S HANDPRINTS.
TUNK TUNK
WHAT THE--IS THIS A PROP GUN?!
WHOA!
GAAAAH!
GOTCHA!
WERT THE--
ER HRND?

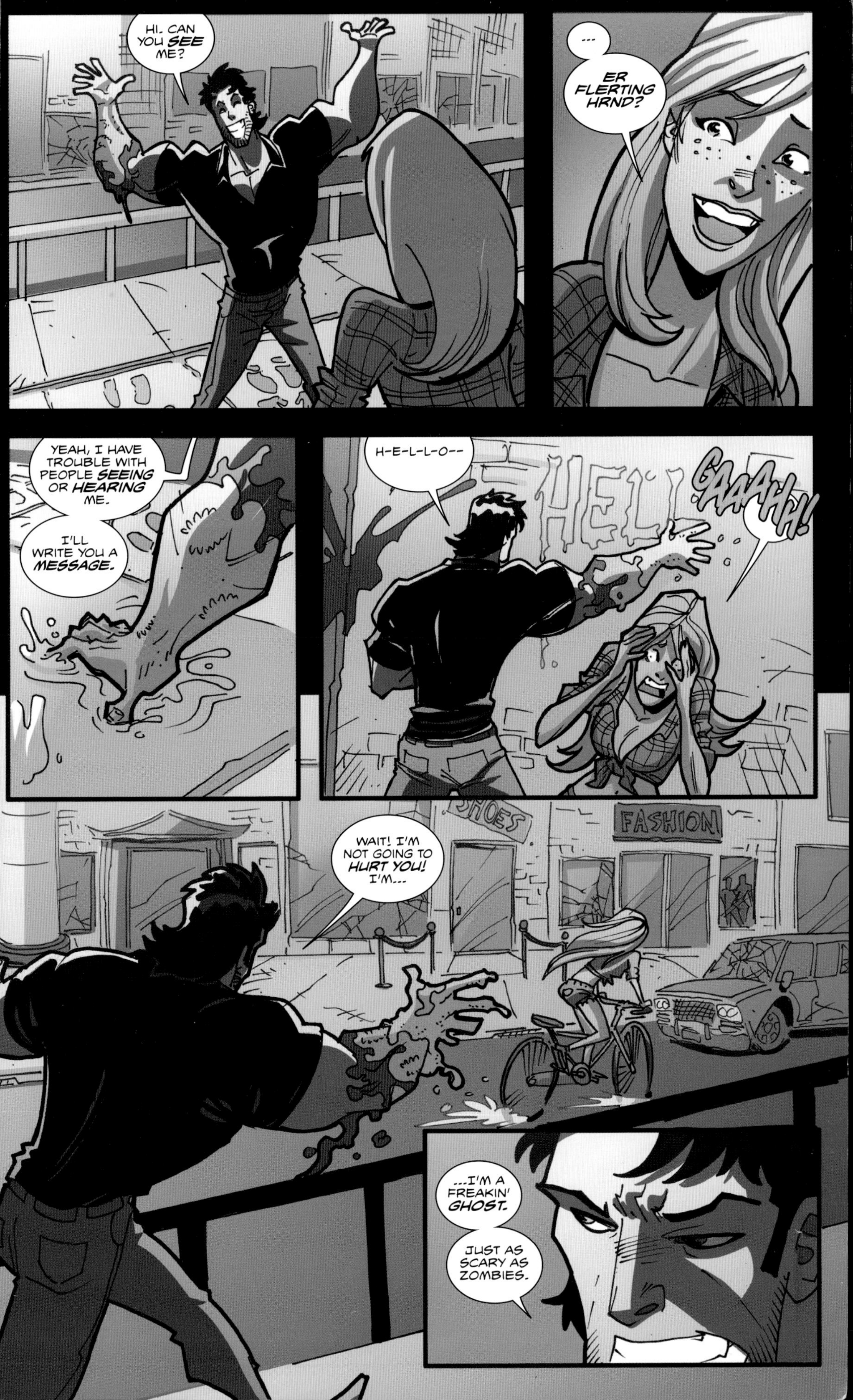

HI. CAN YOU SEE ME?
...
ER FLERTING HRND?
YEAH, I HAVE TROUBLE WITH PEOPLE SEEING OR HEARING ME.
I'LL WRITE YOU A MESSAGE.
H-E-L-L-O--
HELL
GAAAHH!
SHOES
FASHION
WAIT! I'M NOT GOING TO HURT YOU! I'M...
...I'M A FREAKIN' GHOST.
JUST AS SCARY AS ZOMBIES.

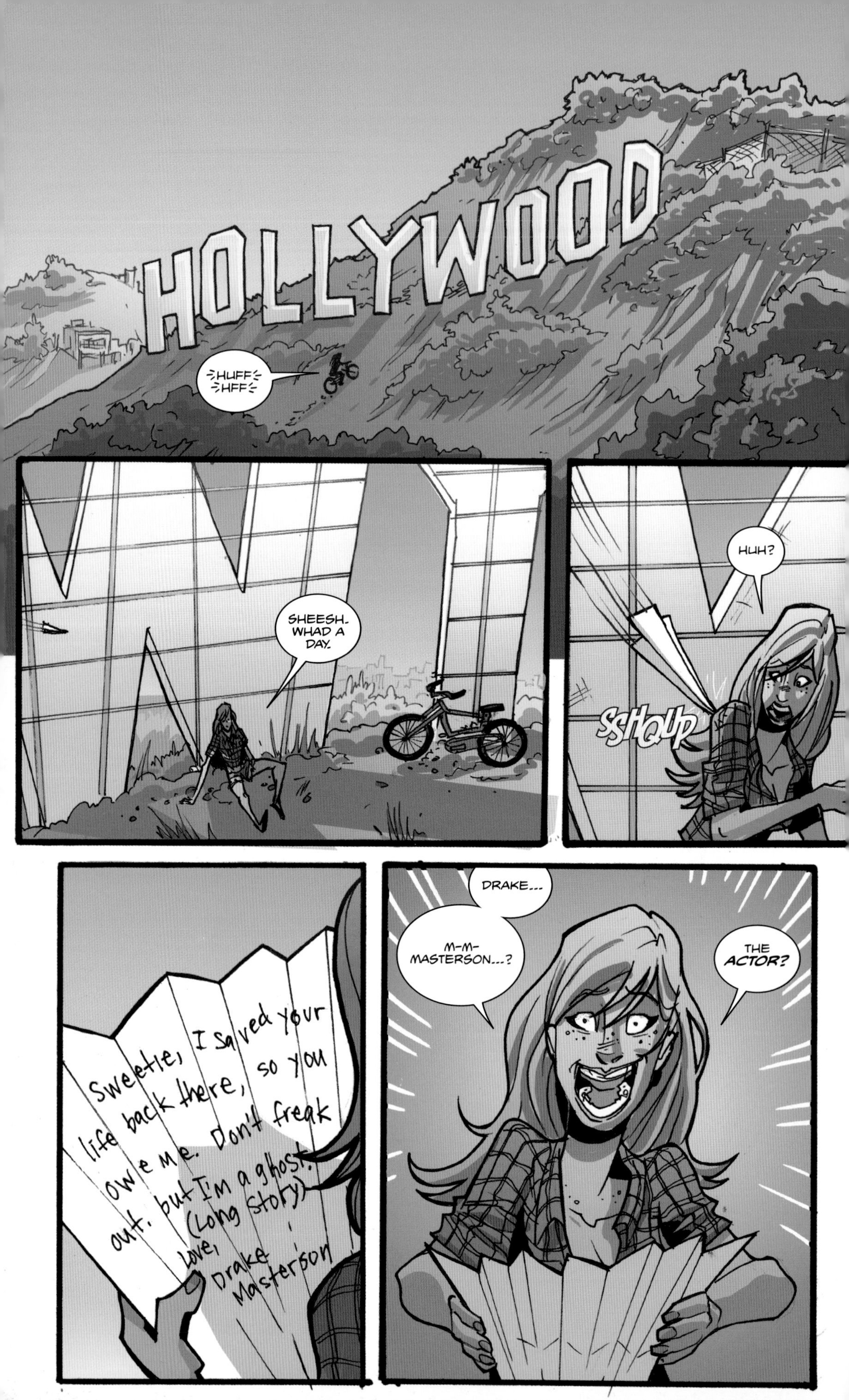

HOLLYWOOD
HUFF HFF
SHEESH. WHAD A DAY.
HUH?
SSHQUP
Sweetie, I saved your life back there, so you owe me. Don't freak out, but I'm a ghost. (Long Story)
Love, Drake Masterson
DRAKE...
M-M-MASTERSON...?
THE ACTOR?

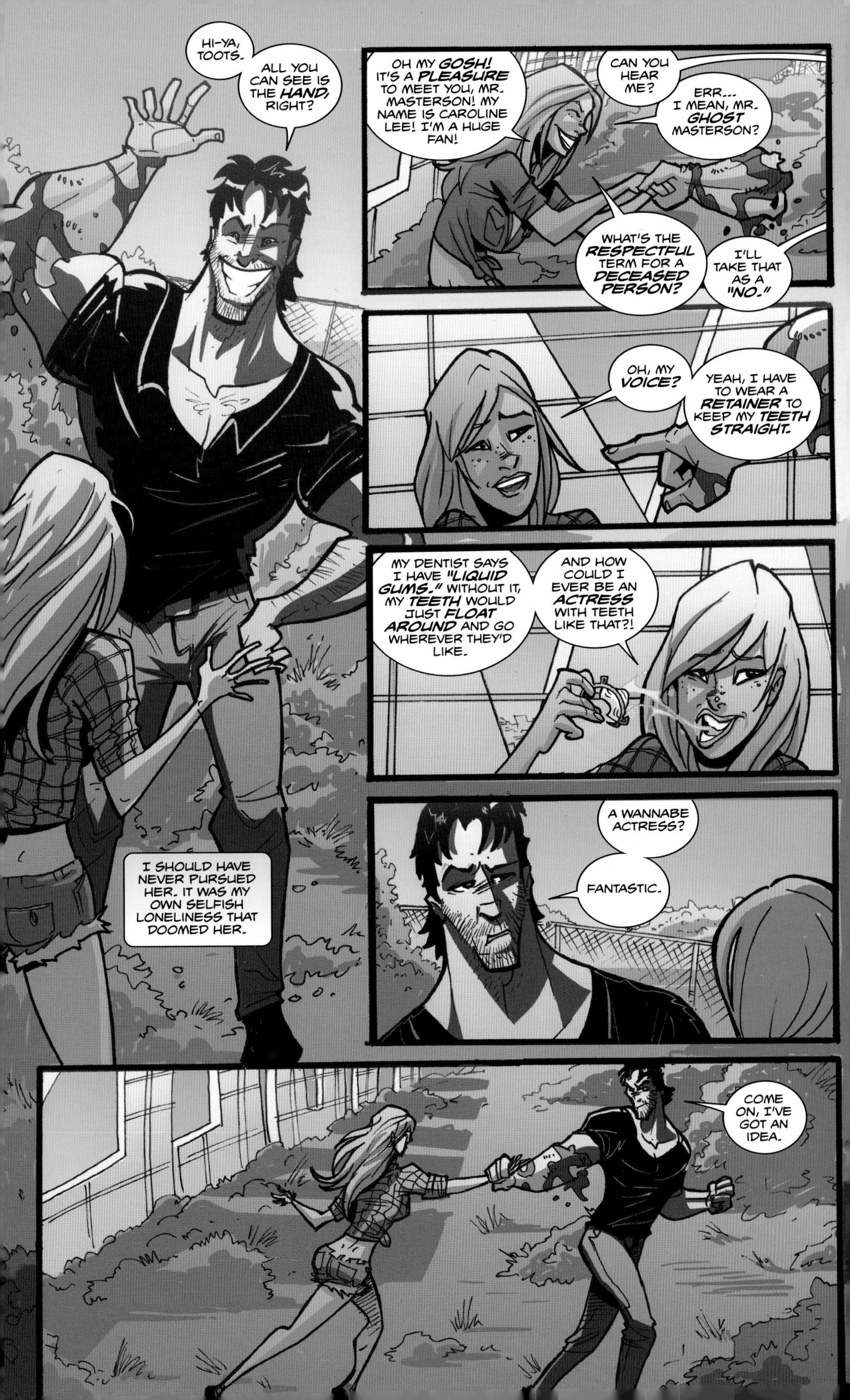

HI-YA, TOOTS.
ALL YOU CAN SEE IS THE HAND, RIGHT?
I SHOULD HAVE NEVER PURSUED HER. IT WAS MY OWN SELFISH LONELINESS THAT DOOMED HER.
OH MY GOSH! IT'S A PLEASURE TO MEET YOU, MR. MASTERSON! MY NAME IS CAROLINE LEE! I'M A HUGE FAN!
CAN YOU HEAR ME?
ERR... I MEAN, MR. GHOST MASTERSON?
WHAT'S THE RESPECTFUL TERM FOR A DECEASED PERSON?
I'LL TAKE THAT AS A "NO."
OH, MY VOICE?
YEAH, I HAVE TO WEAR A RETAINER TO KEEP MY TEETH STRAIGHT.
MY DENTIST SAYS I HAVE "LIQUID GUMS." WITHOUT IT, MY TEETH WOULD JUST FLOAT AROUND AND GO WHEREVER THEY'D LIKE.
AND HOW COULD I EVER BE AN ACTRESS WITH TEETH LIKE THAT?!
A WANNABE ACTRESS?
FANTASTIC.
COME ON, I'VE GOT AN IDEA.

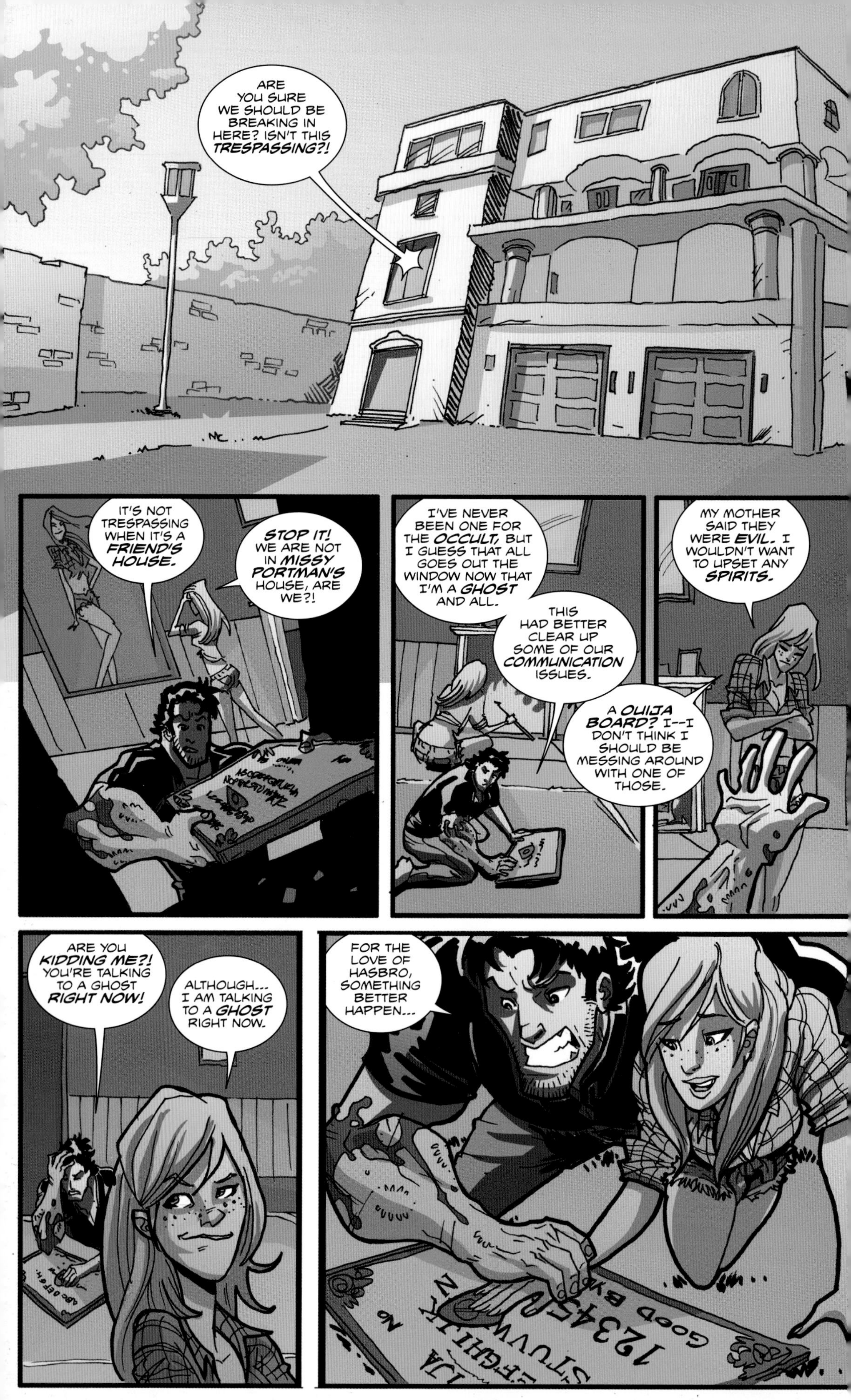

ARE YOU SURE WE SHOULD BE BREAKING IN HERE? ISN'T THIS TRESPASSING?!
IT'S NOT TRESPASSING WHEN IT'S A FRIEND'S HOUSE.
STOP IT! WE ARE NOT IN MISSY PORTMAN'S HOUSE, ARE WE?!
I'VE NEVER BEEN ONE FOR THE OCCULT, BUT I GUESS THAT ALL GOES OUT THE WINDOW NOW THAT I'M A GHOST AND ALL.
THIS HAD BETTER CLEAR UP SOME OF OUR COMMUNICATION ISSUES.
A OUIJA BOARD? I--I DON'T THINK I SHOULD BE MESSING AROUND WITH ONE OF THOSE.
MY MOTHER SAID THEY WERE EVIL. I WOULDN'T WANT TO UPSET ANY SPIRITS.
ARE YOU KIDDING ME?! YOU'RE TALKING TO A GHOST RIGHT NOW!
ALTHOUGH... I AM TALKING TO A GHOST RIGHT NOW.
FOR THE LOVE OF HASBRO, SOMETHING BETTER HAPPEN...

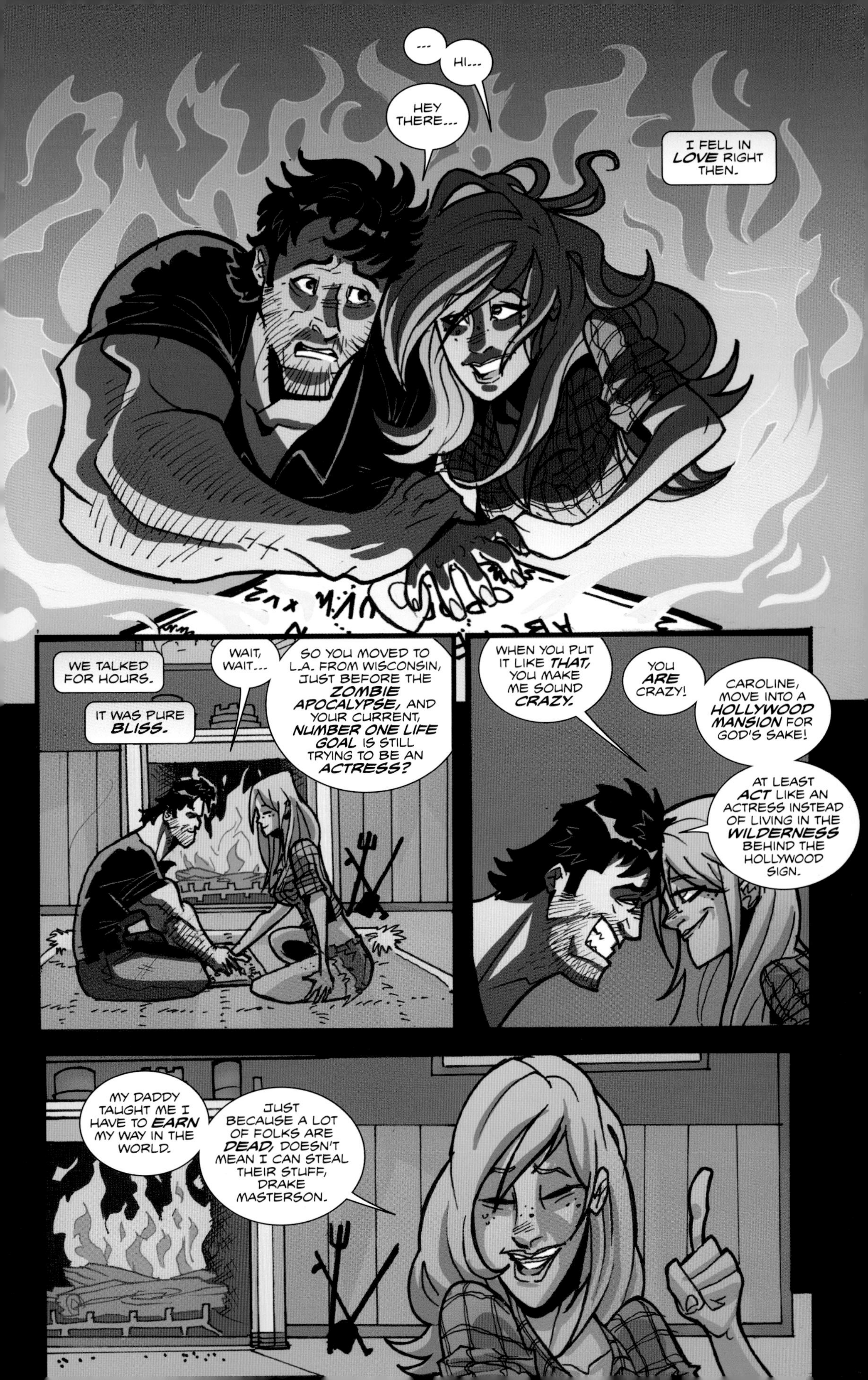
...
HI...
HEY THERE...
I FELL IN LOVE RIGHT THEN.
WE TALKED FOR HOURS.
IT WAS PURE BLISS.
WAIT, WAIT...
SO YOU MOVED TO L.A. FROM WISCONSIN, JUST BEFORE THE ZOMBIE APOCALYPSE, AND YOUR CURRENT, NUMBER ONE LIFE GOAL IS STILL TRYING TO BE AN ACTRESS?
WHEN YOU PUT IT LIKE THAT, YOU MAKE ME SOUND CRAZY.
YOU ARE CRAZY!
CAROLINE, MOVE INTO A HOLLYWOOD MANSION FOR GOD'S SAKE!
AT LEAST ACT LIKE AN ACTRESS INSTEAD OF LIVING IN THE WILDERNESS BEHIND THE HOLLYWOOD SIGN.
MY DADDY TAUGHT ME I HAVE TO EARN MY WAY IN THE WORLD.
JUST BECAUSE A LOT OF FOLKS ARE DEAD, DOESN'T MEAN I CAN STEAL THEIR STUFF, DRAKE MASTERSON.

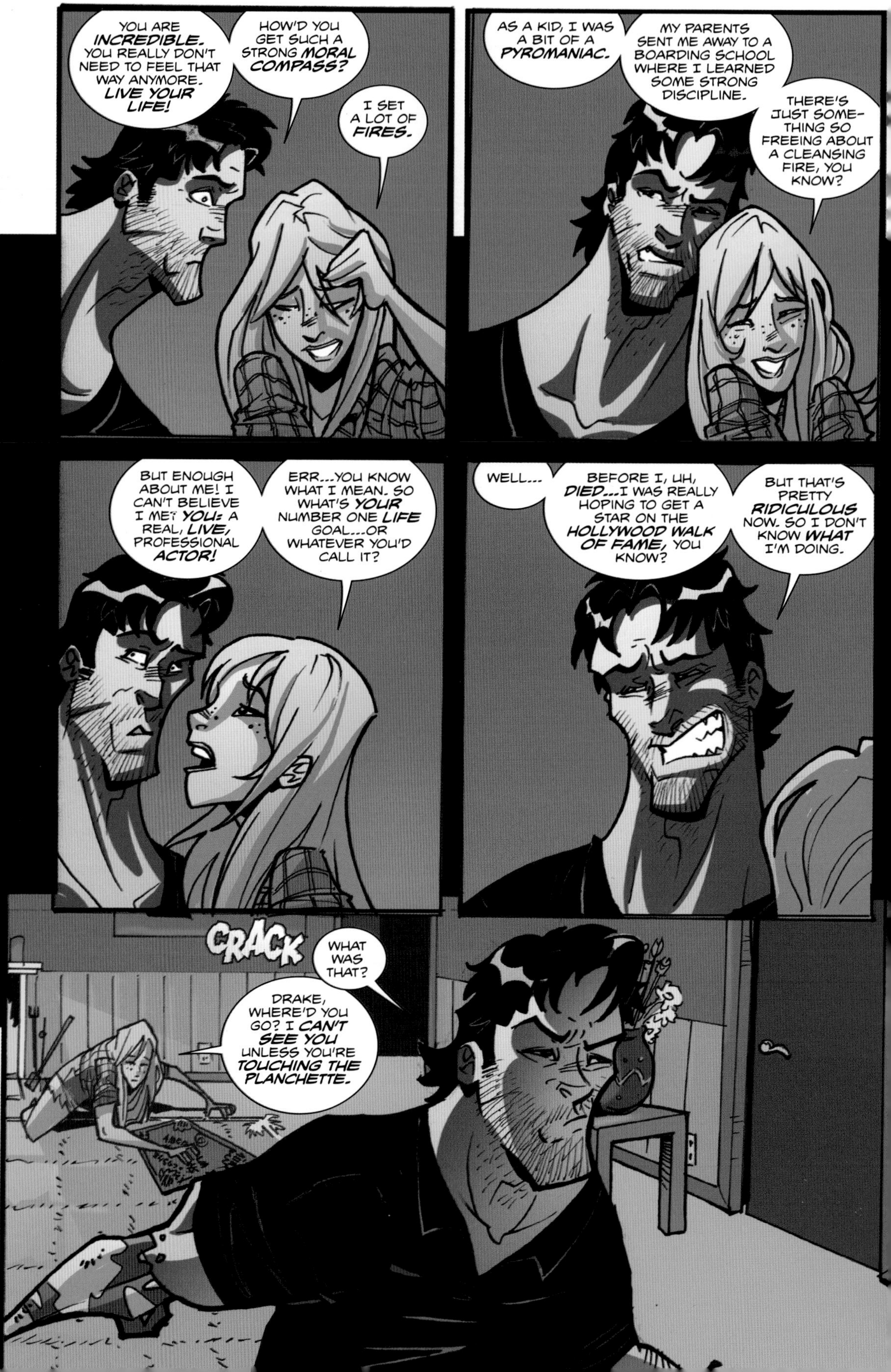

YOU ARE INCREDIBLE. YOU REALLY DON'T NEED TO FEEL THAT WAY ANYMORE. LIVE YOUR LIFE!
HOW'D YOU GET SUCH A STRONG MORAL COMPASS?
I SET A LOT OF FIRES.
AS A KID, I WAS A BIT OF A PYROMANIAC.
MY PARENTS SENT ME AWAY TO A BOARDING SCHOOL WHERE I LEARNED SOME STRONG DISCIPLINE.
THERE'S JUST SOMETHING SO FREEING ABOUT A CLEANSING FIRE, YOU KNOW?
BUT ENOUGH ABOUT ME! I CAN'T BELIEVE I MET YOU: A REAL, LIVE, PROFESSIONAL ACTOR!
ERR...YOU KNOW WHAT I MEAN. SO WHAT'S YOUR NUMBER ONE LIFE GOAL...OR WHATEVER YOU'D CALL IT?
WELL...
BEFORE I, UH, DIED...I WAS REALLY HOPING TO GET A STAR ON THE HOLLYWOOD WALK OF FAME, YOU KNOW?
BUT THAT'S PRETTY RIDICULOUS NOW. SO I DON'T KNOW WHAT I'M DOING.
CRACK
WHAT WAS THAT?
DRAKE, WHERE'D YOU GO? I CAN'T SEE YOU UNLESS YOU'RE TOUCHING THE PLANCHETTE.

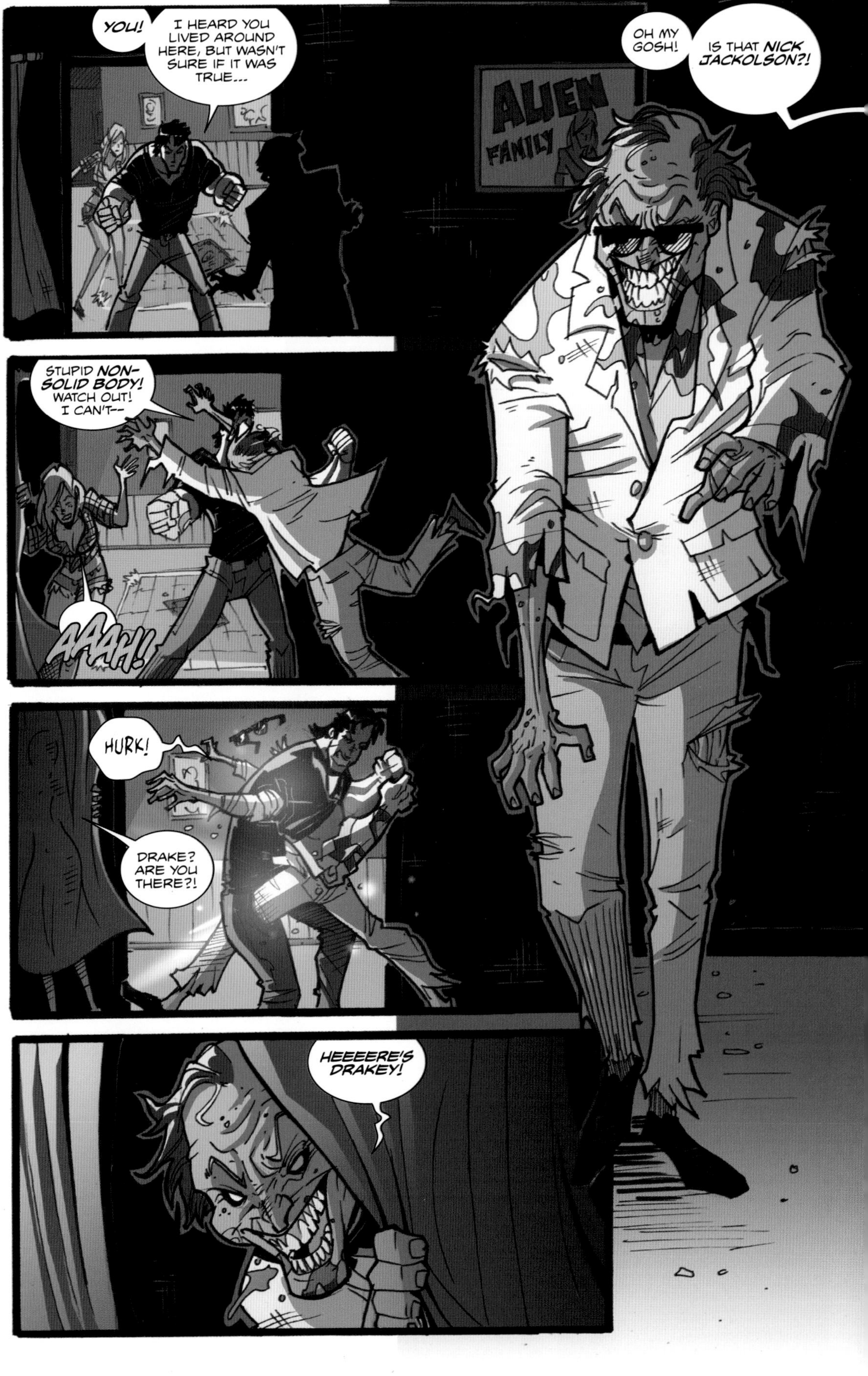
YOU!
I HEARD YOU LIVED AROUND HERE, BUT WASN'T SURE IF IT WAS TRUE...
ALIEN FAMILY
OH MY GOSH!
IS THAT NICK JACKOLSON?!
STUPID NON-SOLID BODY! WATCH OUT! I CAN'T--
AAAH!
HURK!
DRAKE? ARE YOU THERE?!
HEEEERE'S DRAKEY!

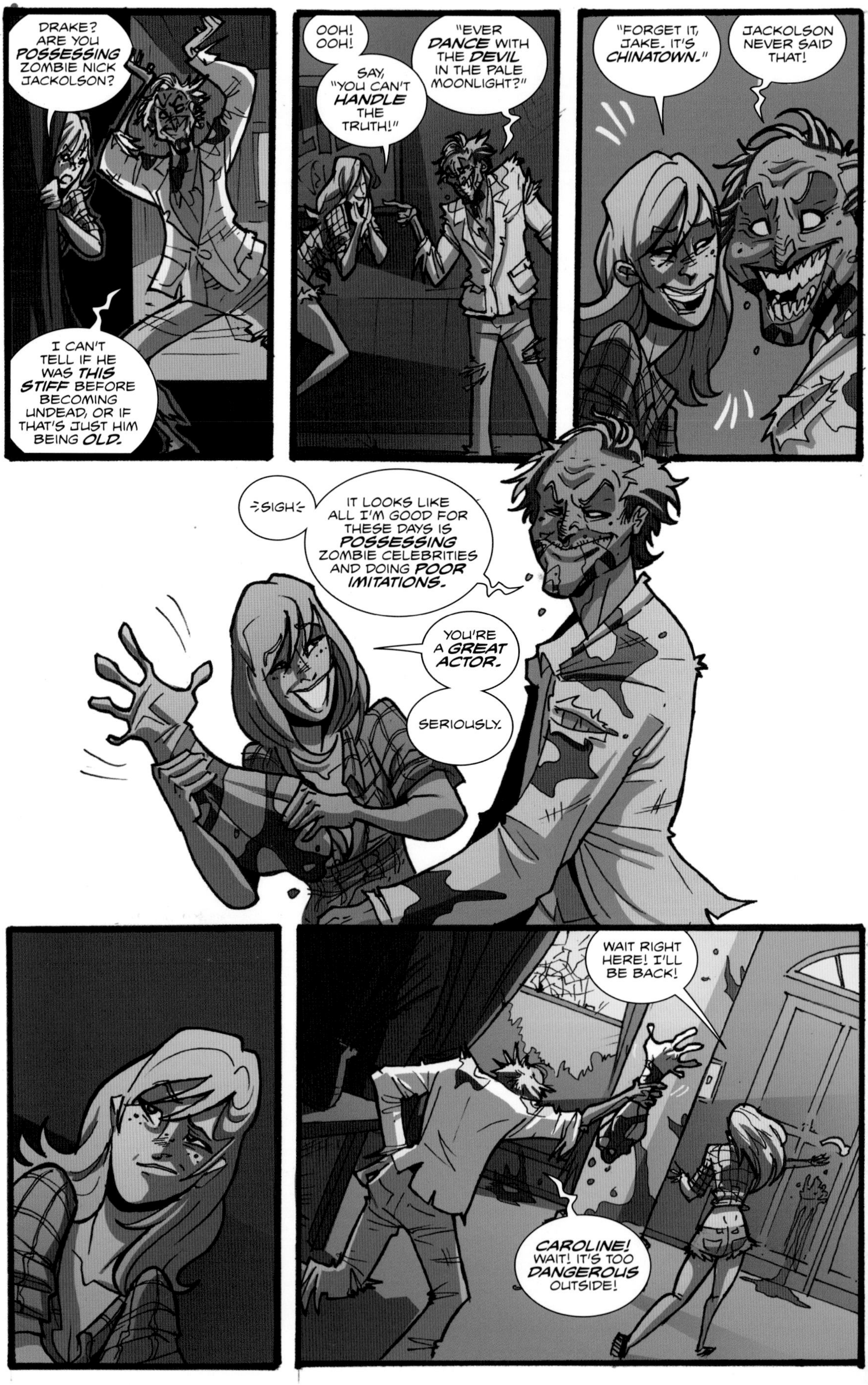
DRAKE? ARE YOU POSSESSING ZOMBIE NICK JACKOLSON?
I CAN'T TELL IF HE WAS THIS STIFF BEFORE BECOMING UNDEAD, OR IF THAT'S JUST HIM BEING OLD.
OOH! OOH!
SAY, "YOU CAN'T HANDLE THE TRUTH!"
"EVER DANCE WITH THE DEVIL IN THE PALE MOONLIGHT?"
"FORGET IT, JAKE. IT'S CHINATOWN."
JACKOLSON NEVER SAID THAT!
SIGH
IT LOOKS LIKE ALL I'M GOOD FOR THESE DAYS IS POSSESSING ZOMBIE CELEBRITIES AND DOING POOR IMITATIONS.
YOU'RE A GREAT ACTOR.
SERIOUSLY.
WAIT RIGHT HERE! I'LL BE BACK!
CAROLINE! WAIT! IT'S TOO DANGEROUS OUTSIDE!

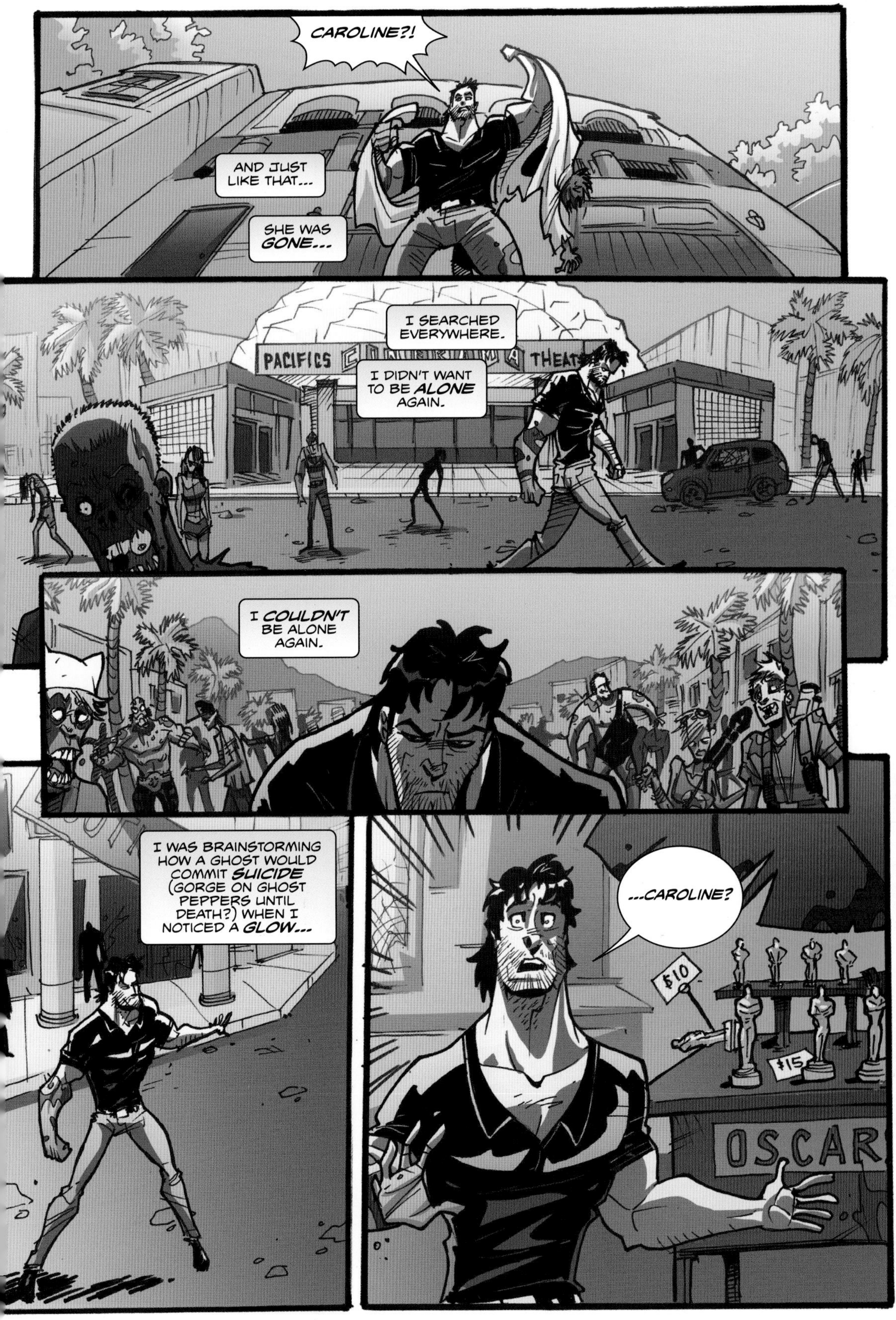
CAROLINE?!
AND JUST LIKE THAT...
SHE WAS GONE...
I SEARCHED EVERYWHERE.
PACIFICS
THEAT
I DIDN'T WANT TO BE ALONE AGAIN.
I COULDN'T BE ALONE AGAIN.
I WAS BRAINSTORMING HOW A GHOST WOULD COMMIT SUICIDE (GORGE ON GHOST PEPPERS UNTIL DEATH?) WHEN I NOTICED A GLOW...
...CAROLINE?
$10
$15
OSCAR

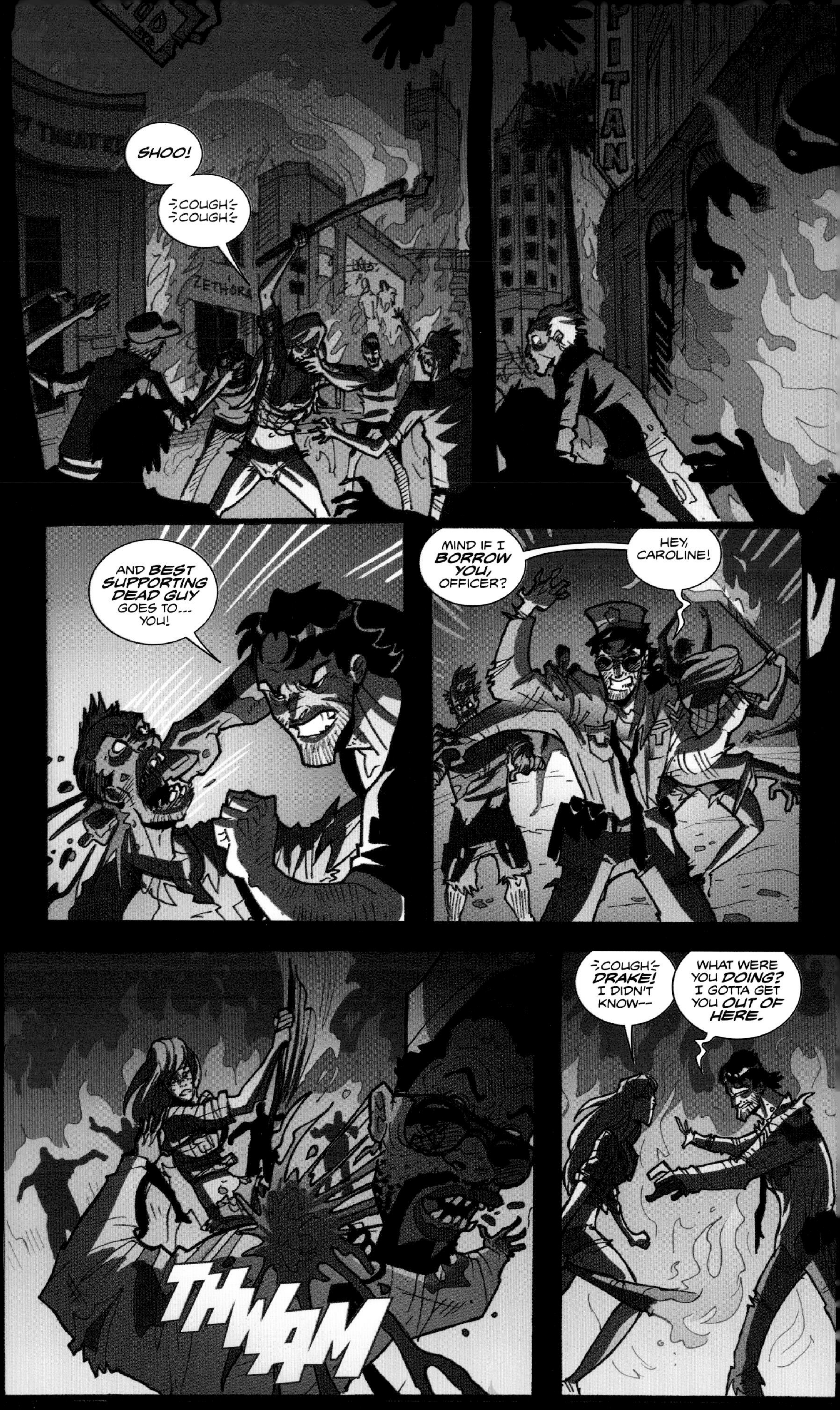

THEATER
ZETHORA
SHOO!
COUGH COUGH
PITAN
AND BEST SUPPORTING DEAD GUY GOES TO... YOU!
MIND IF I BORROW YOU, OFFICER?
HEY, CAROLINE!
THWAM
COUGH DRAKE! I DIDN'T KNOW--
WHAT WERE YOU DOING? I GOTTA GET YOU OUT OF HERE.

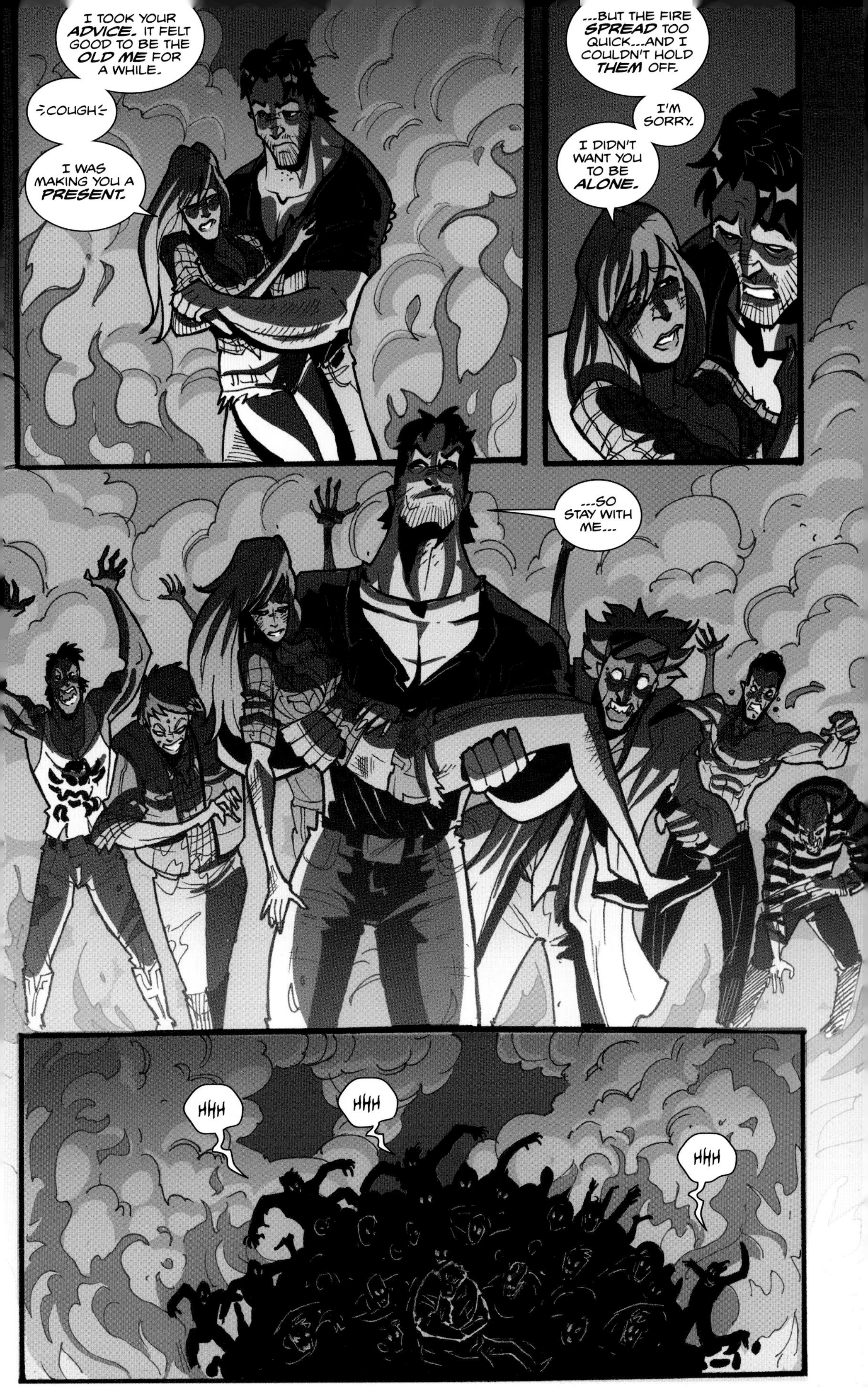

I TOOK YOUR ADVICE. IT FELT GOOD TO BE THE OLD ME FOR A WHILE.
COUGH
I WAS MAKING YOU A PRESENT.
...BUT THE FIRE SPREAD TOO QUICK...AND I COULDN'T HOLD THEM OFF.
I'M SORRY.
I DIDN'T WANT YOU TO BE ALONE.
...SO STAY WITH ME...
HHH
HHH
HHH

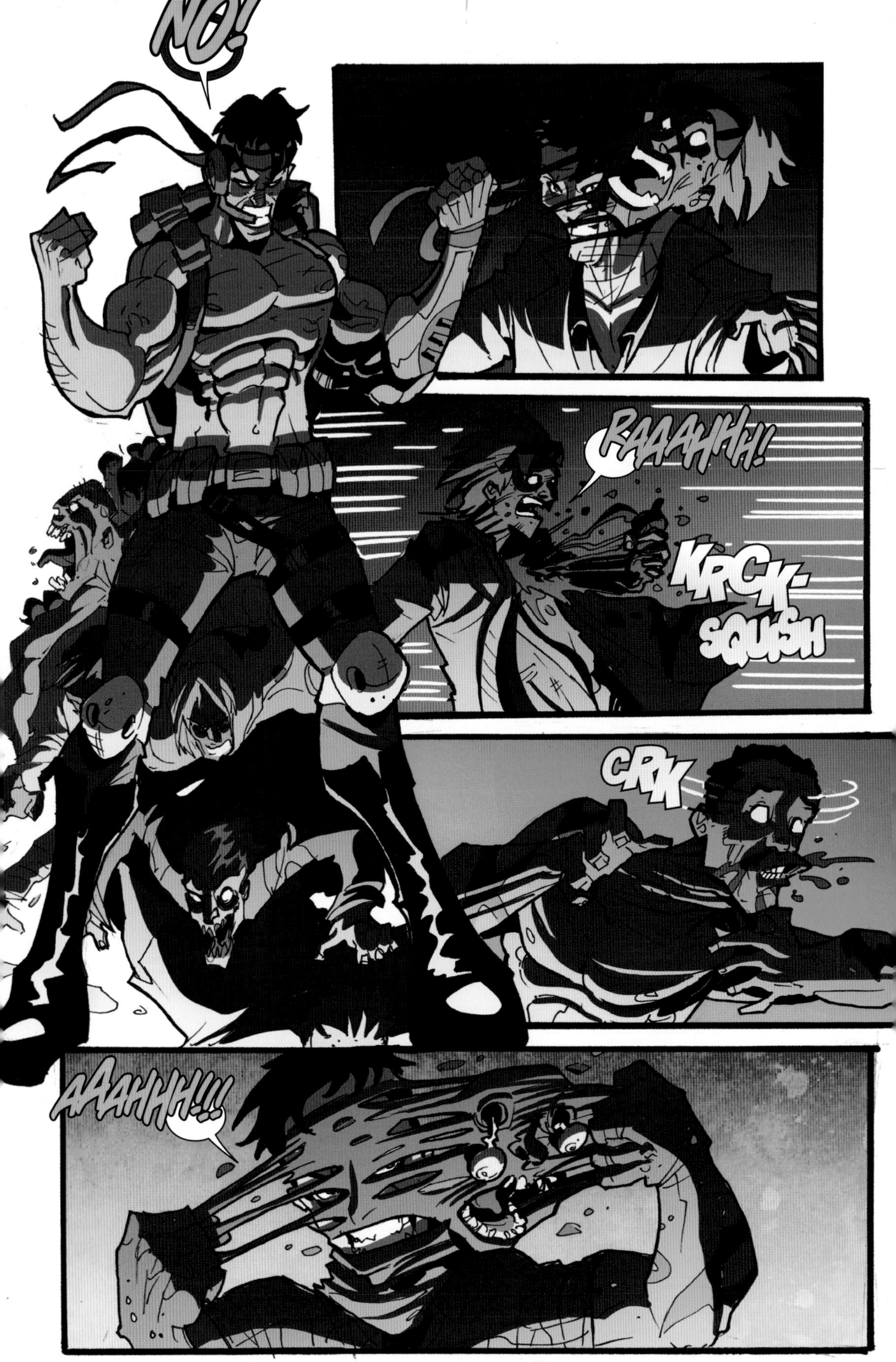
NO!
RAAAHHH!
KRCK-SQUISH
CRK
AAHHH!!!

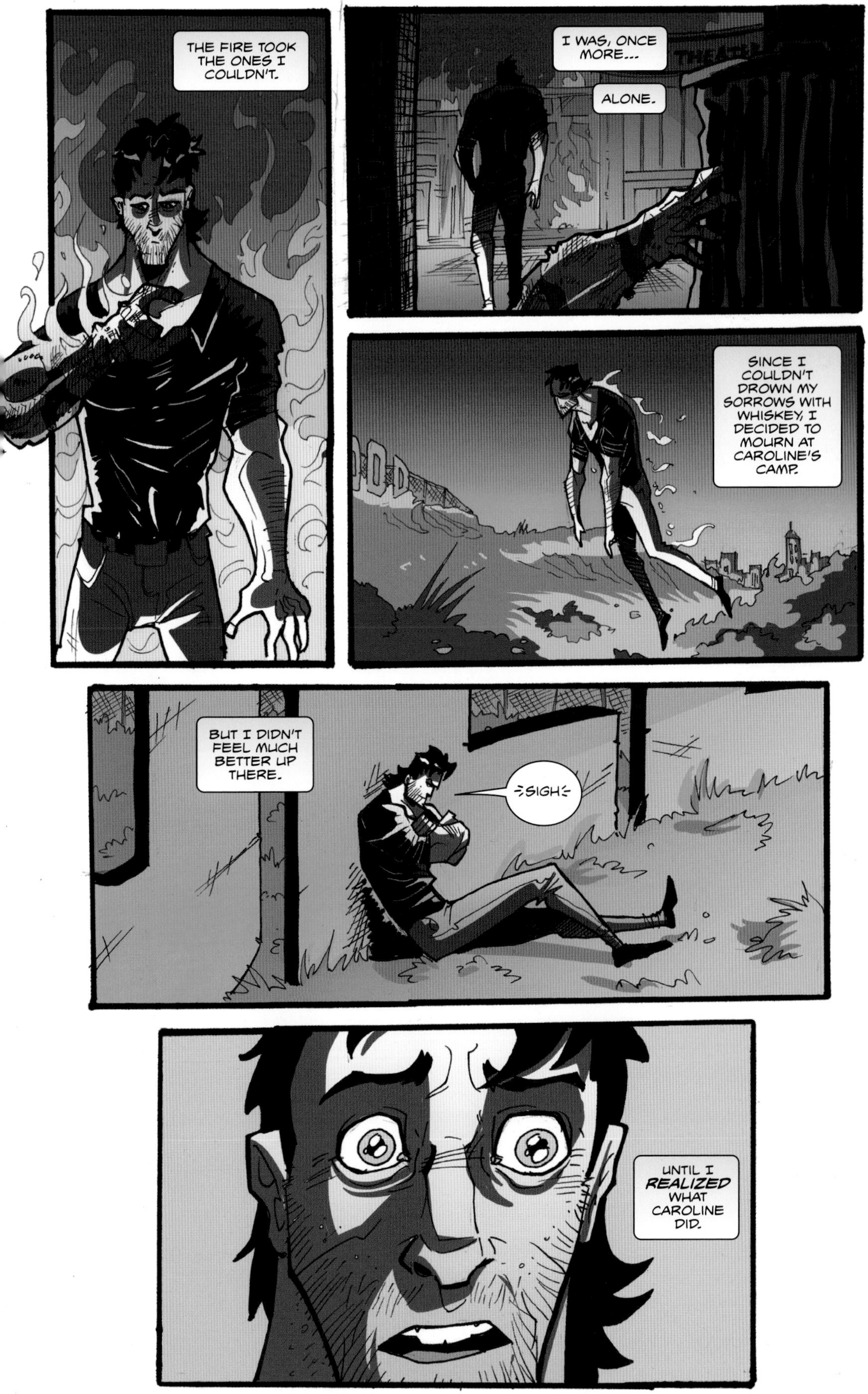
THE FIRE TOOK THE ONES I COULDN'T.
I WAS, ONCE MORE...
ALONE.
THEATE
SINCE I COULDN'T DROWN MY SORROWS WITH WHISKEY, I DECIDED TO MOURN AT CAROLINE'S CAMP.
BUT I DIDN'T FEEL MUCH BETTER UP THERE.
SIGH
UNTIL I REALIZED WHAT CAROLINE DID.

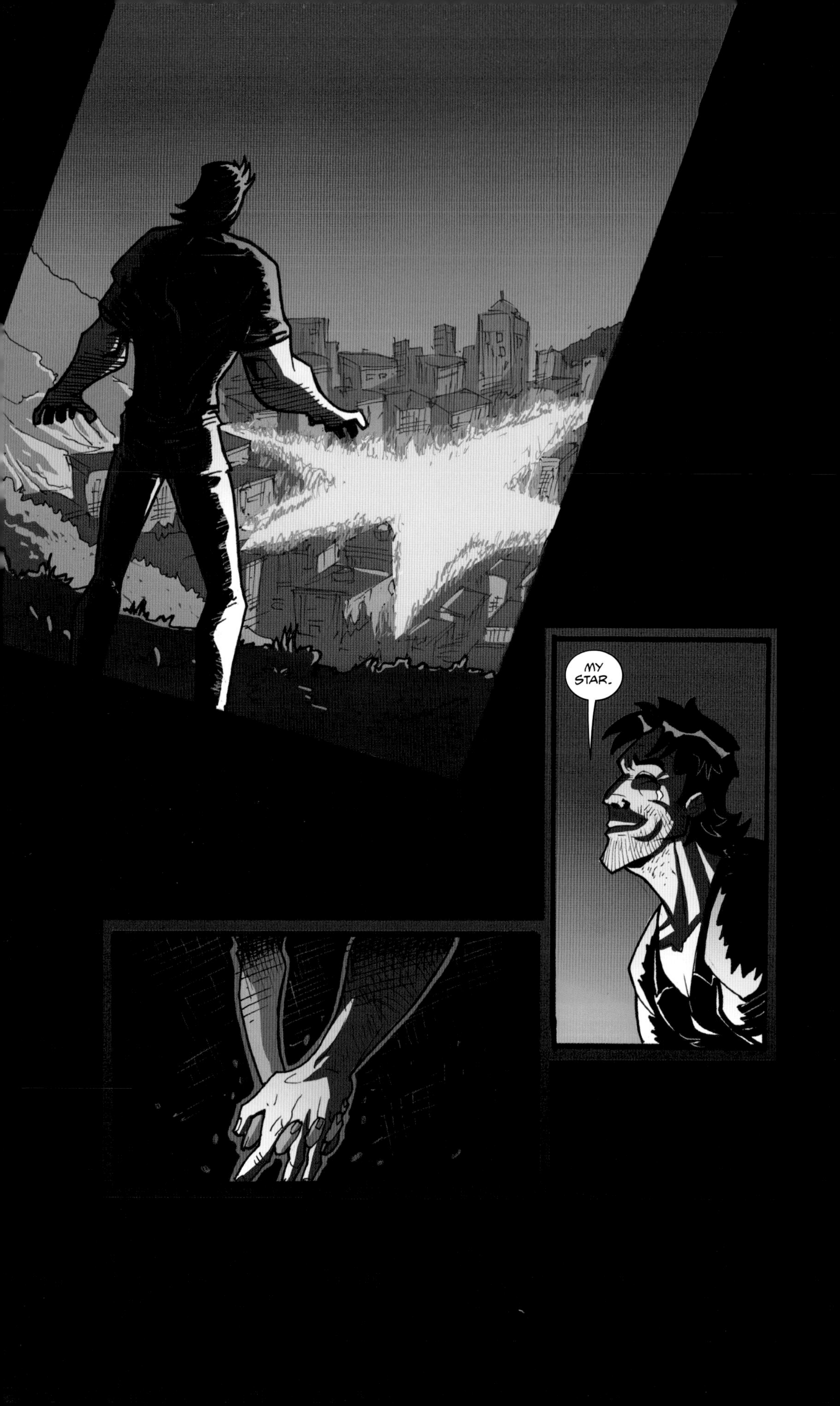
MY STAR.

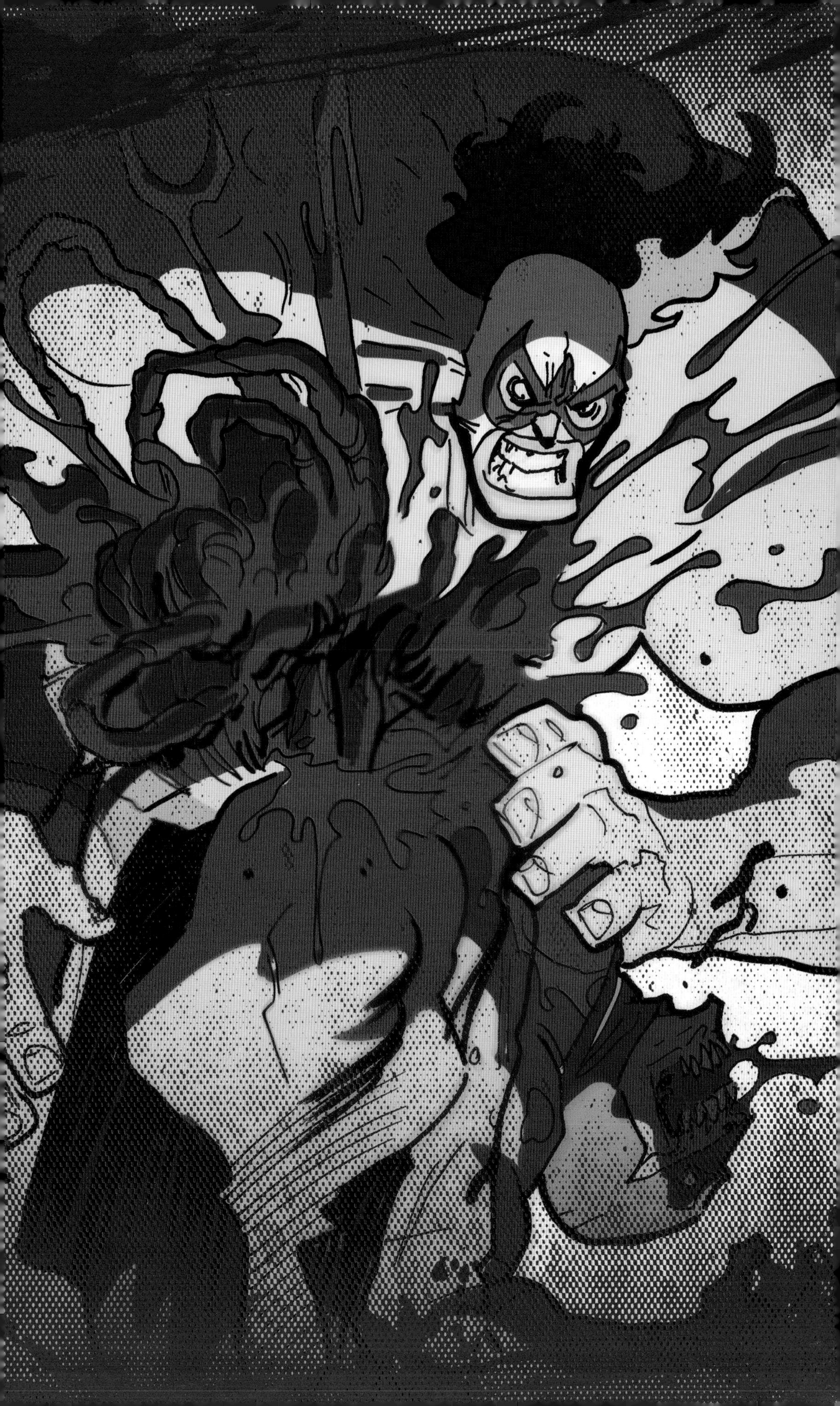

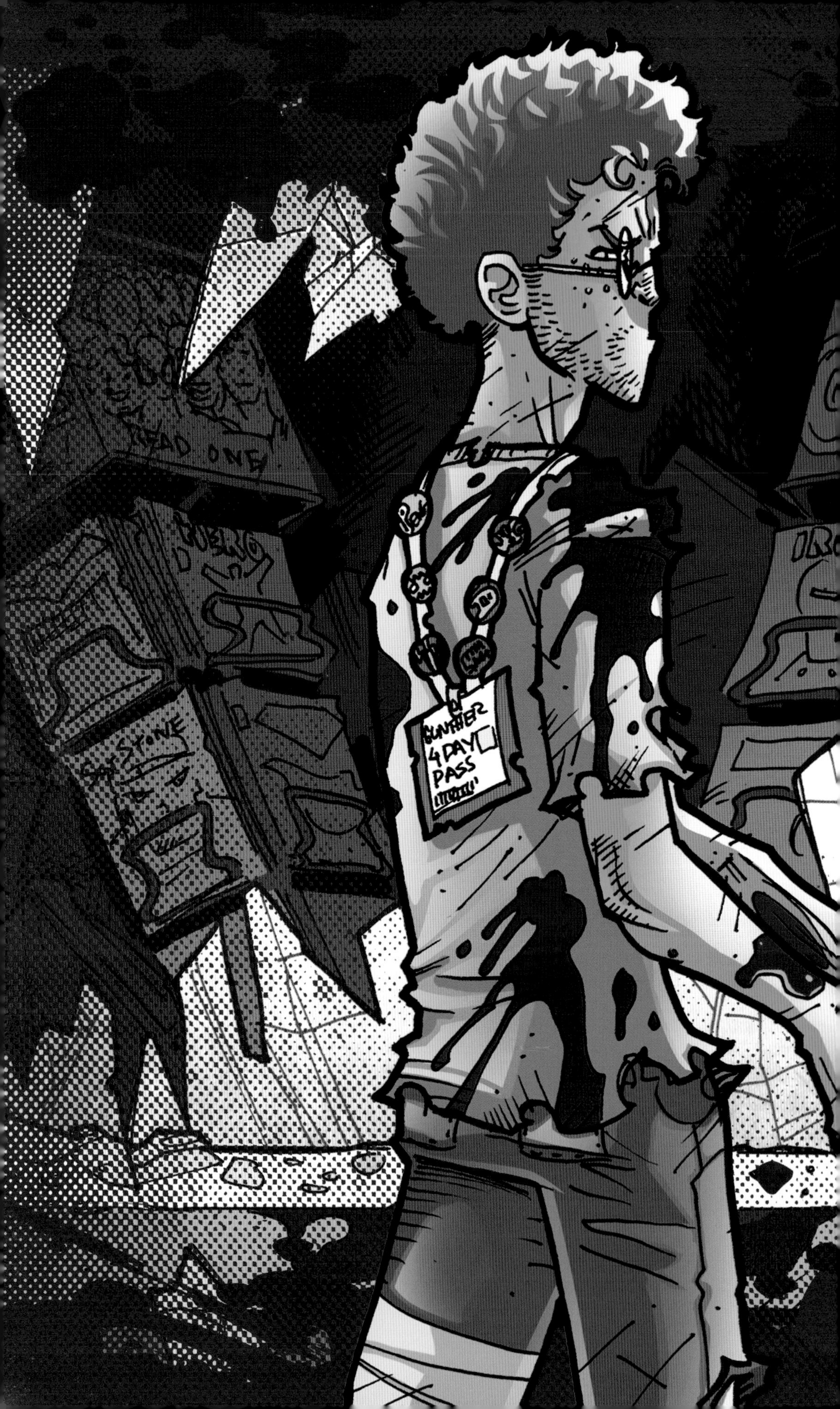
GUNTHER
4 DAY
PASS

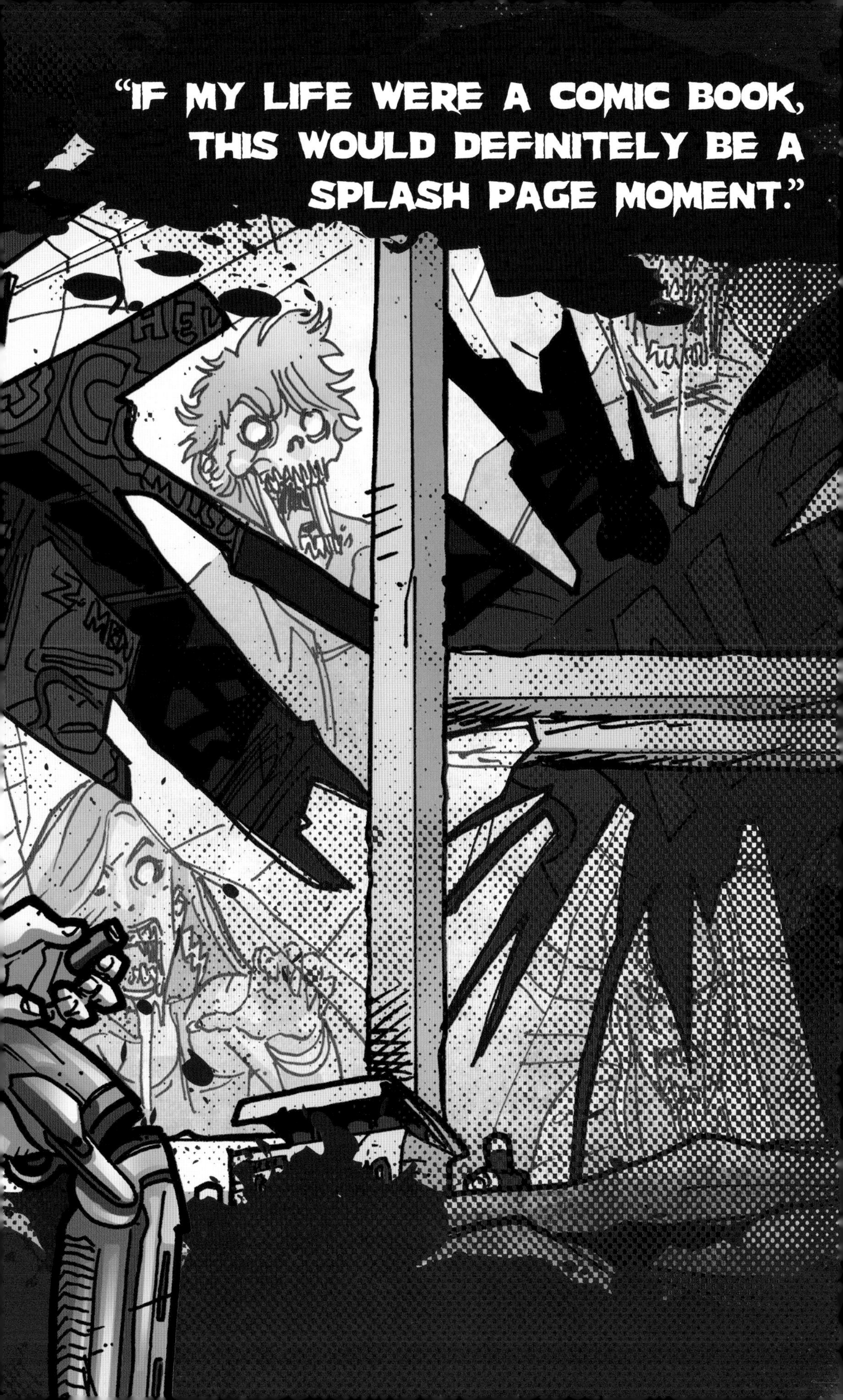
"IF MY LIFE WERE A COMIC BOOK, THIS WOULD DEFINITELY BE A SPLASH PAGE MOMENT."

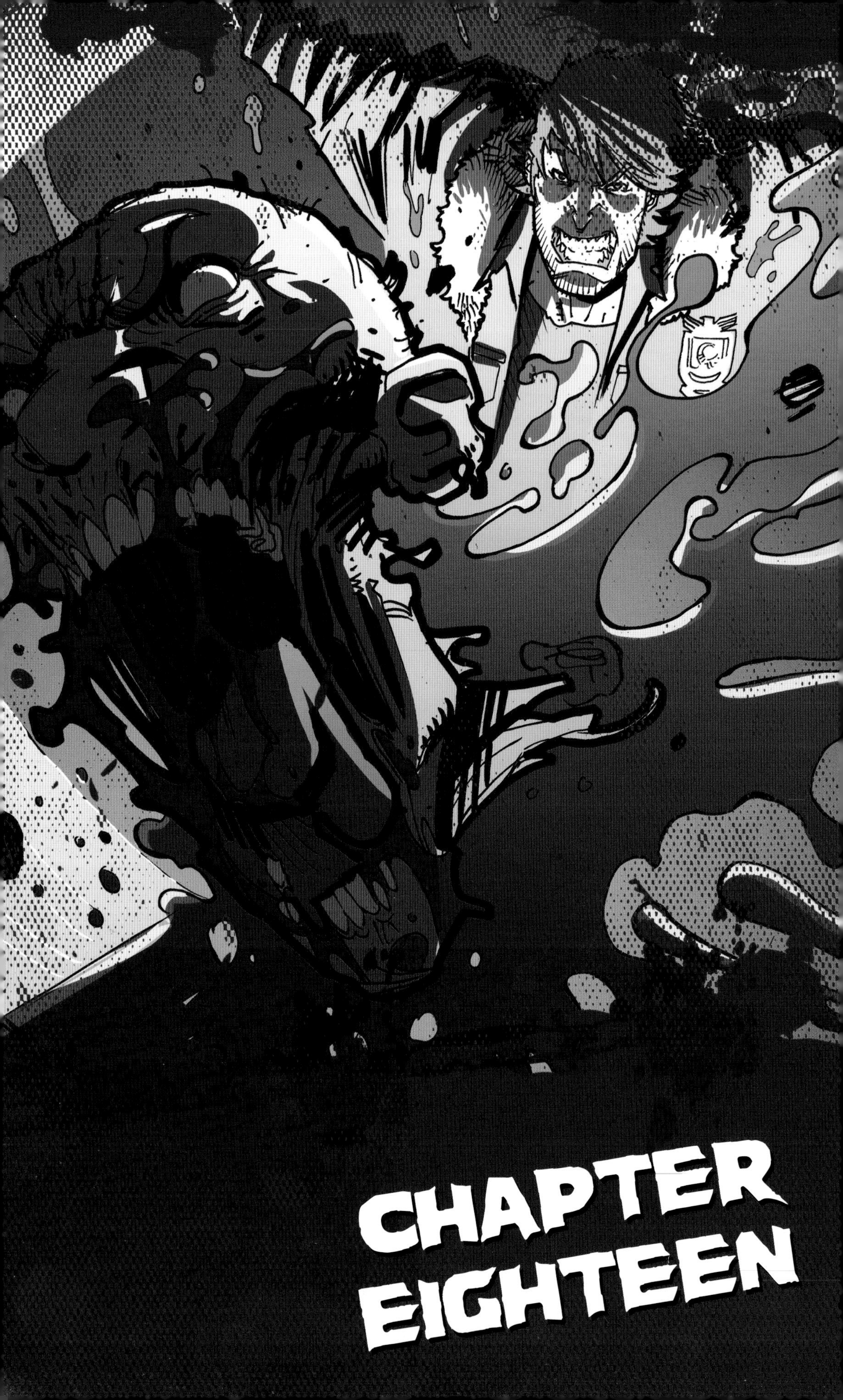
CHAPTER
EIGHTEEN

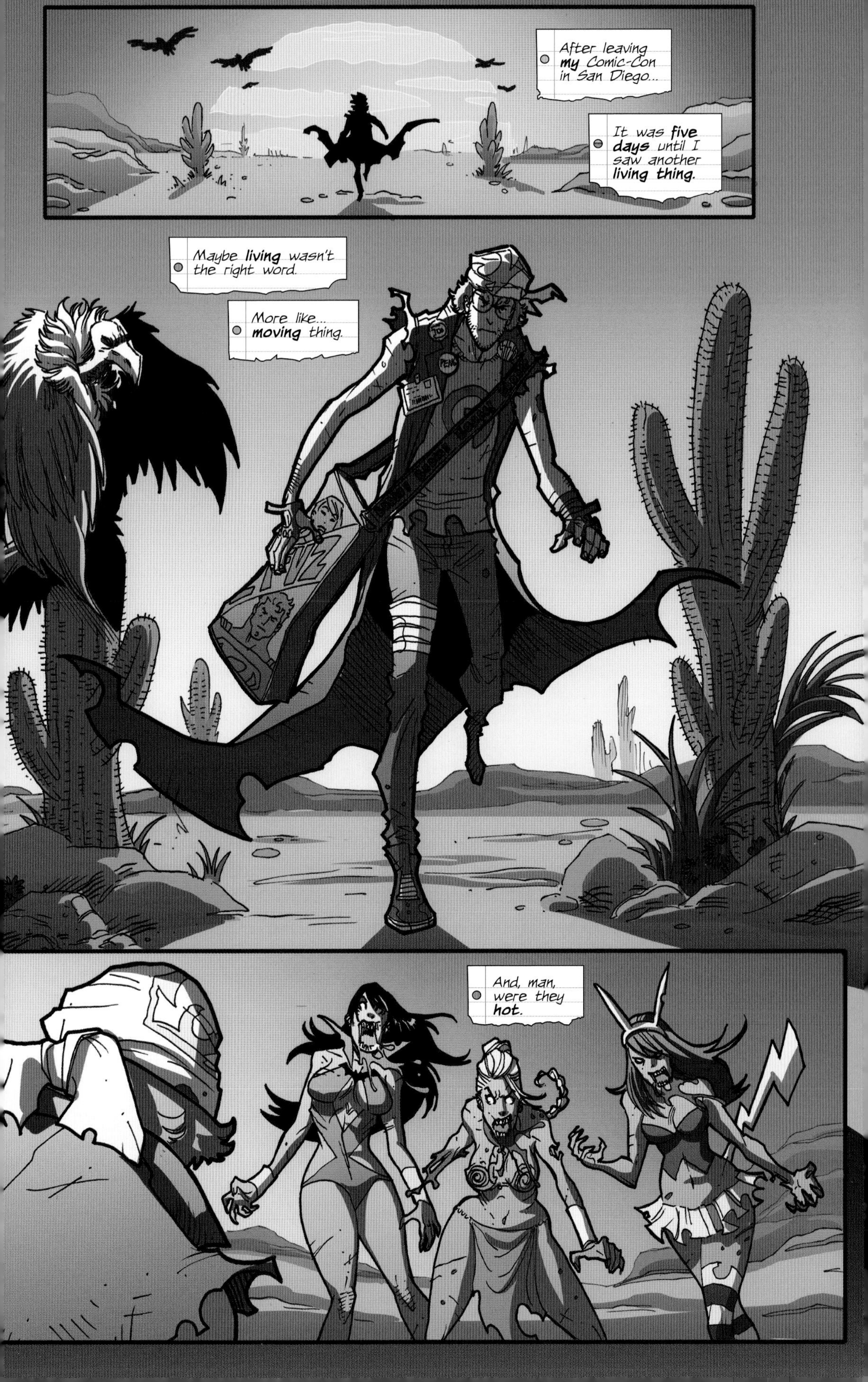
After leaving **my** Comic-Con in San Diego...
It was **five days** until I saw another **living thing.**
Maybe **living** wasn't the right word.
More like... **moving** thing.
And, man, were they **hot.**

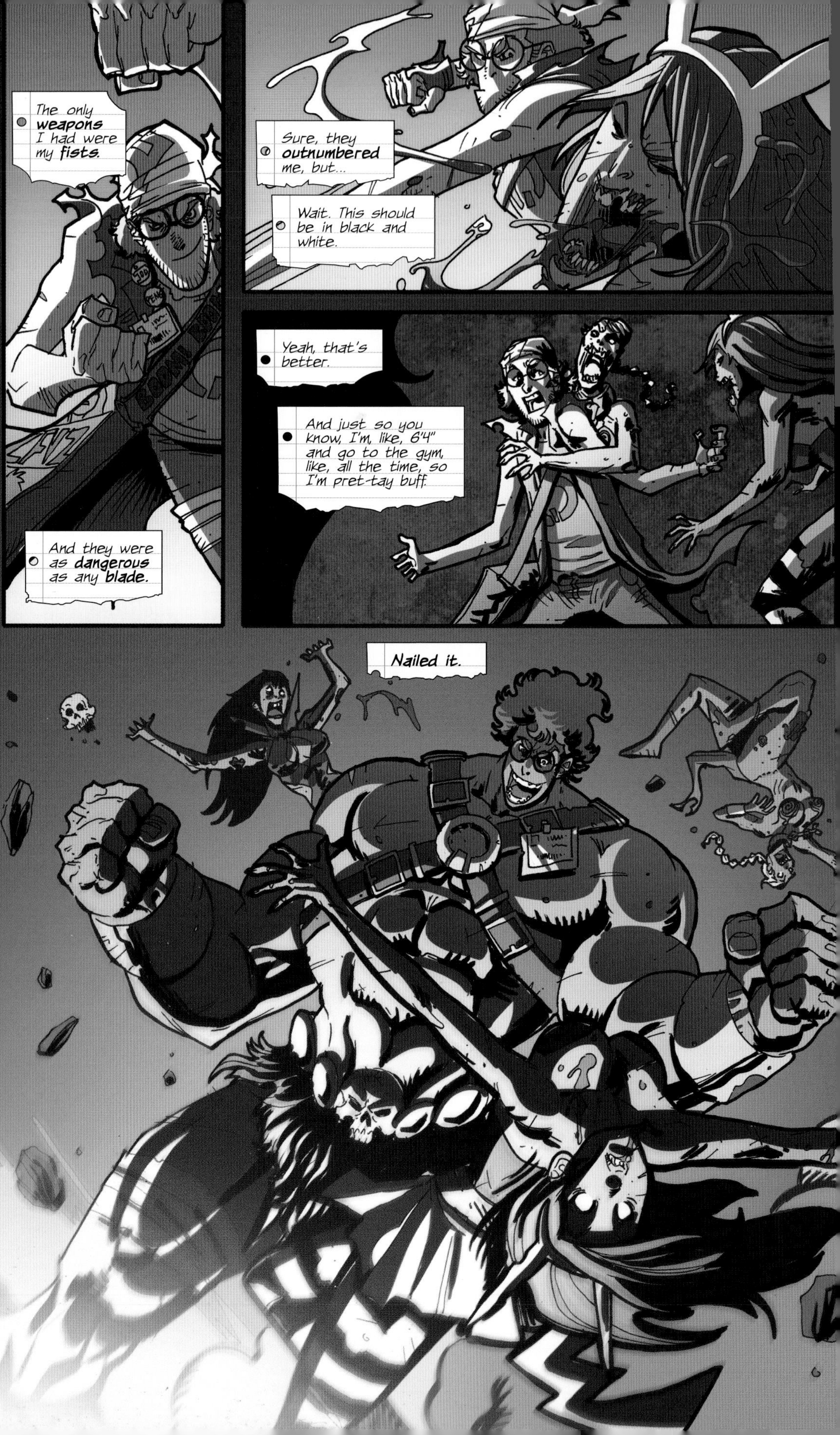

The only **weapons** I had were my **fists.**
Sure, they **outnumbered** me, but...
Wait. This should be in black and white.
Yeah, that's better.
And just so you know, I'm, like, 6'4" and go to the gym, like, all the time, so I'm pret-tay buff.
And they were as **dangerous** as any **blade.**
Nailed it.

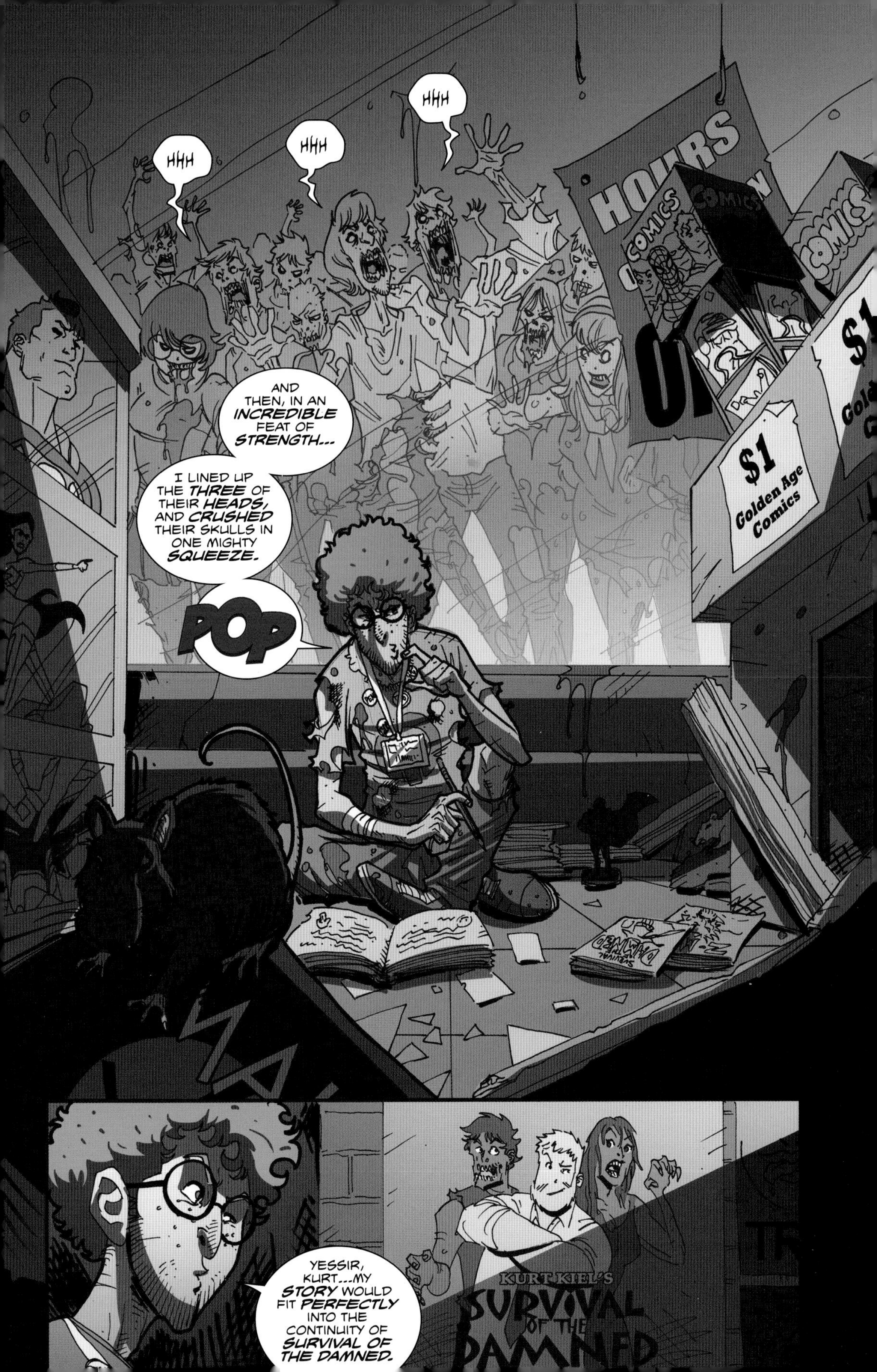
HHH
HHH
HHH
HOURS
COMICS
COMICS
COMICS
$1
$1 Golden Age Comics
AND THEN, IN AN INCREDIBLE FEAT OF STRENGTH...
I LINED UP THE THREE OF THEIR HEADS, AND CRUSHED THEIR SKULLS IN ONE MIGHTY SQUEEZE.
POP
YESSIR, KURT...MY STORY WOULD FIT PERFECTLY INTO THE CONTINUITY OF SURVIVAL OF THE DAMNED.
KURT KIEL'S SURVIVAL OF THE DAMNED

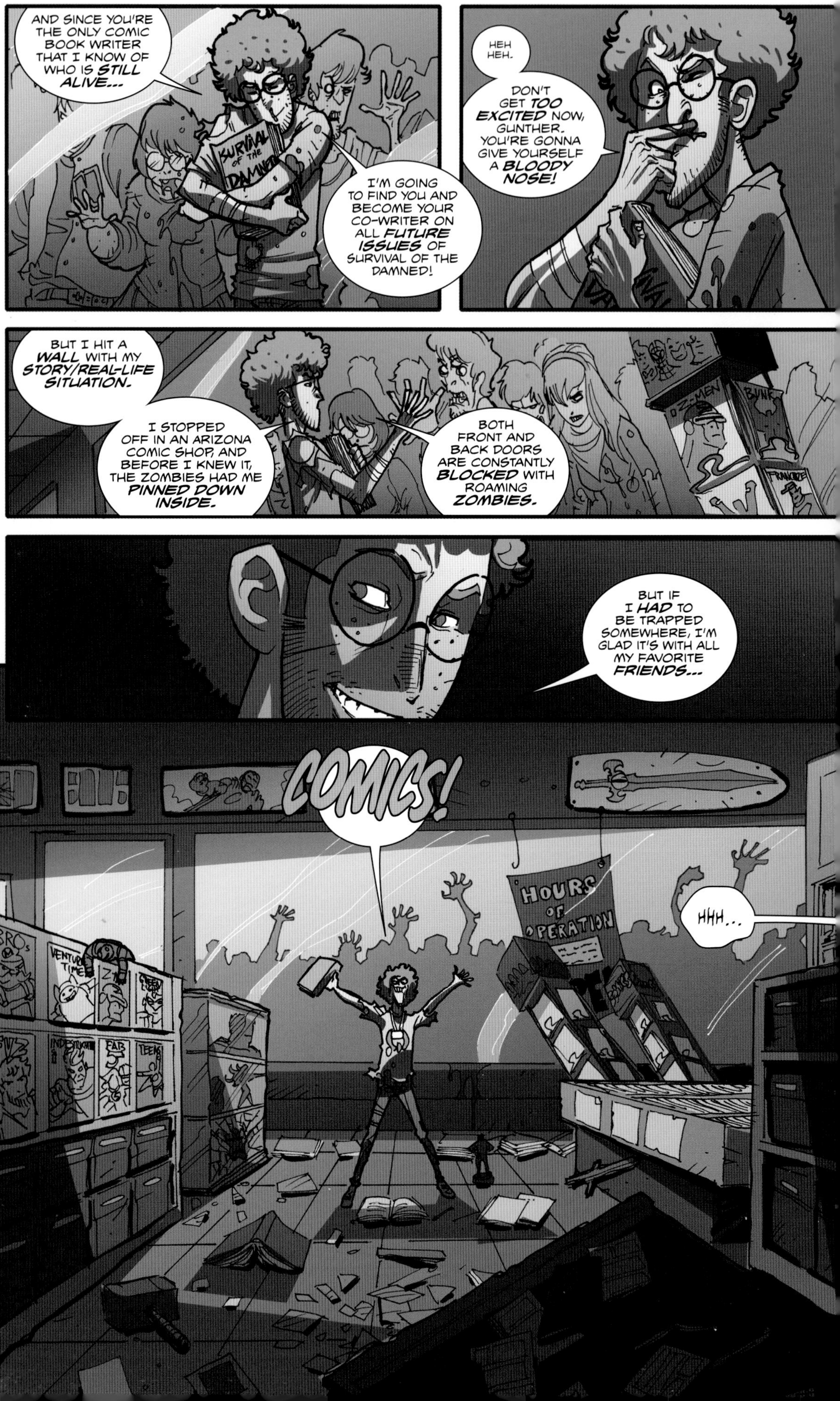

AND SINCE YOU'RE THE ONLY COMIC BOOK WRITER THAT I KNOW OF WHO IS STILL ALIVE...
SURVIVAL OF THE DAMNED
I'M GOING TO FIND YOU AND BECOME YOUR CO-WRITER ON ALL FUTURE ISSUES OF SURVIVAL OF THE DAMNED!
HEH HEH.
DON'T GET TOO EXCITED NOW, GUNTHER. YOU'RE GONNA GIVE YOURSELF A BLOODY NOSE!
BUT I HIT A WALL WITH MY STORY/REAL-LIFE SITUATION.
I STOPPED OFF IN AN ARIZONA COMIC SHOP, AND BEFORE I KNEW IT, THE ZOMBIES HAD ME PINNED DOWN INSIDE.
BOTH FRONT AND BACK DOORS ARE CONSTANTLY BLOCKED WITH ROAMING ZOMBIES.
BUT IF I HAD TO BE TRAPPED SOMEWHERE, I'M GLAD IT'S WITH ALL MY FAVORITE FRIENDS...
COMICS!
HOURS OF OPERATION
HHH...

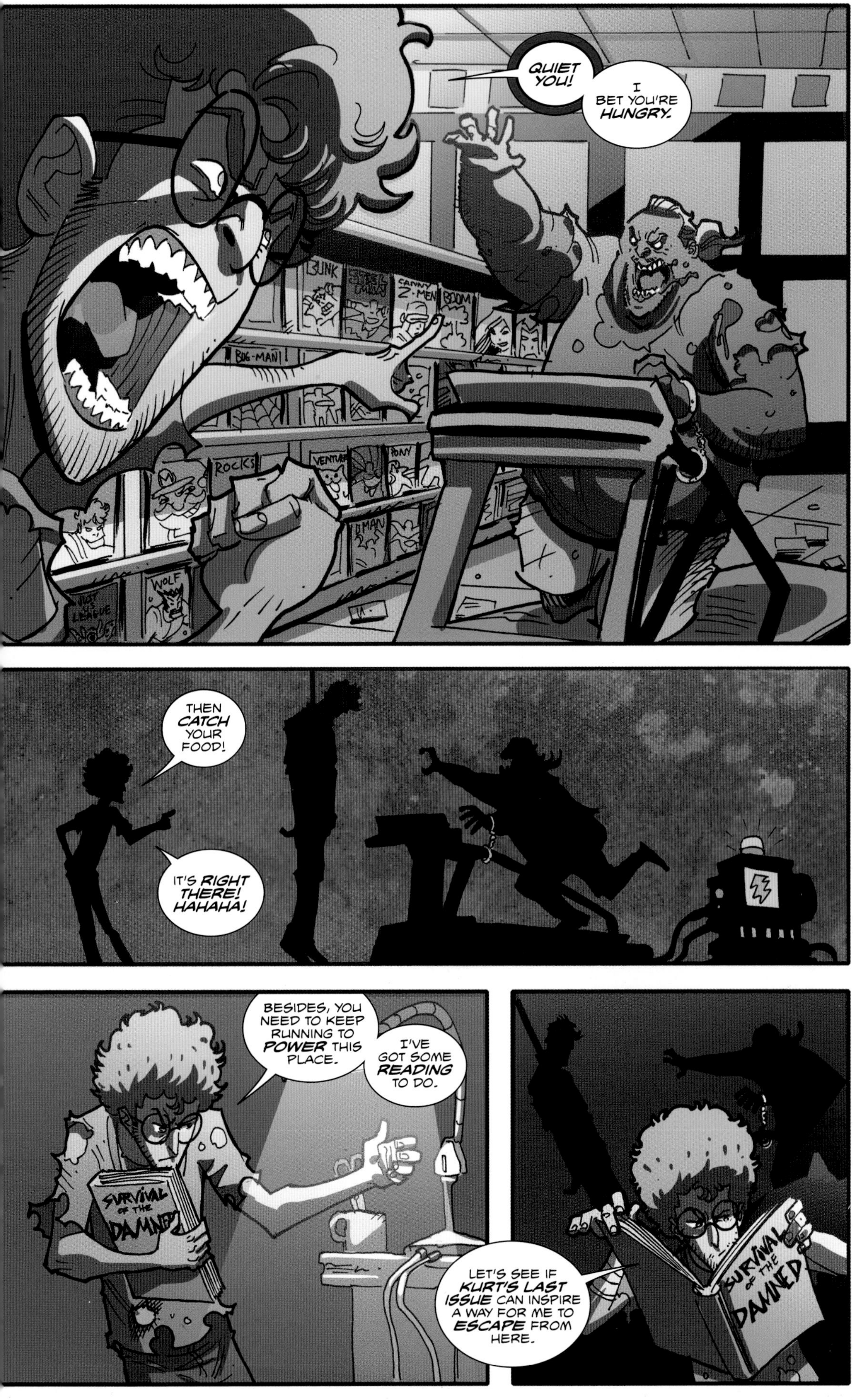

QUIET YOU!
I BET YOU'RE HUNGRY.
BUNK
STEEL MAN
CANNY Z-MEN
BOOM
BOG-MAN
ROCKS
VENTURE
PONY
WOLF
LEAGUE
THEN CATCH YOUR FOOD!
IT'S RIGHT THERE! HAHAHA!
BESIDES, YOU NEED TO KEEP RUNNING TO POWER THIS PLACE.
I'VE GOT SOME READING TO DO.
SURVIVAL OF THE DAMNED
LET'S SEE IF KURT'S LAST ISSUE CAN INSPIRE A WAY FOR ME TO ESCAPE FROM HERE.
SURVIVAL OF THE DAMNED

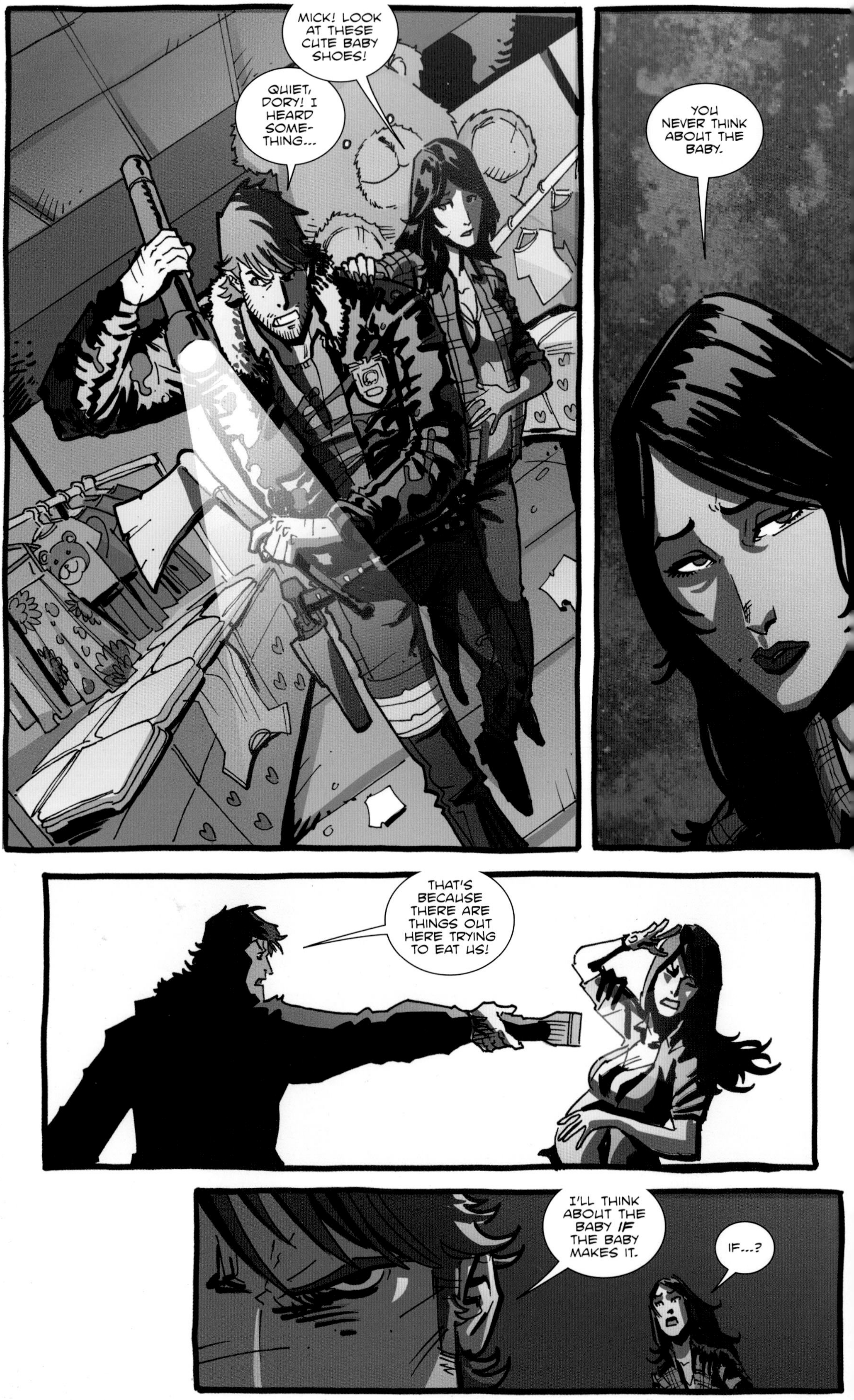
MICK! LOOK AT THESE CUTE BABY SHOES!
QUIET, DORY! I HEARD SOME-THING...
YOU NEVER THINK ABOUT THE BABY.
THAT'S BECAUSE THERE ARE THINGS OUT HERE TRYING TO EAT US!
I'LL THINK ABOUT THE BABY *IF* THE BABY MAKES IT.
IF...?

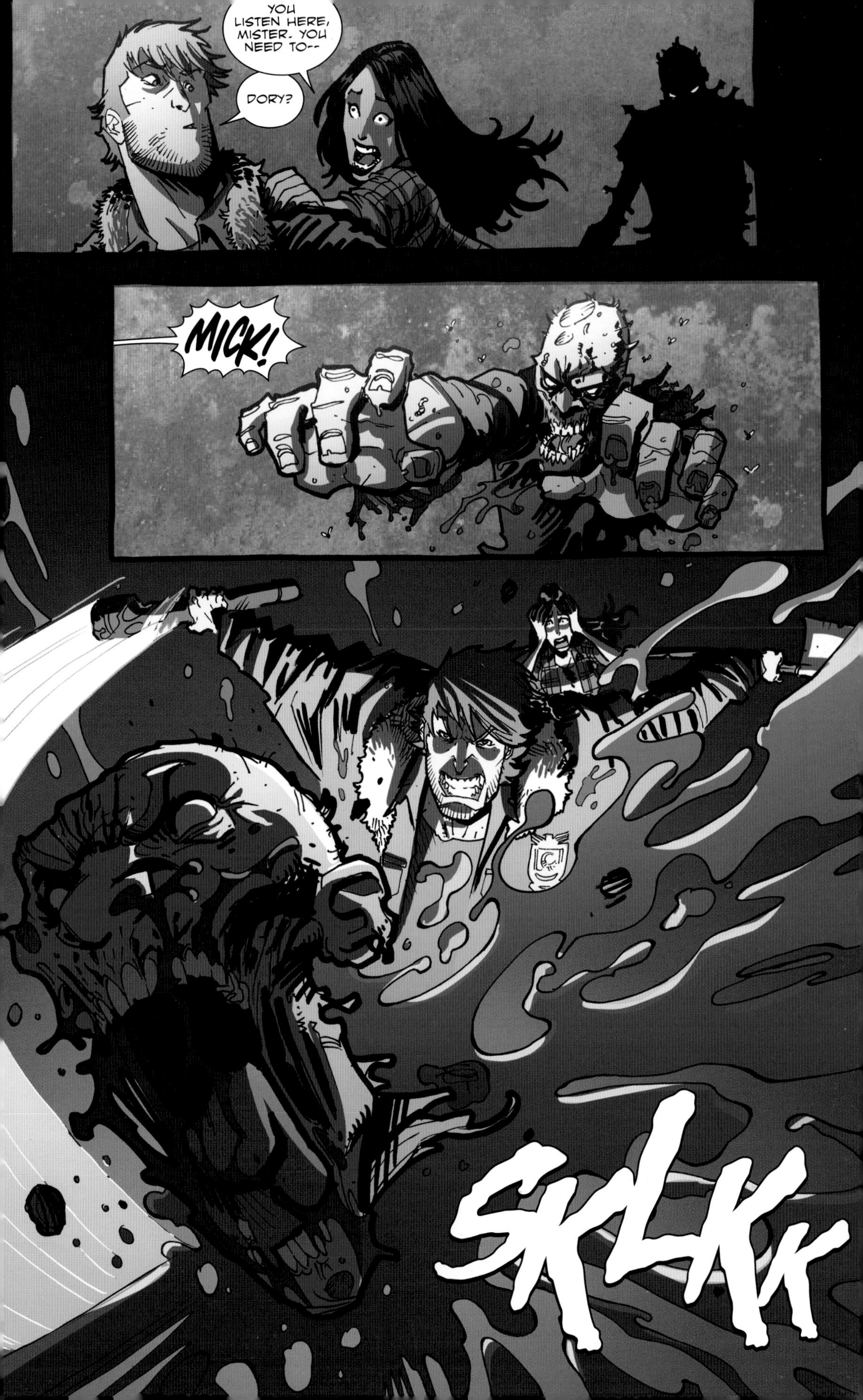
YOU LISTEN HERE, MISTER. YOU NEED TO--
DORY?
MICK!
SKLKK

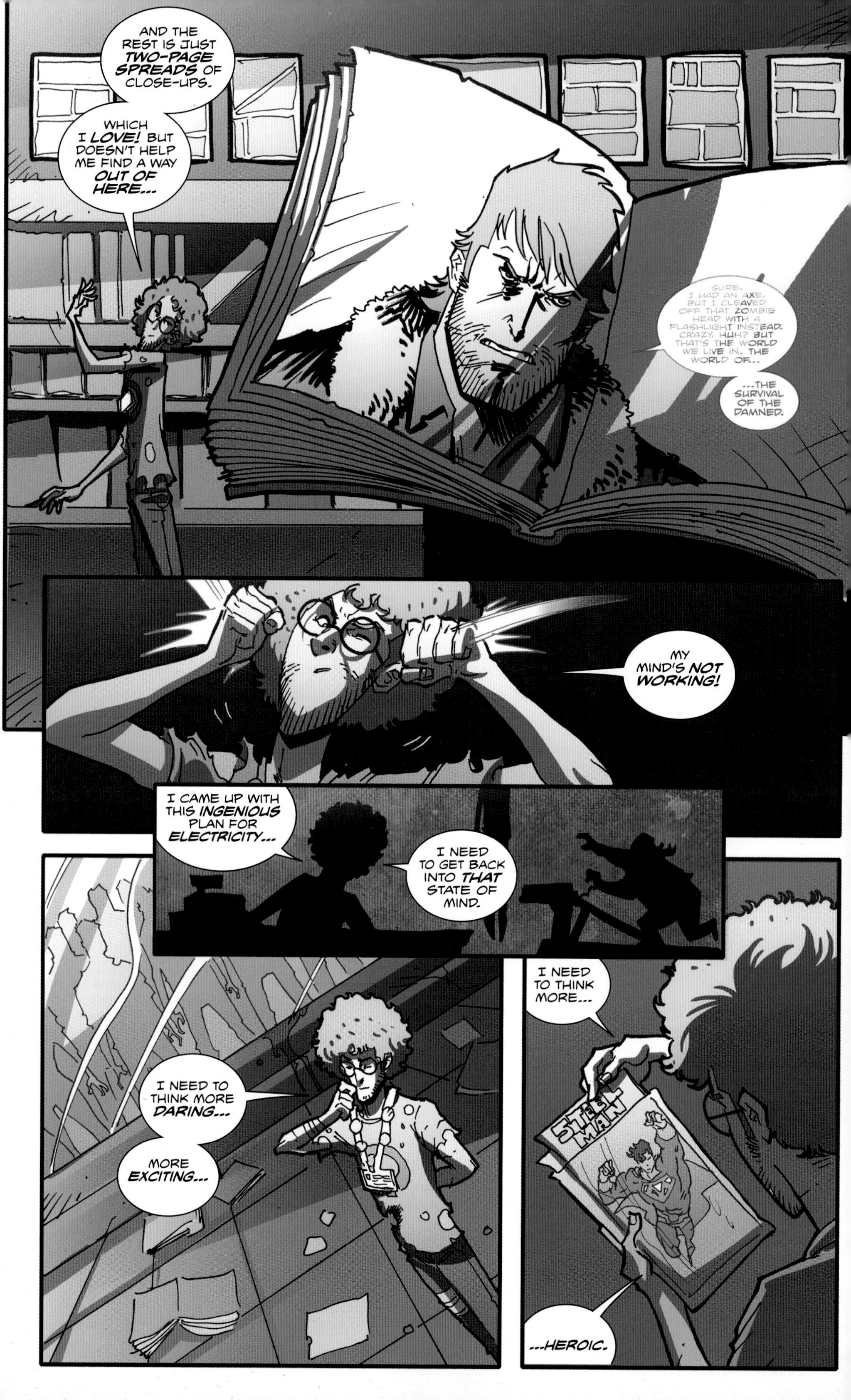
AND THE REST IS JUST TWO-PAGE SPREADS OF CLOSE-UPS.
WHICH I LOVE! BUT DOESN'T HELP ME FIND A WAY OUT OF HERE...
SURE, I HAD AN AXE, BUT I CLEAVED OFF THAT ZOMBIE HEAD WITH A FLASHLIGHT INSTEAD. CRAZY, HUH? BUT THAT'S THE WORLD WE LIVE IN. THE WORLD OF...
...THE SURVIVAL OF THE DAMNED.
MY MIND'S NOT WORKING!
I CAME UP WITH THIS INGENIOUS PLAN FOR ELECTRICITY...
I NEED TO GET BACK INTO THAT STATE OF MIND.
I NEED TO THINK MORE DARING...
MORE EXCITING...
I NEED TO THINK MORE...
...HEROIC.

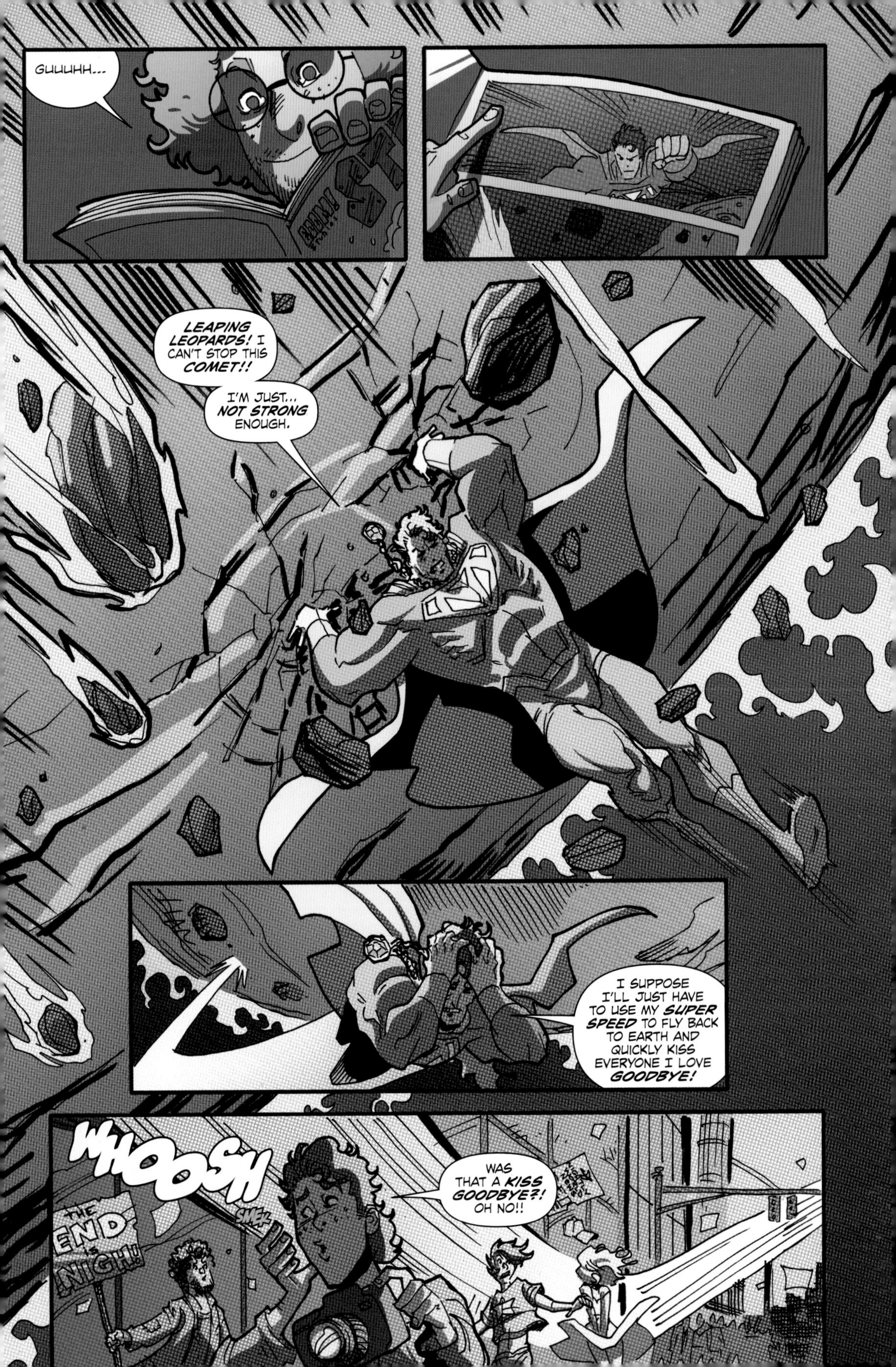
GUUUHH...
LEAPING LEOPARDS! I CAN'T STOP THIS COMET!!
I'M JUST... NOT STRONG ENOUGH.
I SUPPOSE I'LL JUST HAVE TO USE MY SUPER SPEED TO FLY BACK TO EARTH AND QUICKLY KISS EVERYONE I LOVE GOODBYE!
WHOOSH
THE END is NIGH!
SMEK
WAS THAT A KISS GOODBYE?! OH NO!!

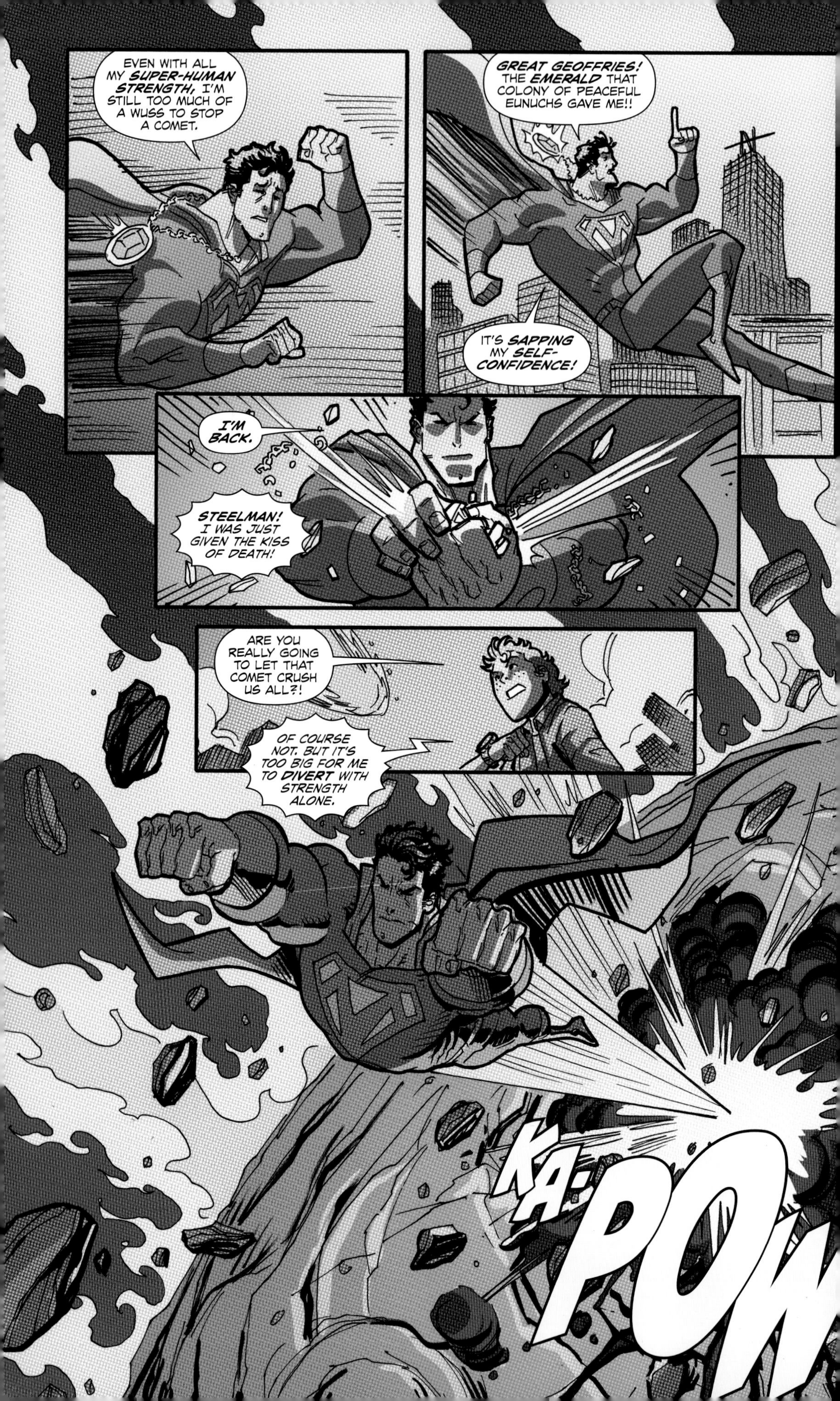

EVEN WITH ALL MY SUPER-HUMAN STRENGTH, I'M STILL TOO MUCH OF A WUSS TO STOP A COMET.
GREAT GEOFFRIES! THE EMERALD THAT COLONY OF PEACEFUL EUNUCHS GAVE ME!!
IT'S SAPPING MY SELF-CONFIDENCE!
I'M BACK.
STEELMAN! I WAS JUST GIVEN THE KISS OF DEATH!
ARE YOU REALLY GOING TO LET THAT COMET CRUSH US ALL?!
OF COURSE NOT. BUT IT'S TOO BIG FOR ME TO DIVERT WITH STRENGTH ALONE.
KA-POW

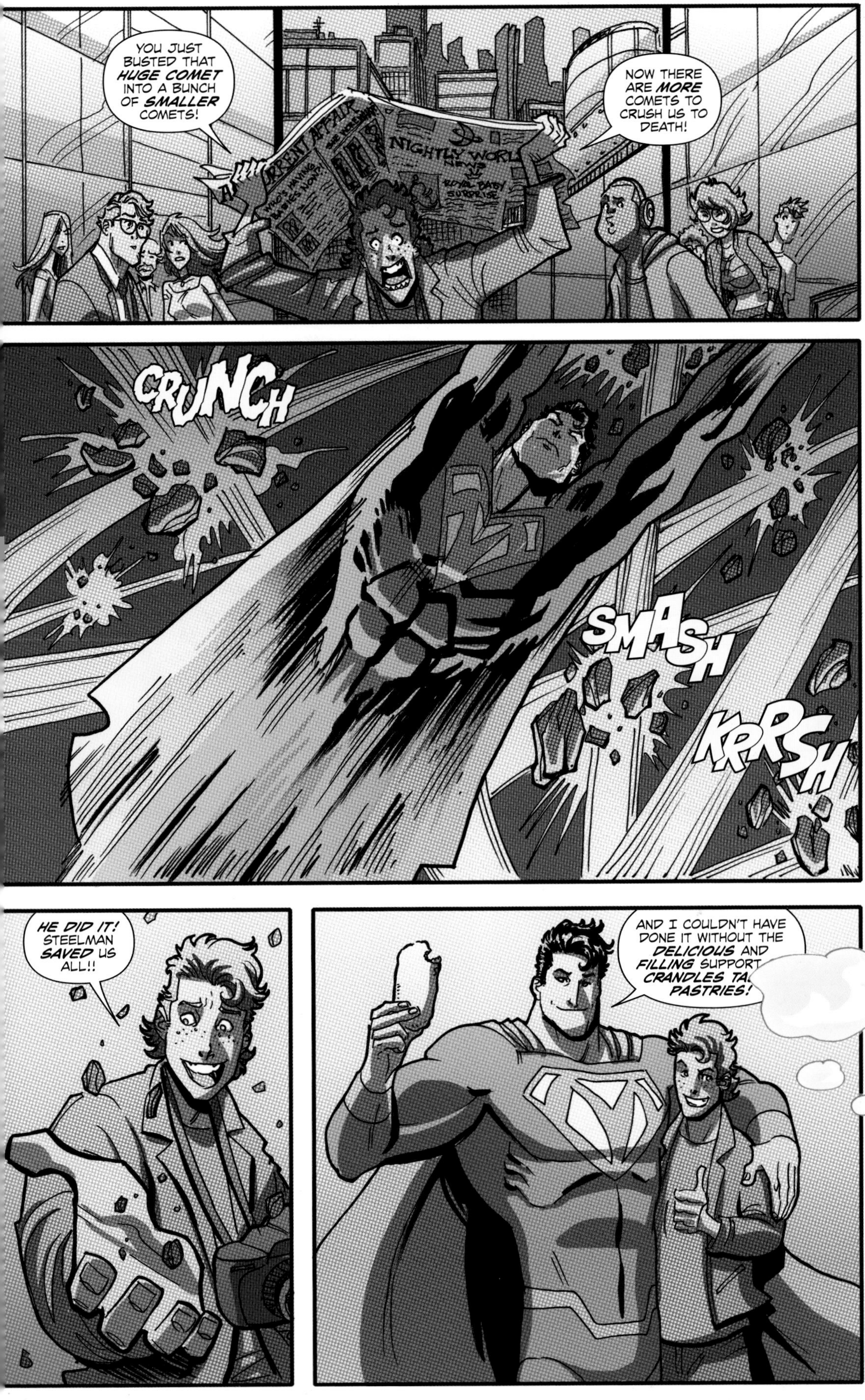
YOU JUST BUSTED THAT *HUGE COMET* INTO A BUNCH OF *SMALLER* COMETS!
NOW THERE ARE *MORE* COMETS TO CRUSH US TO DEATH!
CRUNCH
SMASH
KRRSH
HE DID IT! STEELMAN *SAVED* US ALL!!
AND I COULDN'T HAVE DONE IT WITHOUT THE *DELICIOUS* AND *FILLING* SUPPORT
CRANDLES TA
PASTRIES!

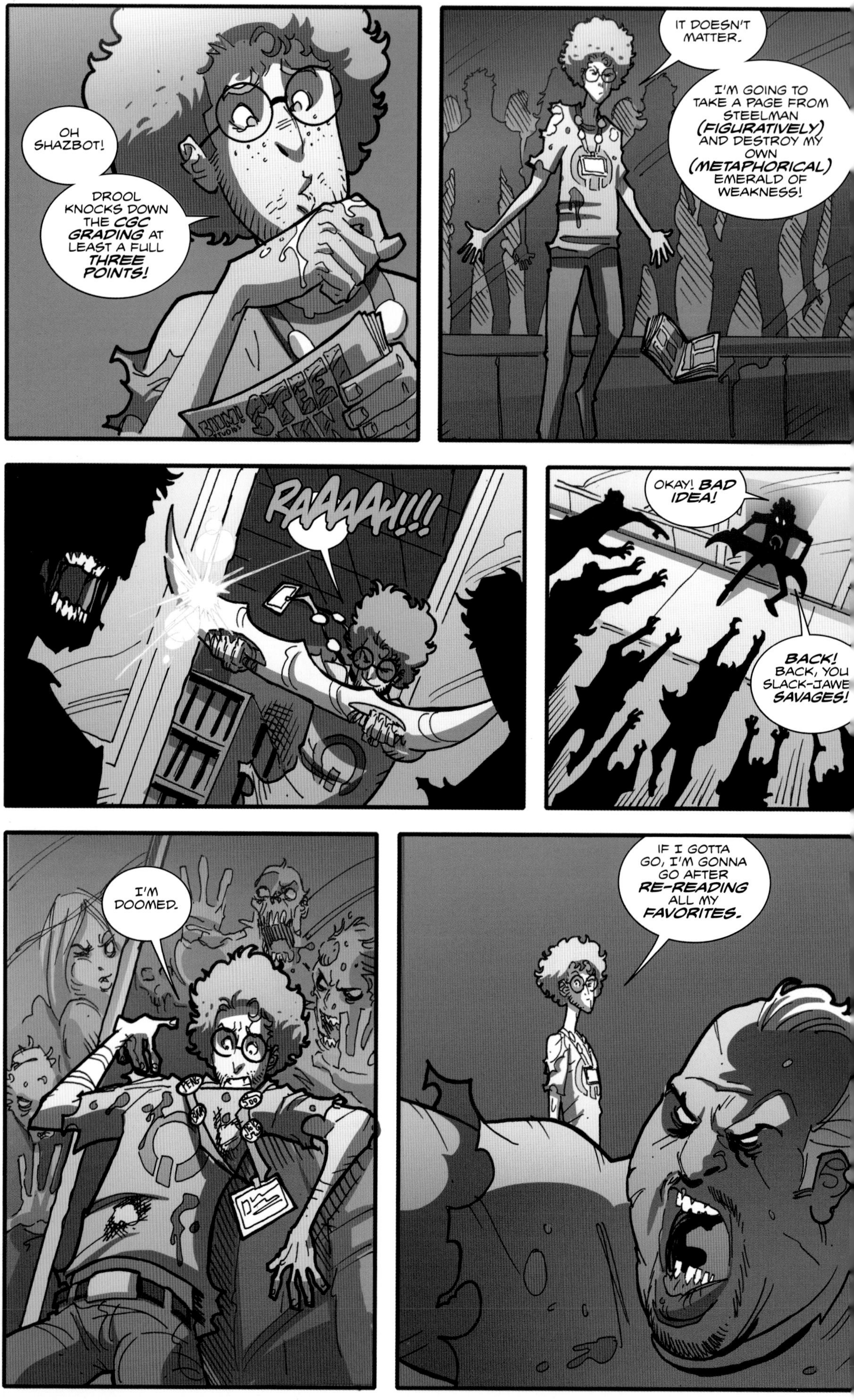

OH SHAZBOT!
DROOL KNOCKS DOWN THE CGC GRADING AT LEAST A FULL THREE POINTS!
IT DOESN'T MATTER.
I'M GOING TO TAKE A PAGE FROM STEELMAN (FIGURATIVELY) AND DESTROY MY OWN (METAPHORICAL) EMERALD OF WEAKNESS!
RAAAAH!!!
OKAY! BAD IDEA!
BACK! BACK, YOU SLACK-JAWE SAVAGES!
I'M DOOMED.
IF I GOTTA GO, I'M GONNA GO AFTER RE-READING ALL MY FAVORITES.

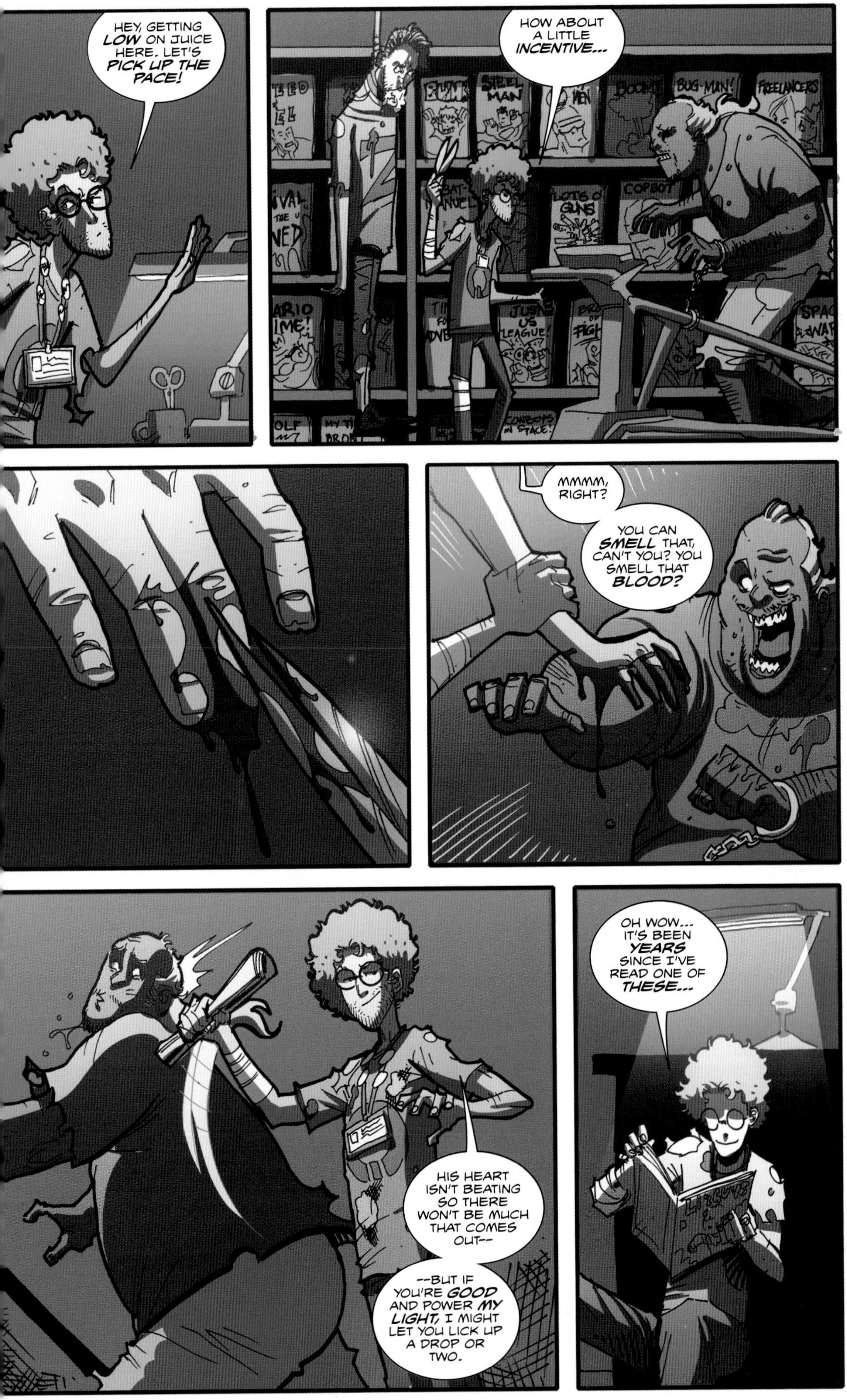

HEY, GETTING LOW ON JUICE HERE. LET'S PICK UP THE PACE!
HOW ABOUT A LITTLE INCENTIVE...
MMMM, RIGHT?
YOU CAN SMELL THAT, CAN'T YOU? YOU SMELL THAT BLOOD?
HIS HEART ISN'T BEATING SO THERE WON'T BE MUCH THAT COMES OUT--
--BUT IF YOU'RE GOOD AND POWER MY LIGHT, I MIGHT LET YOU LICK UP A DROP OR TWO.
OH WOW... IT'S BEEN YEARS SINCE I'VE READ ONE OF THESE...

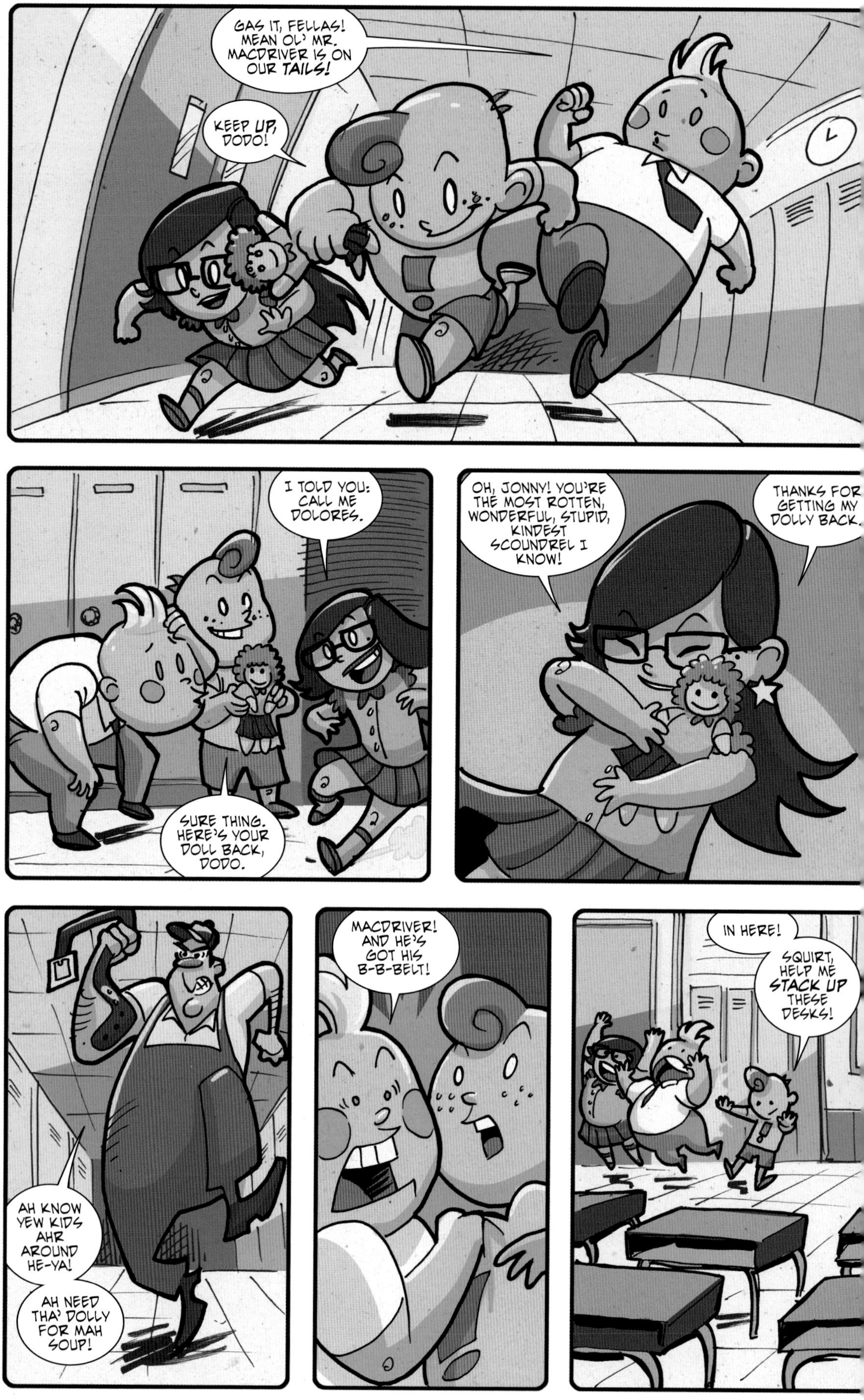
GAS IT, FELLAS! MEAN OL' MR. MACDRIVER IS ON OUR TAILS!
KEEP UP, DODO!
I TOLD YOU: CALL ME DOLORES.
SURE THING. HERE'S YOUR DOLL BACK, DODO.
OH, JONNY! YOU'RE THE MOST ROTTEN, WONDERFUL, STUPID, KINDEST SCOUNDREL I KNOW!
THANKS FOR GETTING MY DOLLY BACK.
AH KNOW YEW KIDS AHR AROUND HE-YA!
AH NEED THA' DOLLY FOR MAH SOUP!
MACDRIVER! AND HE'S GOT HIS B-B-BELT!
IN HERE!
SQUIRT, HELP ME STACK UP THESE DESKS!

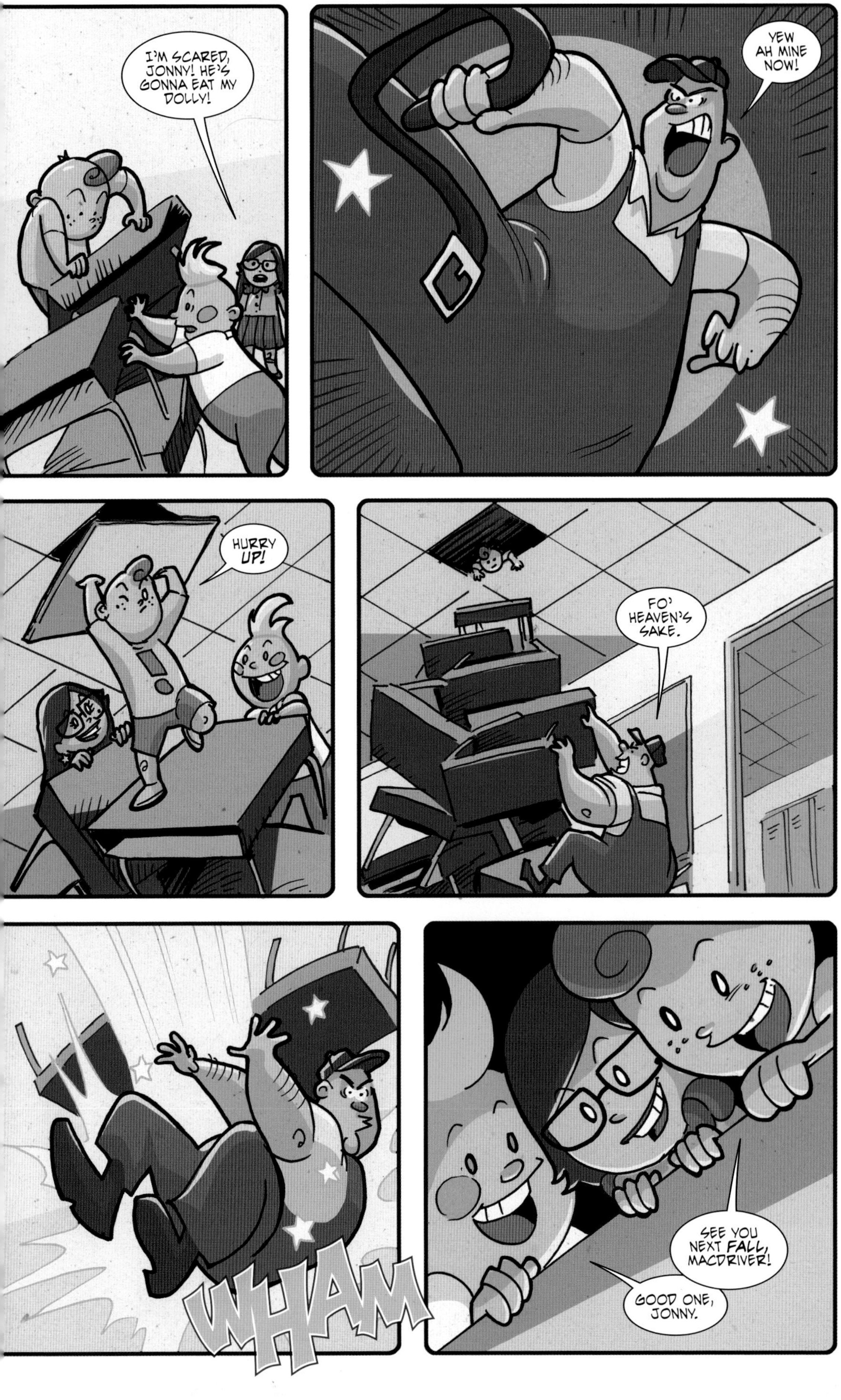
I'M SCARED, JONNY! HE'S GONNA EAT MY DOLLY!
YEW AH MINE NOW!
HURRY UP!
FO' HEAVEN'S SAKE.
WHAM
SEE YOU NEXT FALL, MACDRIVER!
GOOD ONE, JONNY.

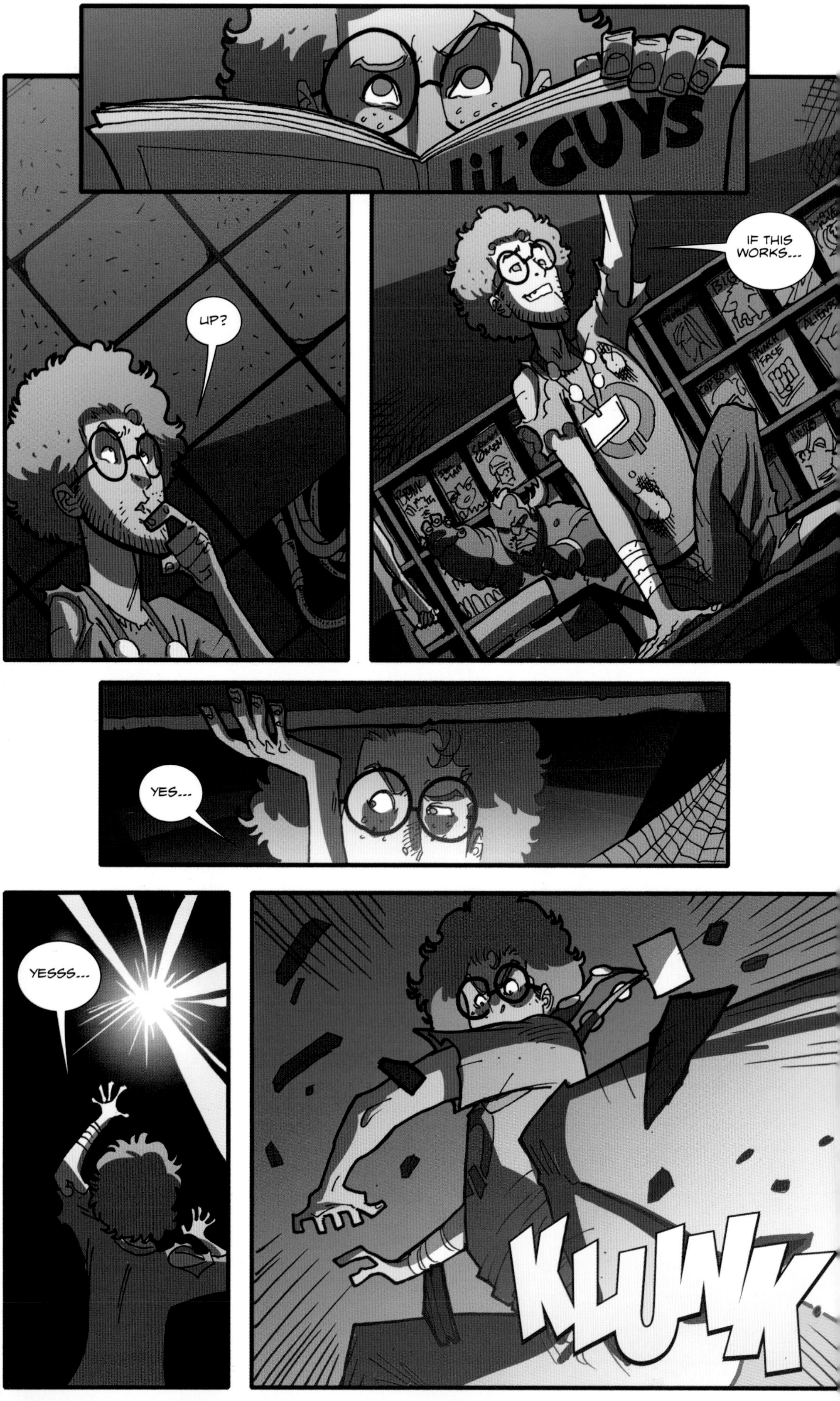
LIL' GUYS
UP?
IF THIS WORKS...
YES...
YESSS...
KLUNK

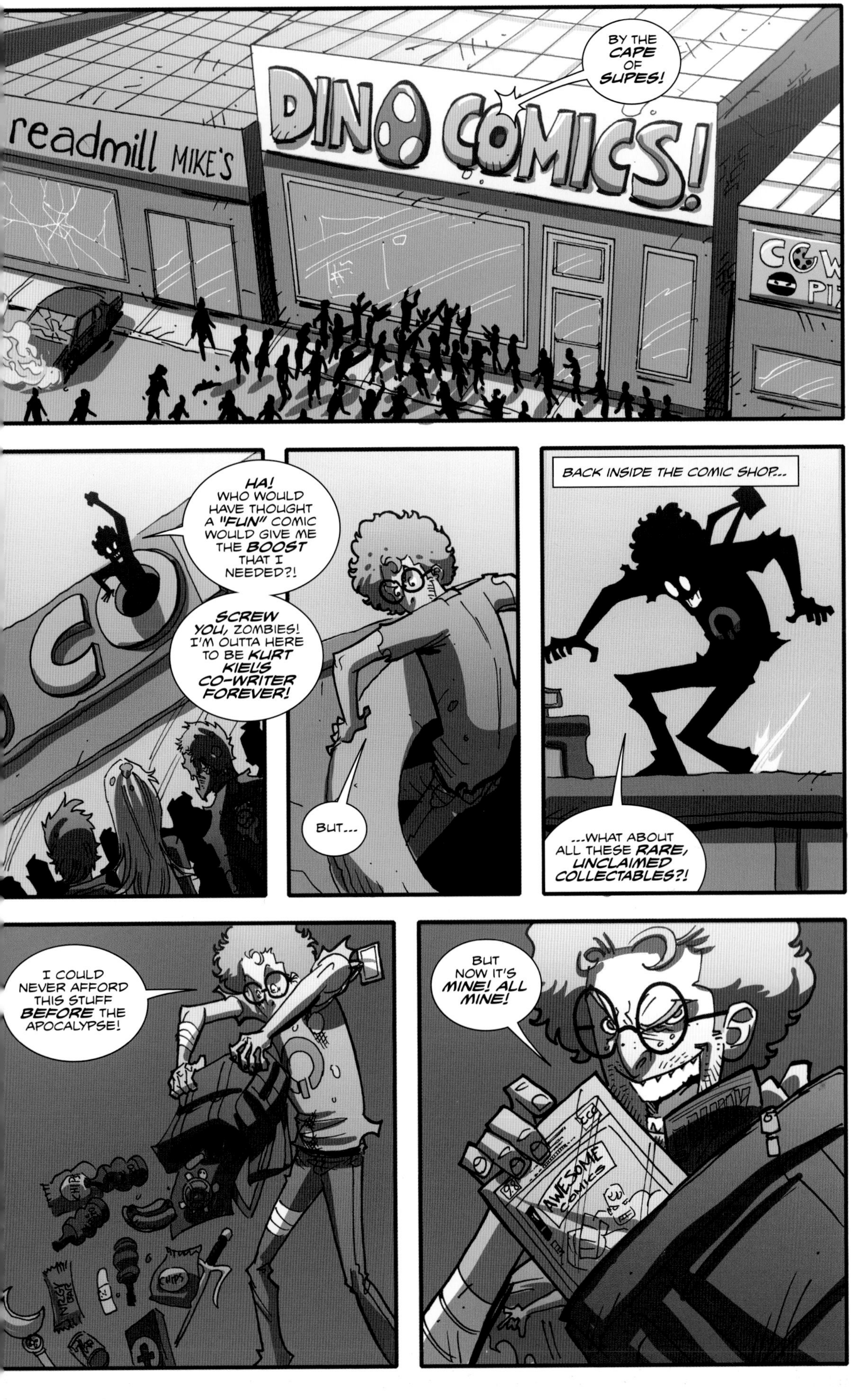
BY THE CAPE OF SUPES!
readmill MIKE'S
DINO COMICS!
HA! WHO WOULD HAVE THOUGHT A "FUN" COMIC WOULD GIVE ME THE BOOST THAT I NEEDED?!
SCREW YOU, ZOMBIES! I'M OUTTA HERE TO BE KURT KIEL'S CO-WRITER FOREVER!
BUT...
BACK INSIDE THE COMIC SHOP...
...WHAT ABOUT ALL THESE RARE, UNCLAIMED COLLECTABLES?!
I COULD NEVER AFFORD THIS STUFF BEFORE THE APOCALYPSE!
CHIPS
BUT NOW IT'S MINE! ALL MINE!
AWESOME COMICS

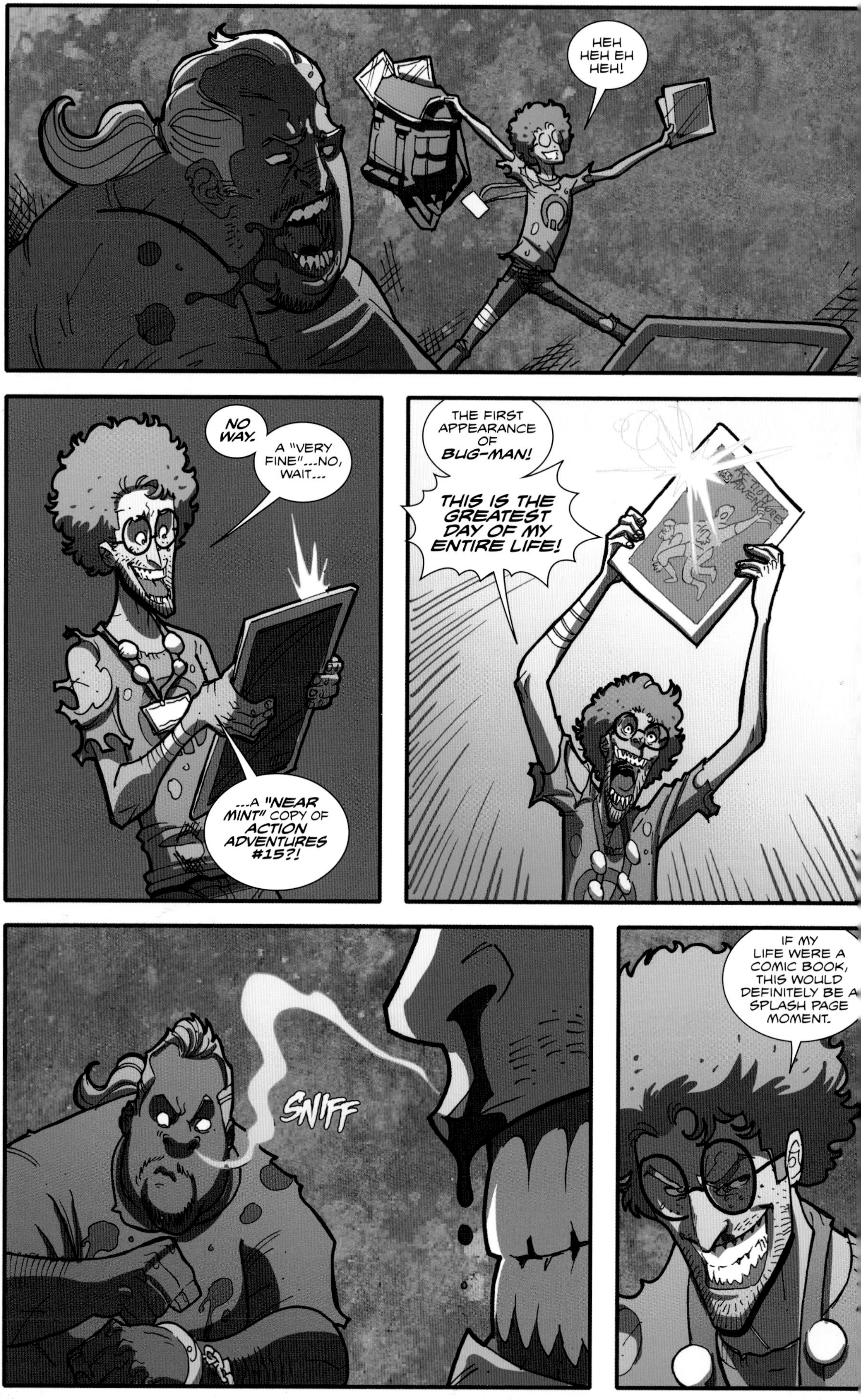
HEH HEH EH HEH!
NO WAY.
A "VERY FINE"...NO, WAIT...
...A "NEAR MINT" COPY OF ACTION ADVENTURES #15?!
THE FIRST APPEARANCE OF BUG-MAN!
THIS IS THE GREATEST DAY OF MY ENTIRE LIFE!
SNIFF
IF MY LIFE WERE A COMIC BOOK, THIS WOULD DEFINITELY BE A SPLASH PAGE MOMENT.

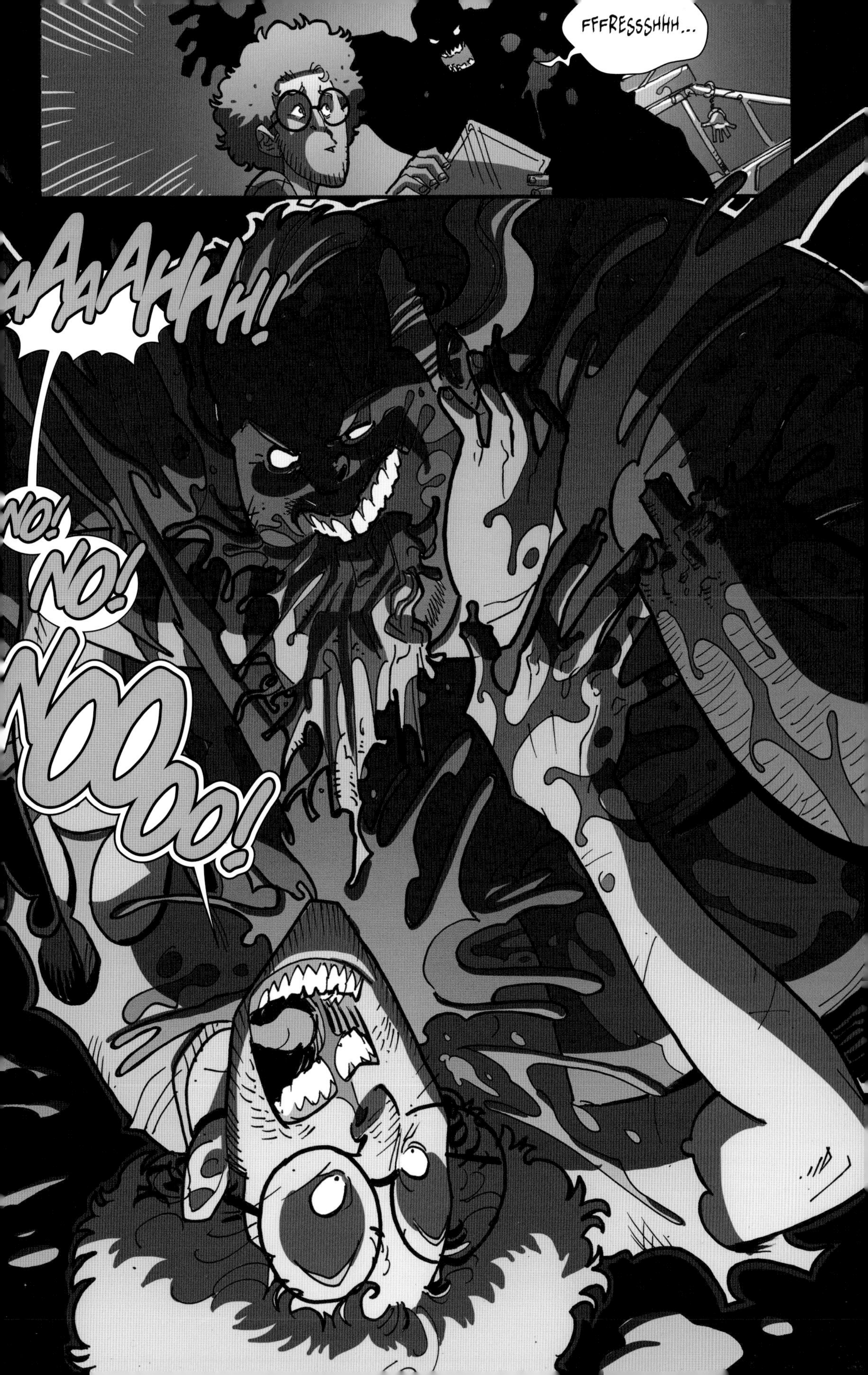
FFFRESSSHHH...
AAAAAHHH!
NO!
NO!
NOOOOO!

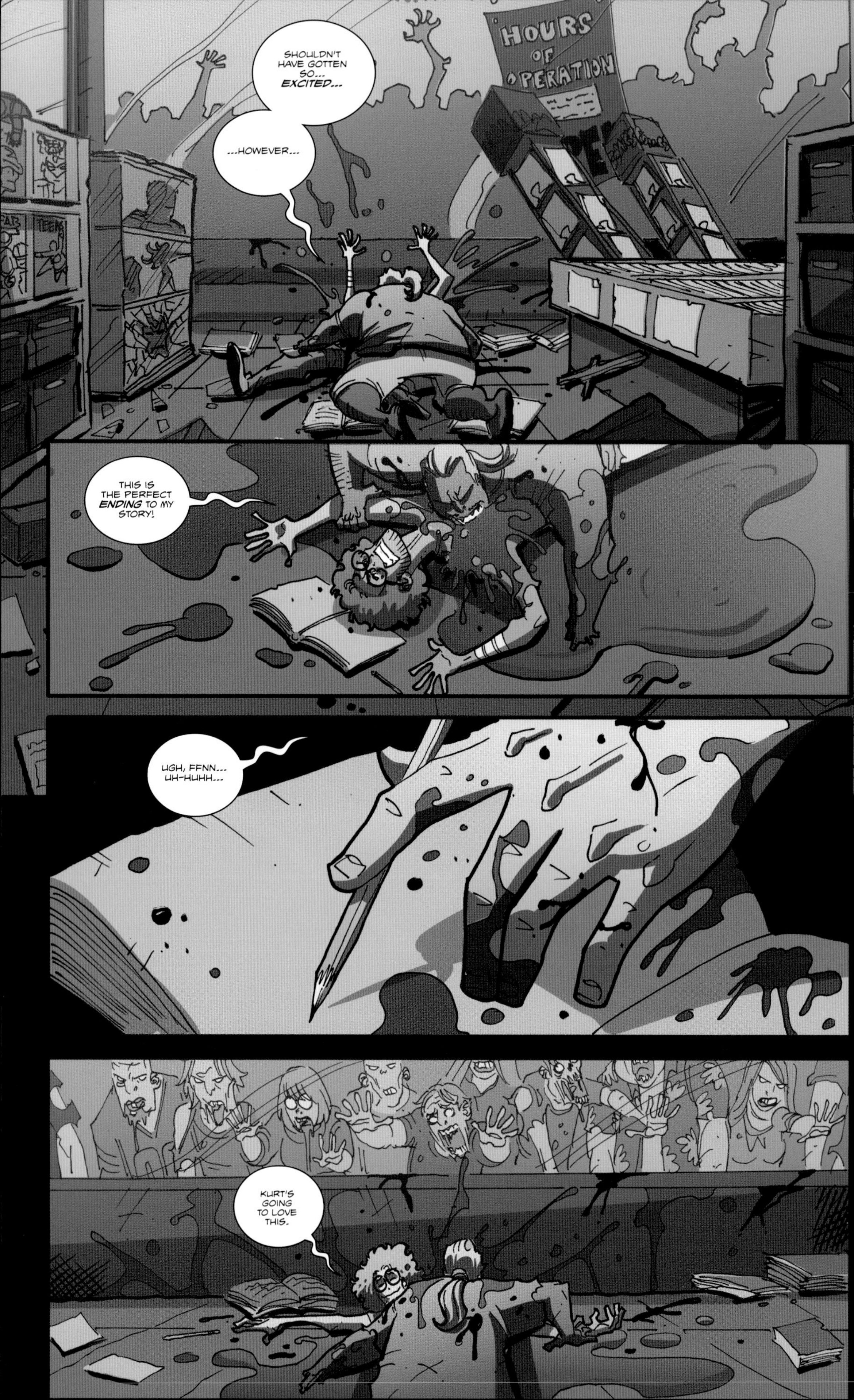
SHOULDN'T HAVE GOTTEN SO... EXCITED...
...HOWEVER...
HOURS OF OPERATION
THIS IS THE PERFECT ENDING TO MY STORY!
UGH, FFNN... UH-HUHH...
KURT'S GOING TO LOVE THIS.

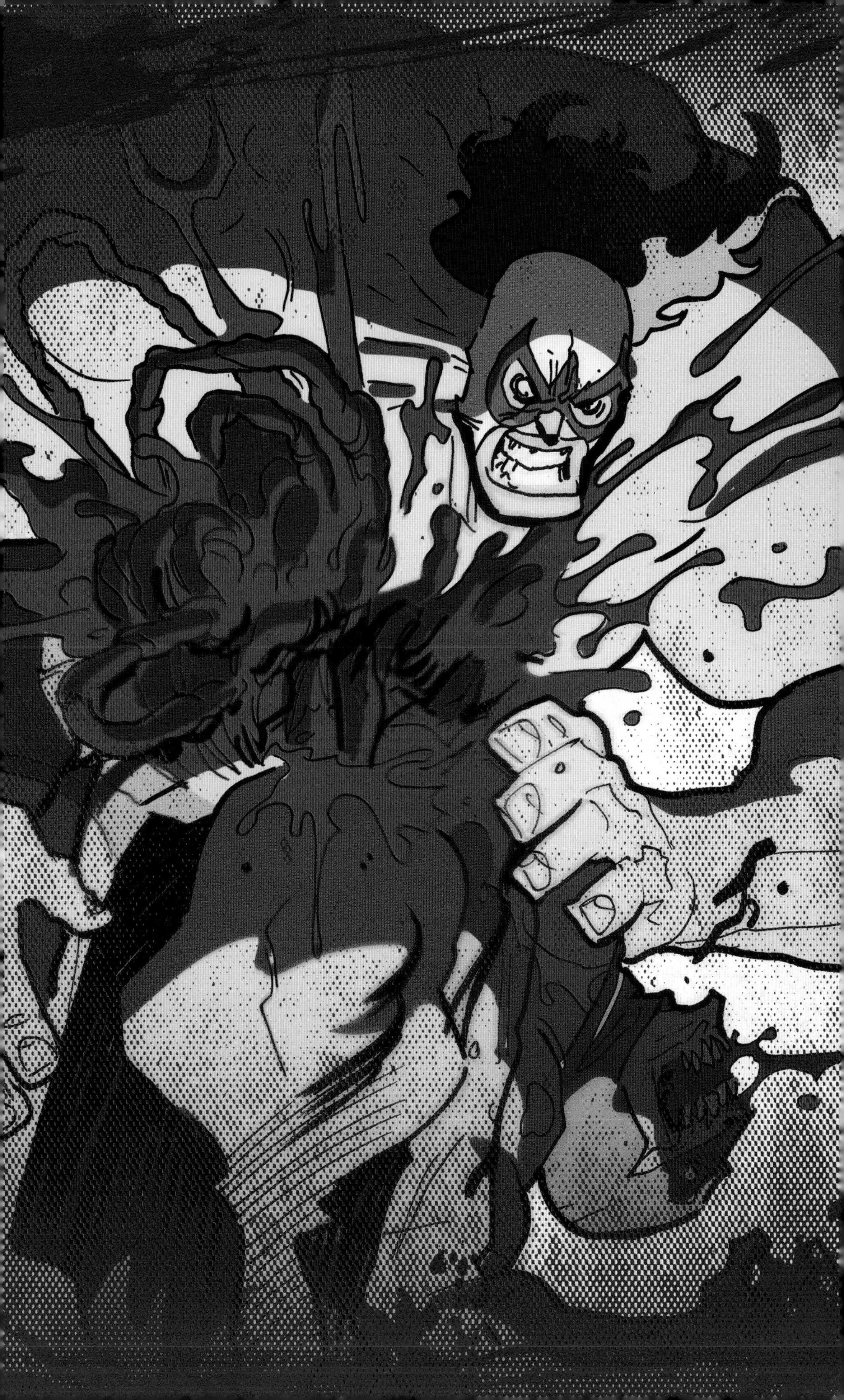

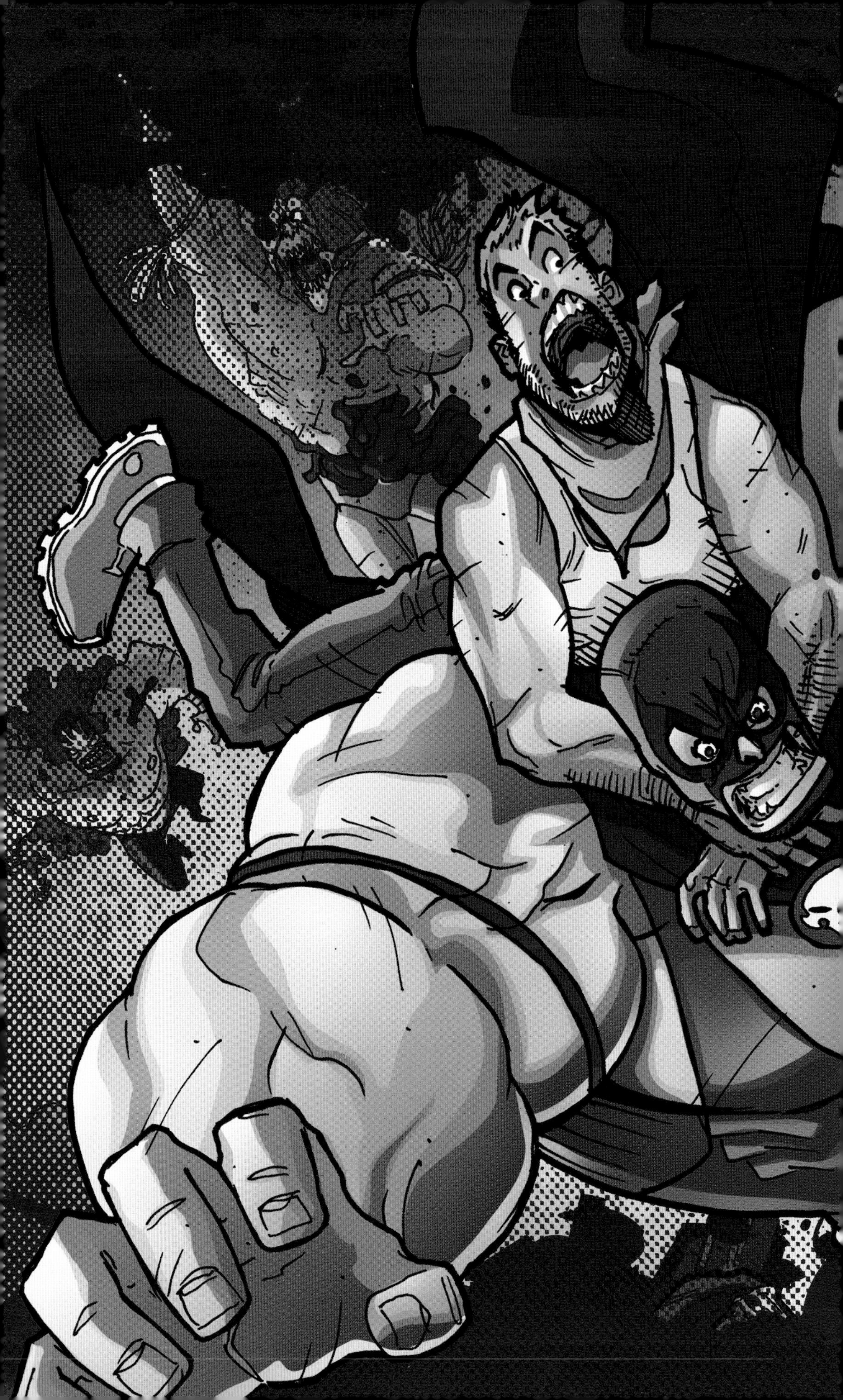

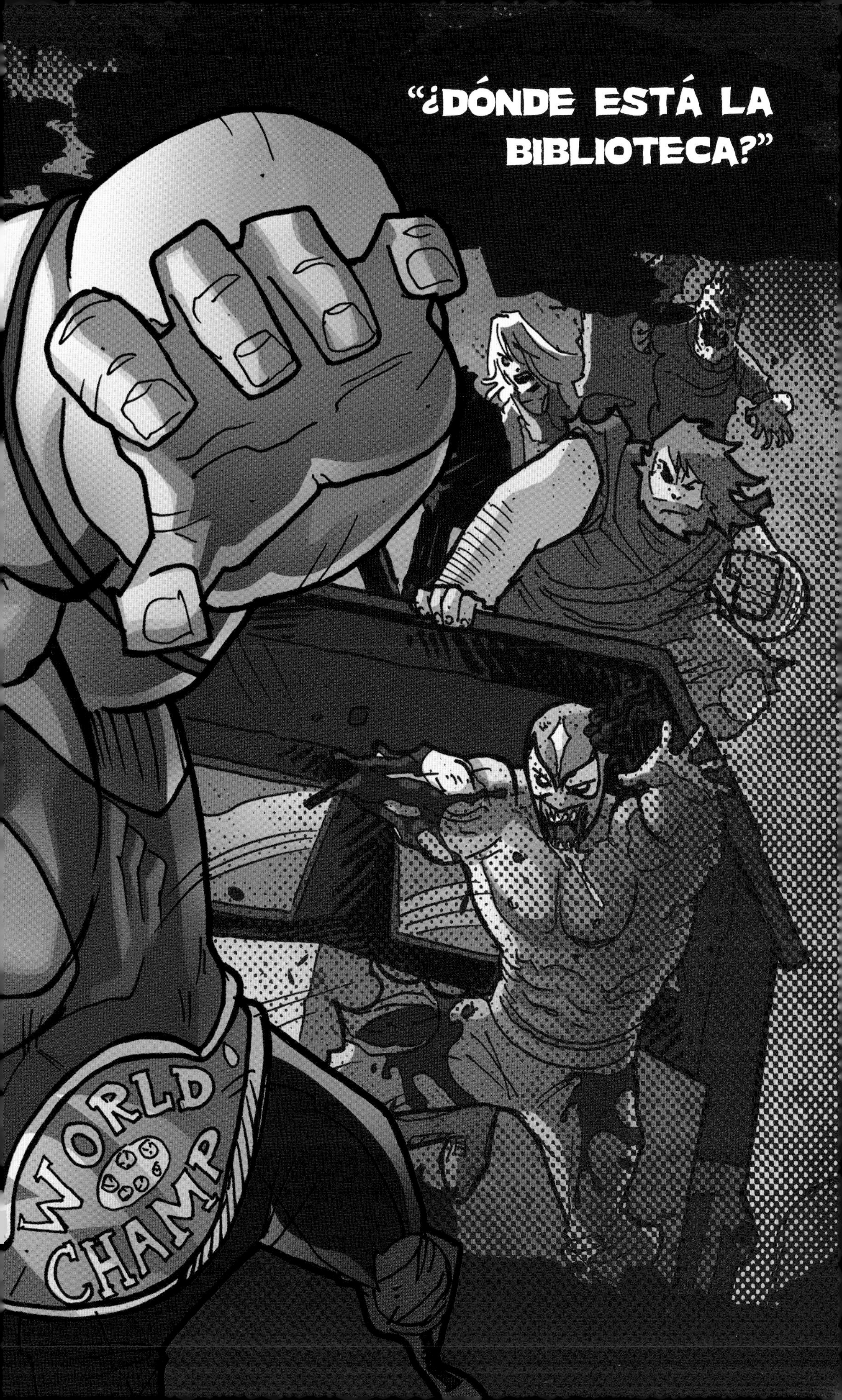
“¿DÓNDE ESTÁ LA BIBLIOTECA?”
WORLD CHAMP

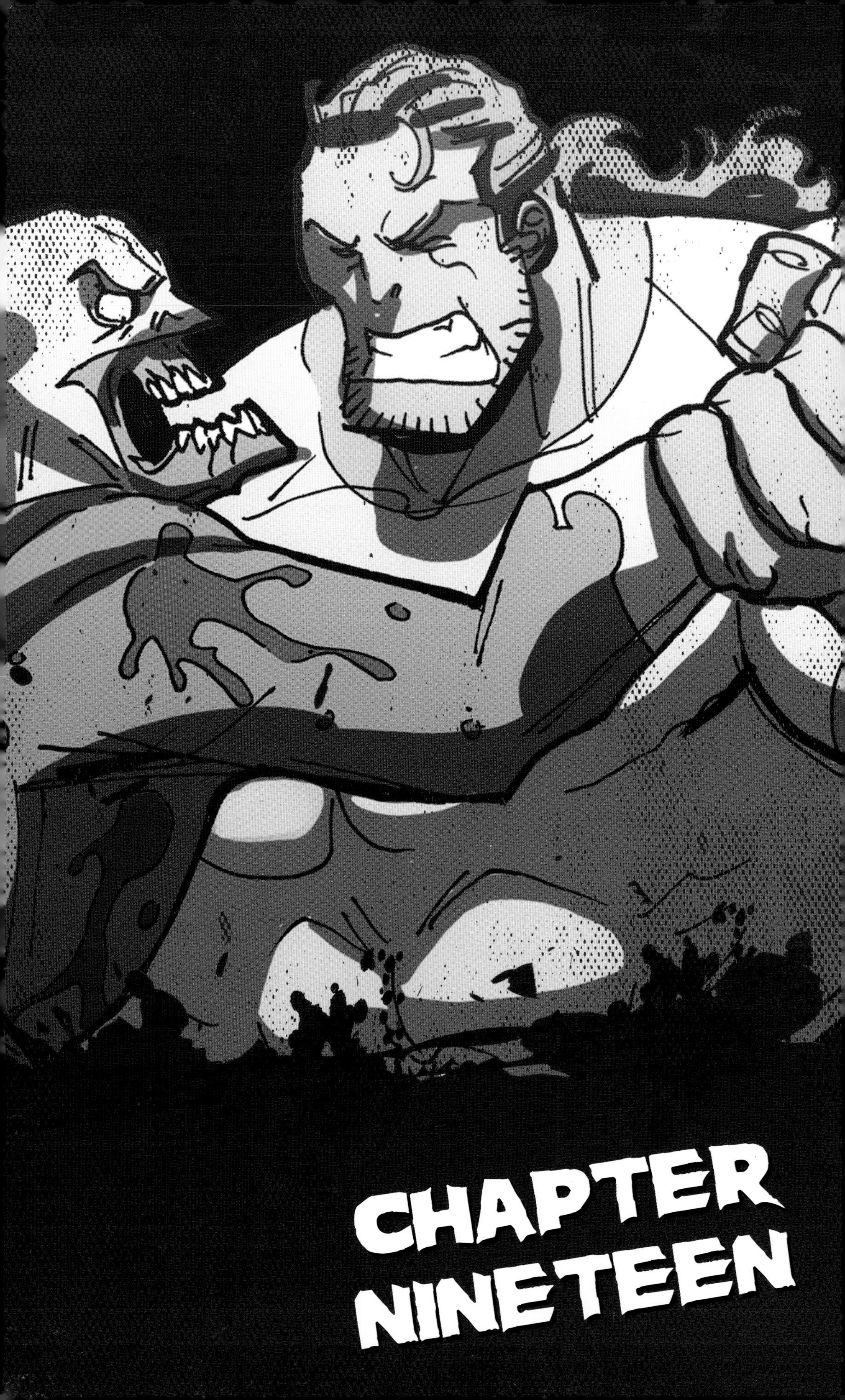

CHAPTER NINETEEN

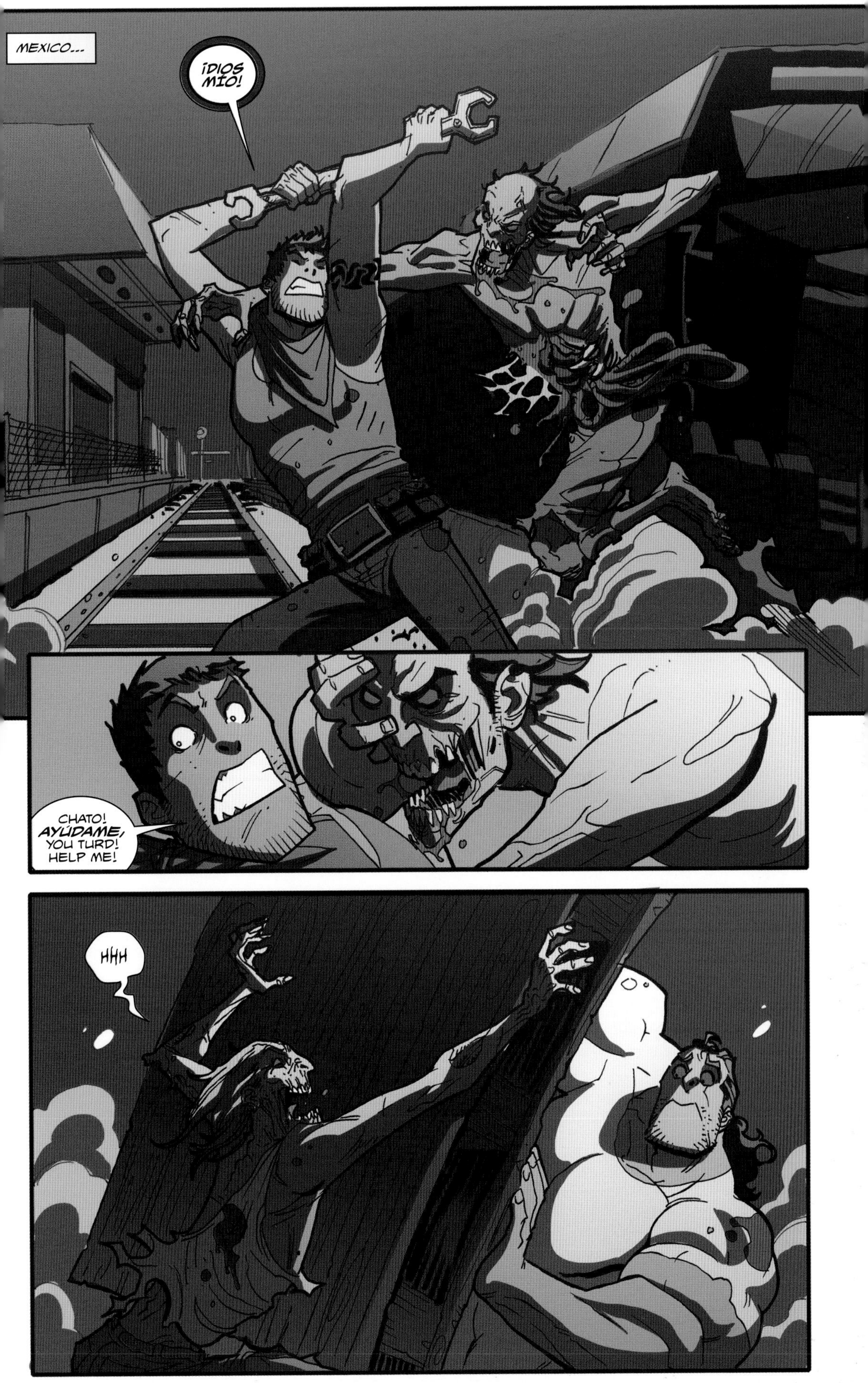

MEXICO...
¡DIOS MÍO!
CHATO! AYÚDAME, YOU TURD! HELP ME!
HHH

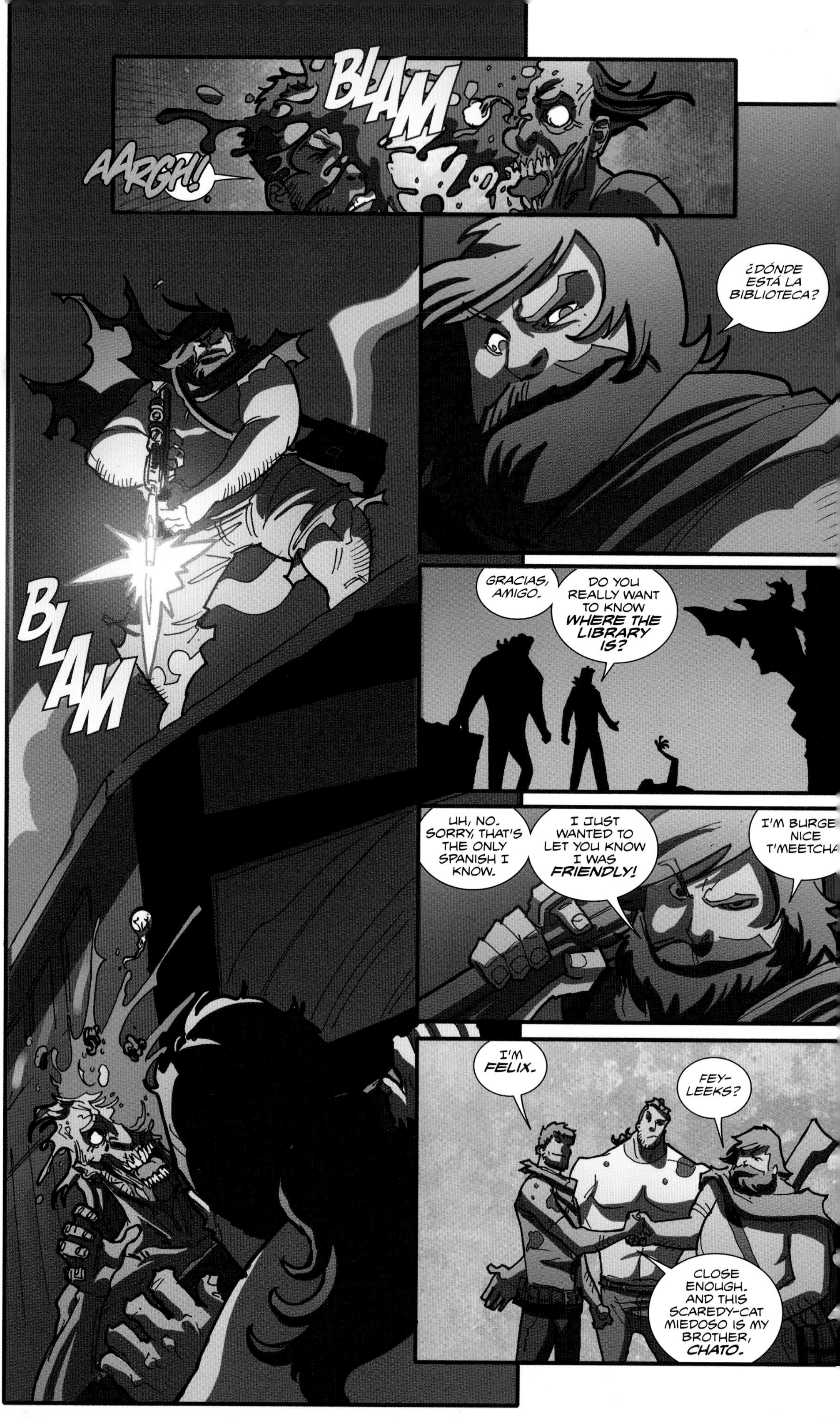

BLAM
AARGH!
BLAM
¿DÓNDE ESTÁ LA BIBLIOTECA?
GRACIAS, AMIGO.
DO YOU REALLY WANT TO KNOW WHERE THE LIBRARY IS?
UH, NO. SORRY, THAT'S THE ONLY SPANISH I KNOW.
I JUST WANTED TO LET YOU KNOW I WAS FRIENDLY!
I'M BURGE
NICE T'MEETCHA
I'M FELIX.
FEY-LEEKS?
CLOSE ENOUGH. AND THIS SCAREDY-CAT MIEDOSO IS MY BROTHER, CHATO.

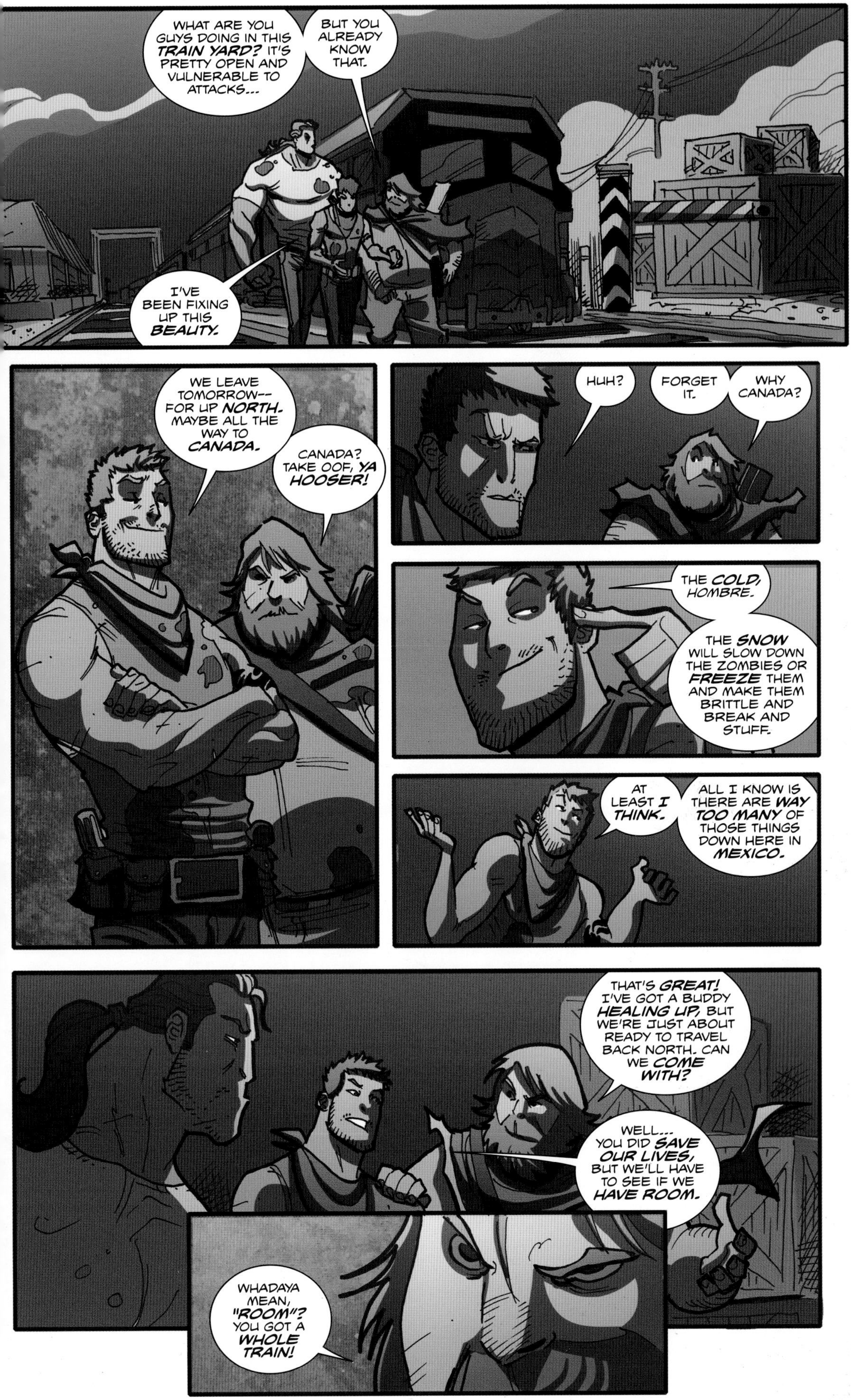
WHAT ARE YOU GUYS DOING IN THIS TRAIN YARD? IT'S PRETTY OPEN AND VULNERABLE TO ATTACKS...
BUT YOU ALREADY KNOW THAT.
I'VE BEEN FIXING UP THIS BEAUTY.
WE LEAVE TOMORROW-- FOR UP NORTH. MAYBE ALL THE WAY TO CANADA.
CANADA? TAKE OOF, YA HOOSER!
HUH?
FORGET IT.
WHY CANADA?
THE COLD, HOMBRE.
THE SNOW WILL SLOW DOWN THE ZOMBIES OR FREEZE THEM AND MAKE THEM BRITTLE AND BREAK AND STUFF.
AT LEAST I THINK.
ALL I KNOW IS THERE ARE WAY TOO MANY OF THOSE THINGS DOWN HERE IN MEXICO.
THAT'S GREAT! I'VE GOT A BUDDY HEALING UP, BUT WE'RE JUST ABOUT READY TO TRAVEL BACK NORTH. CAN WE COME WITH?
WELL... YOU DID SAVE OUR LIVES, BUT WE'LL HAVE TO SEE IF WE HAVE ROOM.
WHADAYA MEAN, "ROOM"? YOU GOT A WHOLE TRAIN!

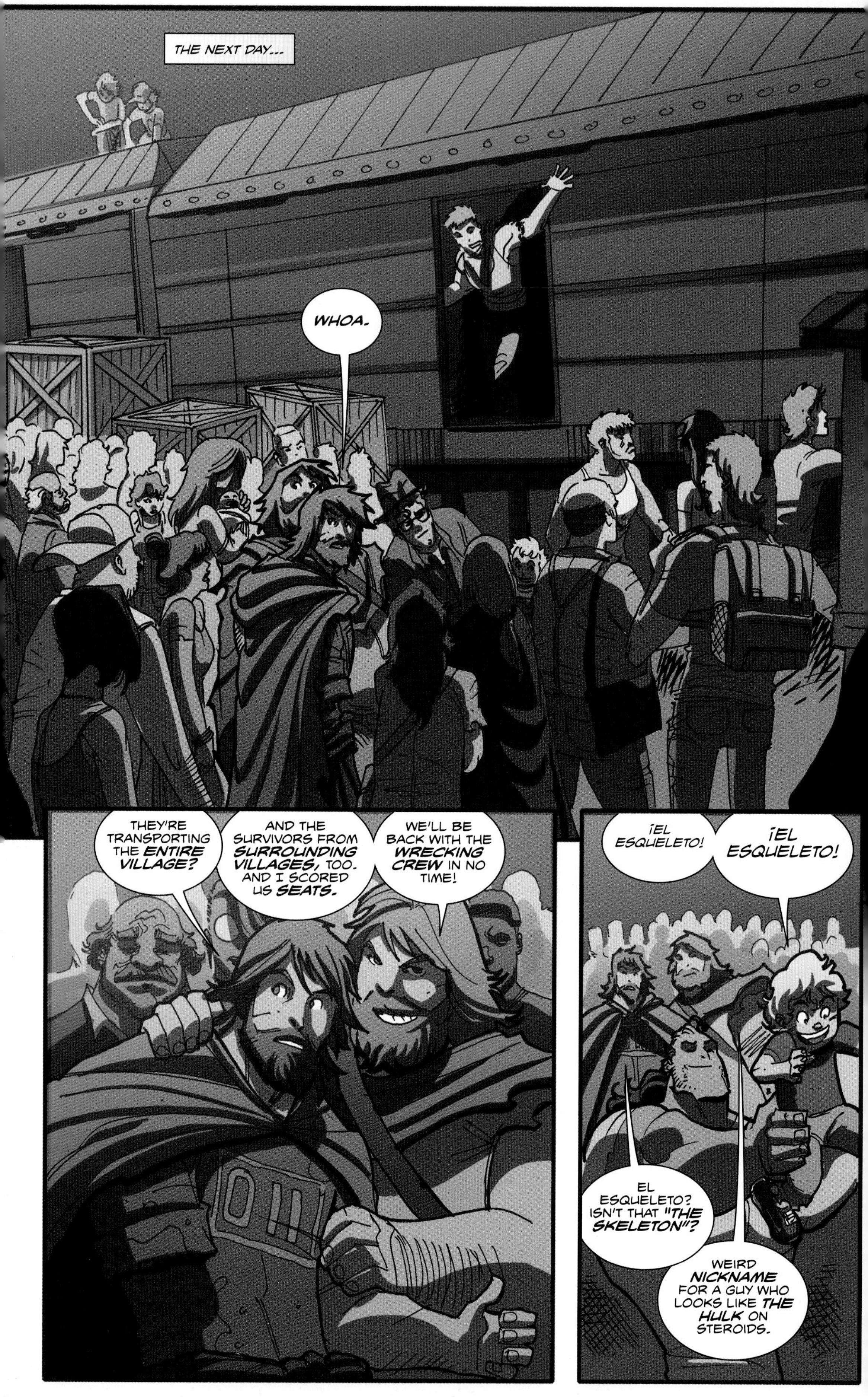
THE NEXT DAY...
WHOA.
THEY'RE TRANSPORTING THE ENTIRE VILLAGE?
AND THE SURVIVORS FROM SURROUNDING VILLAGES, TOO. AND I SCORED US SEATS.
WE'LL BE BACK WITH THE WRECKING CREW IN NO TIME!
¡EL ESQUELETO!
¡EL ESQUELETO!
EL ESQUELETO? ISN'T THAT "THE SKELETON"?
WEIRD NICKNAME FOR A GUY WHO LOOKS LIKE THE HULK ON STEROIDS.

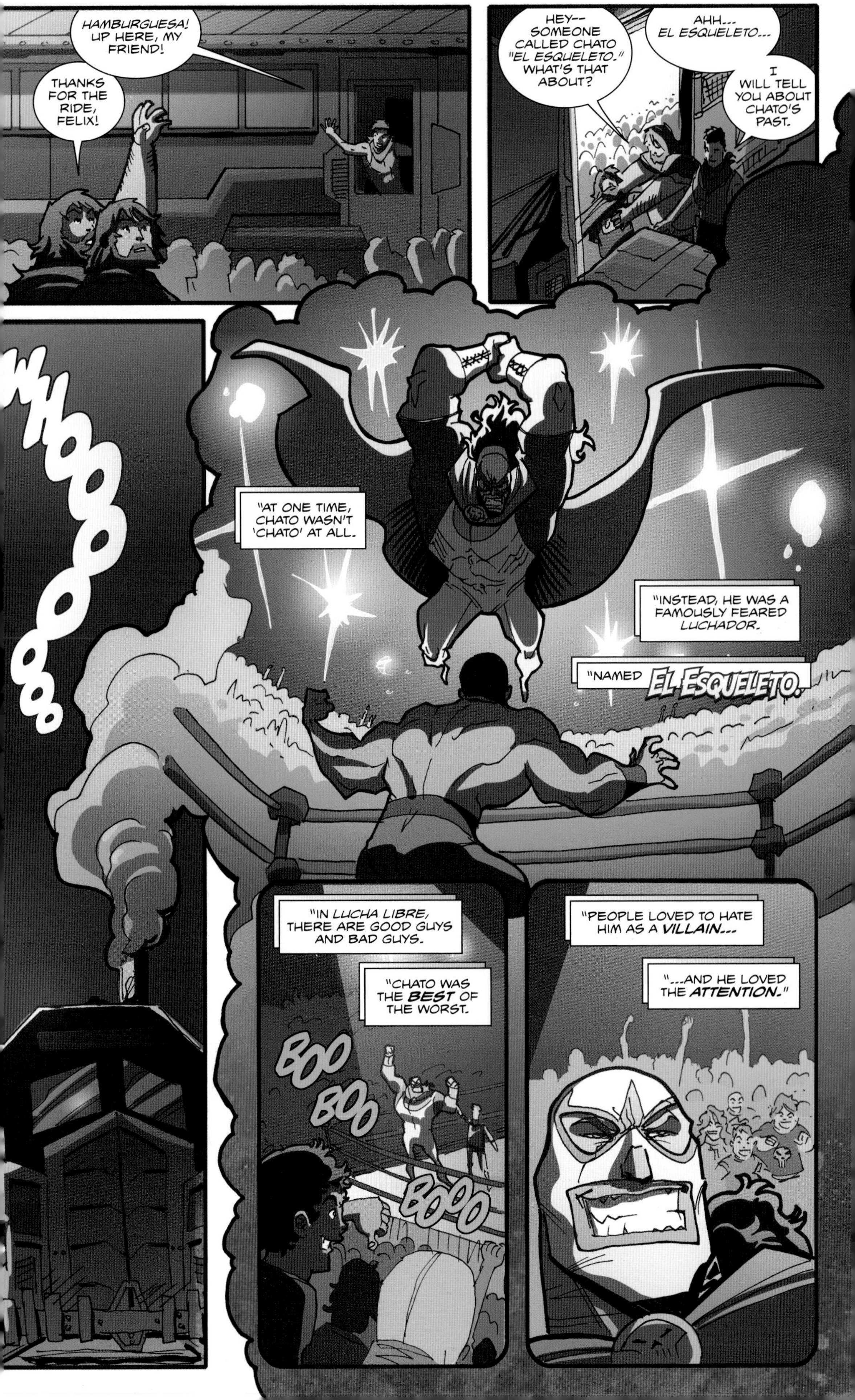
HAMBURGUESA! UP HERE, MY FRIEND!
THANKS FOR THE RIDE, FELIX!
HEY-- SOMEONE CALLED CHATO "EL ESQUELETO." WHAT'S THAT ABOUT?
AHH... EL ESQUELETO...
I WILL TELL YOU ABOUT CHATO'S PAST.
WHOOOOOOOOOO
"AT ONE TIME, CHATO WASN'T 'CHATO' AT ALL.
"INSTEAD, HE WAS A FAMOUSLY FEARED LUCHADOR.
"NAMED EL ESQUELETO.
"IN LUCHA LIBRE, THERE ARE GOOD GUYS AND BAD GUYS.
"CHATO WAS THE BEST OF THE WORST.
BOO
BOO
BOOO
"PEOPLE LOVED TO HATE HIM AS A VILLAIN...
"...AND HE LOVED THE ATTENTION."

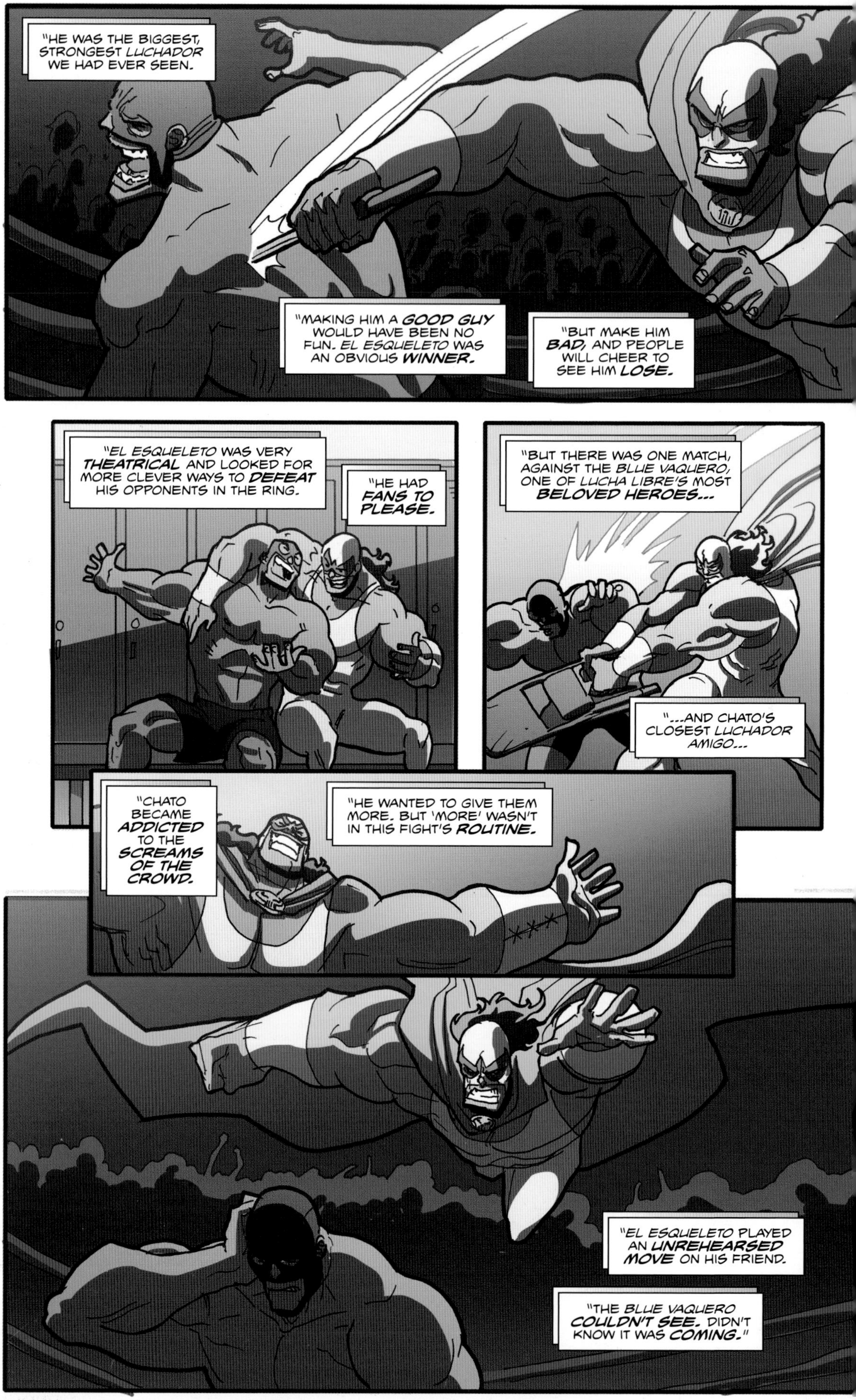
"HE WAS THE BIGGEST, STRONGEST LUCHADOR WE HAD EVER SEEN.
"MAKING HIM A GOOD GUY WOULD HAVE BEEN NO FUN. EL ESQUELETO WAS AN OBVIOUS WINNER.
"BUT MAKE HIM BAD, AND PEOPLE WILL CHEER TO SEE HIM LOSE.
"EL ESQUELETO WAS VERY THEATRICAL AND LOOKED FOR MORE CLEVER WAYS TO DEFEAT HIS OPPONENTS IN THE RING.
"HE HAD FANS TO PLEASE.
"BUT THERE WAS ONE MATCH, AGAINST THE BLUE VAQUERO, ONE OF LUCHA LIBRE'S MOST BELOVED HEROES...
"...AND CHATO'S CLOSEST LUCHADOR AMIGO...
"CHATO BECAME ADDICTED TO THE SCREAMS OF THE CROWD.
"HE WANTED TO GIVE THEM MORE. BUT 'MORE' WASN'T IN THIS FIGHT'S ROUTINE.
"EL ESQUELETO PLAYED AN UNREHEARSED MOVE ON HIS FRIEND.
"THE BLUE VAQUERO COULDN'T SEE. DIDN'T KNOW IT WAS COMING."

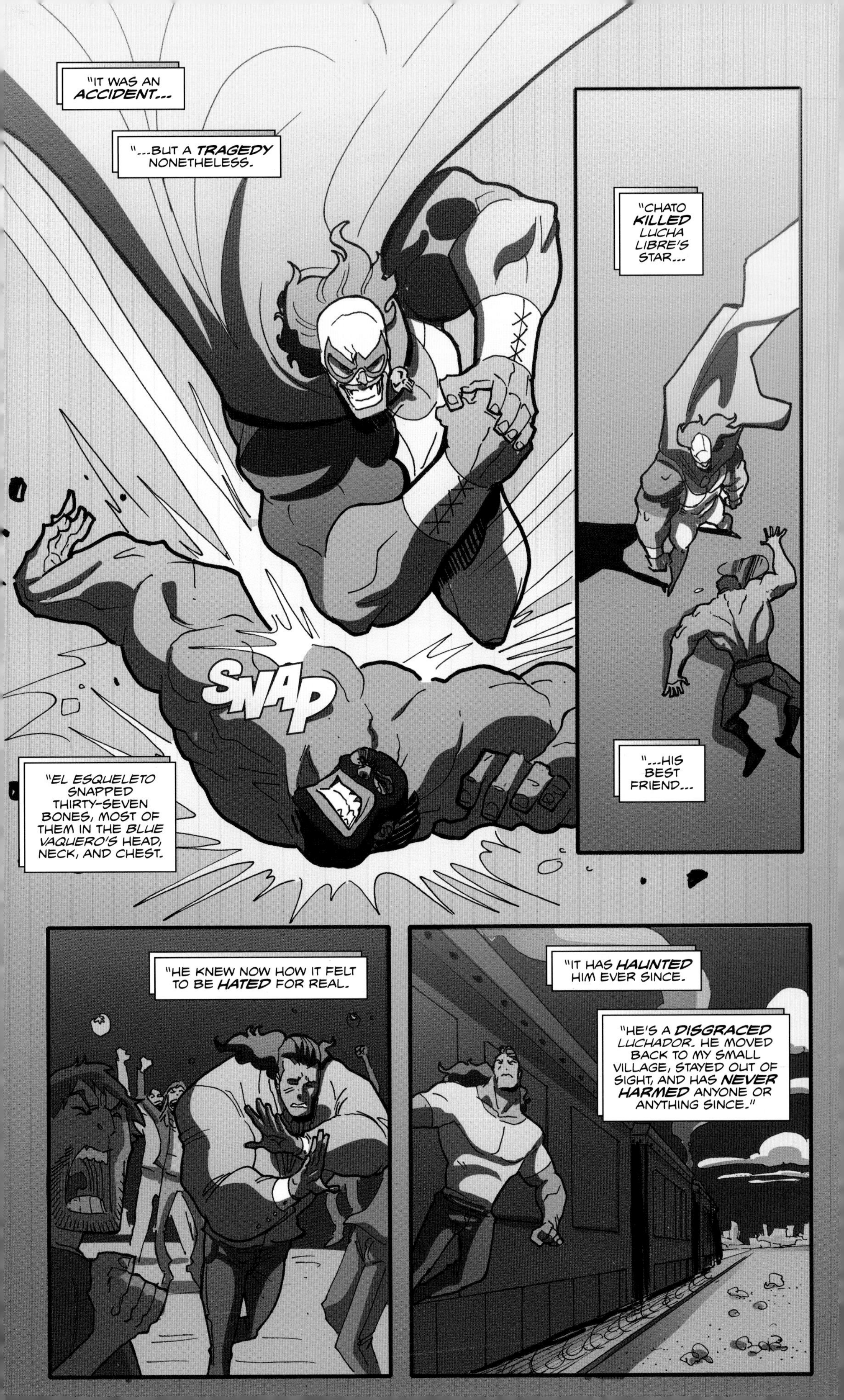
"IT WAS AN *ACCIDENT*...
"...BUT A *TRAGEDY* NONETHELESS.
SNAP
"*EL ESQUELETO* SNAPPED THIRTY-SEVEN BONES, MOST OF THEM IN THE *BLUE VAQUERO'S* HEAD, NECK, AND CHEST.
"CHATO **KILLED** *LUCHA LIBRE'S* STAR...
"...HIS BEST FRIEND...
"HE KNEW NOW HOW IT FELT TO BE ***HATED*** FOR REAL.
"IT HAS ***HAUNTED*** HIM EVER SINCE.
"HE'S A ***DISGRACED*** *LUCHADOR*. HE MOVED BACK TO MY SMALL VILLAGE, STAYED OUT OF SIGHT, AND HAS ***NEVER HARMED*** ANYONE OR ANYTHING SINCE."

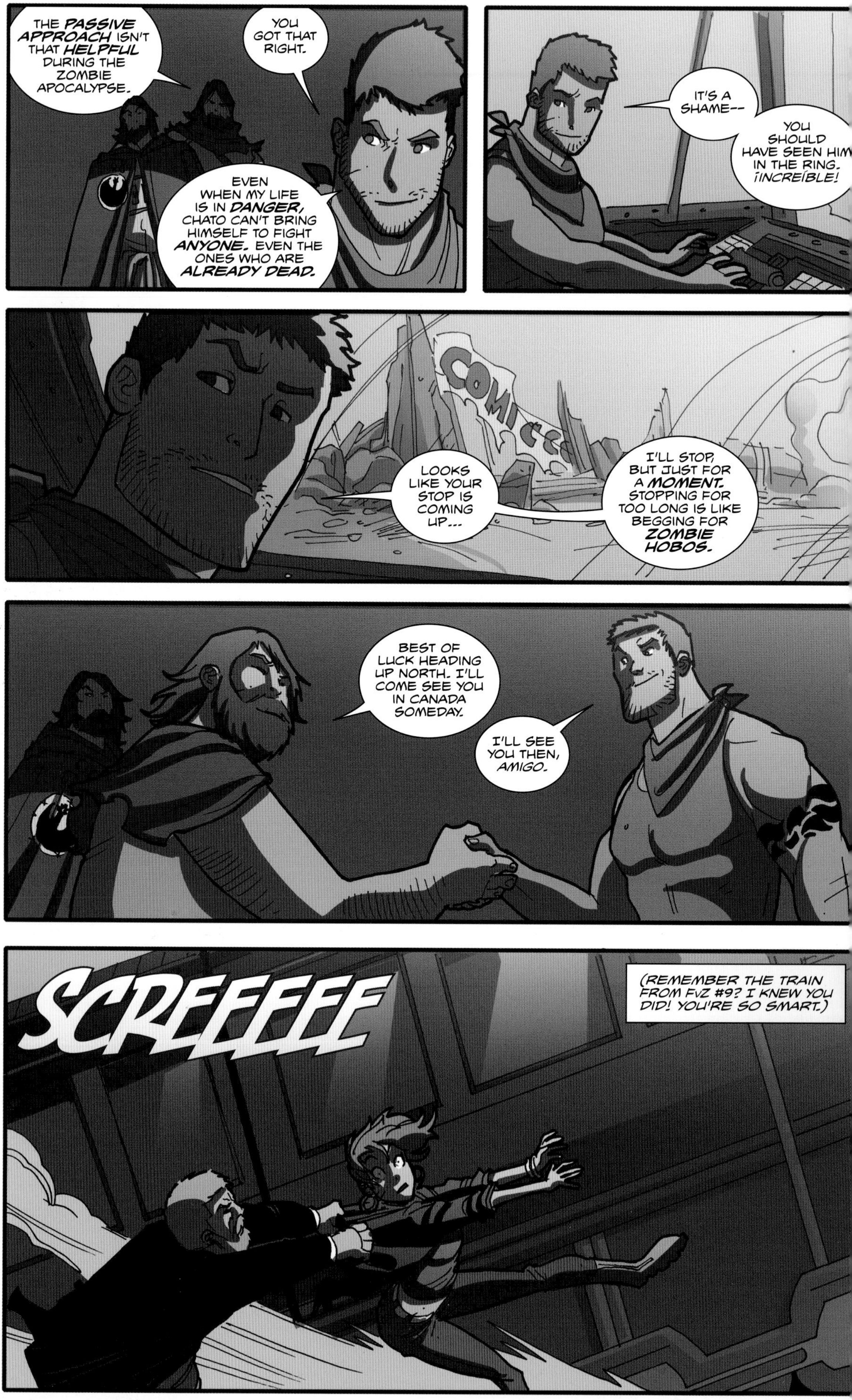
THE PASSIVE APPROACH ISN'T THAT HELPFUL DURING THE ZOMBIE APOCALYPSE.
YOU GOT THAT RIGHT.
EVEN WHEN MY LIFE IS IN DANGER, CHATO CAN'T BRING HIMSELF TO FIGHT ANYONE. EVEN THE ONES WHO ARE ALREADY DEAD.
IT'S A SHAME--
YOU SHOULD HAVE SEEN HIM IN THE RING. ¡INCREÍBLE!
COMIC
LOOKS LIKE YOUR STOP IS COMING UP...
I'LL STOP, BUT JUST FOR A MOMENT. STOPPING FOR TOO LONG IS LIKE BEGGING FOR ZOMBIE HOBOS.
BEST OF LUCK HEADING UP NORTH. I'LL COME SEE YOU IN CANADA SOMEDAY.
I'LL SEE YOU THEN, AMIGO.
SCREEEEE
(REMEMBER THE TRAIN FROM FvZ #9? I KNEW YOU DID! YOU'RE SO SMART.)

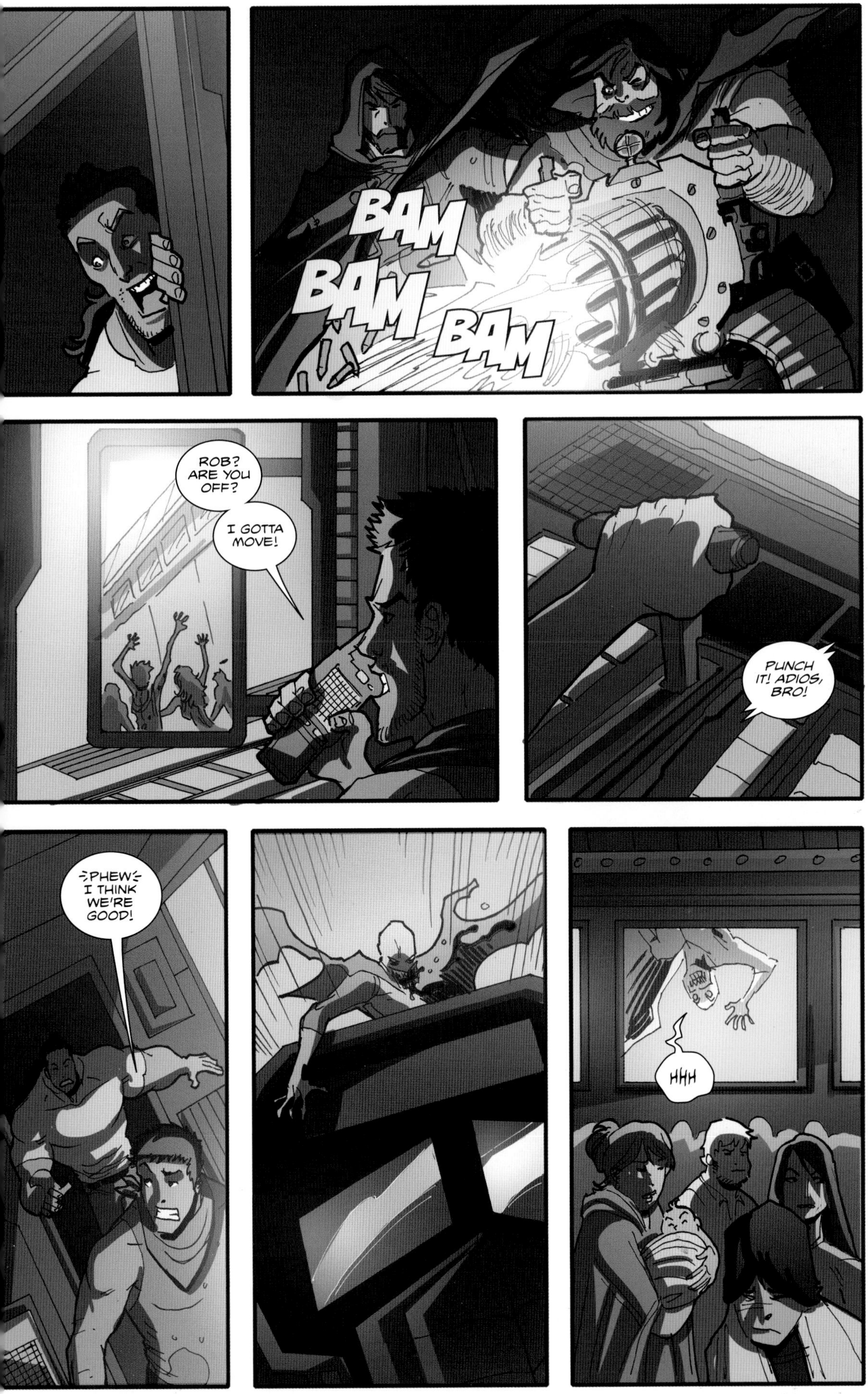
BAM
BAM
BAM
ROB? ARE YOU OFF?
I GOTTA MOVE!
PUNCH IT! ADIOS, BRO!
PHEW I THINK WE'RE GOOD!
HHH

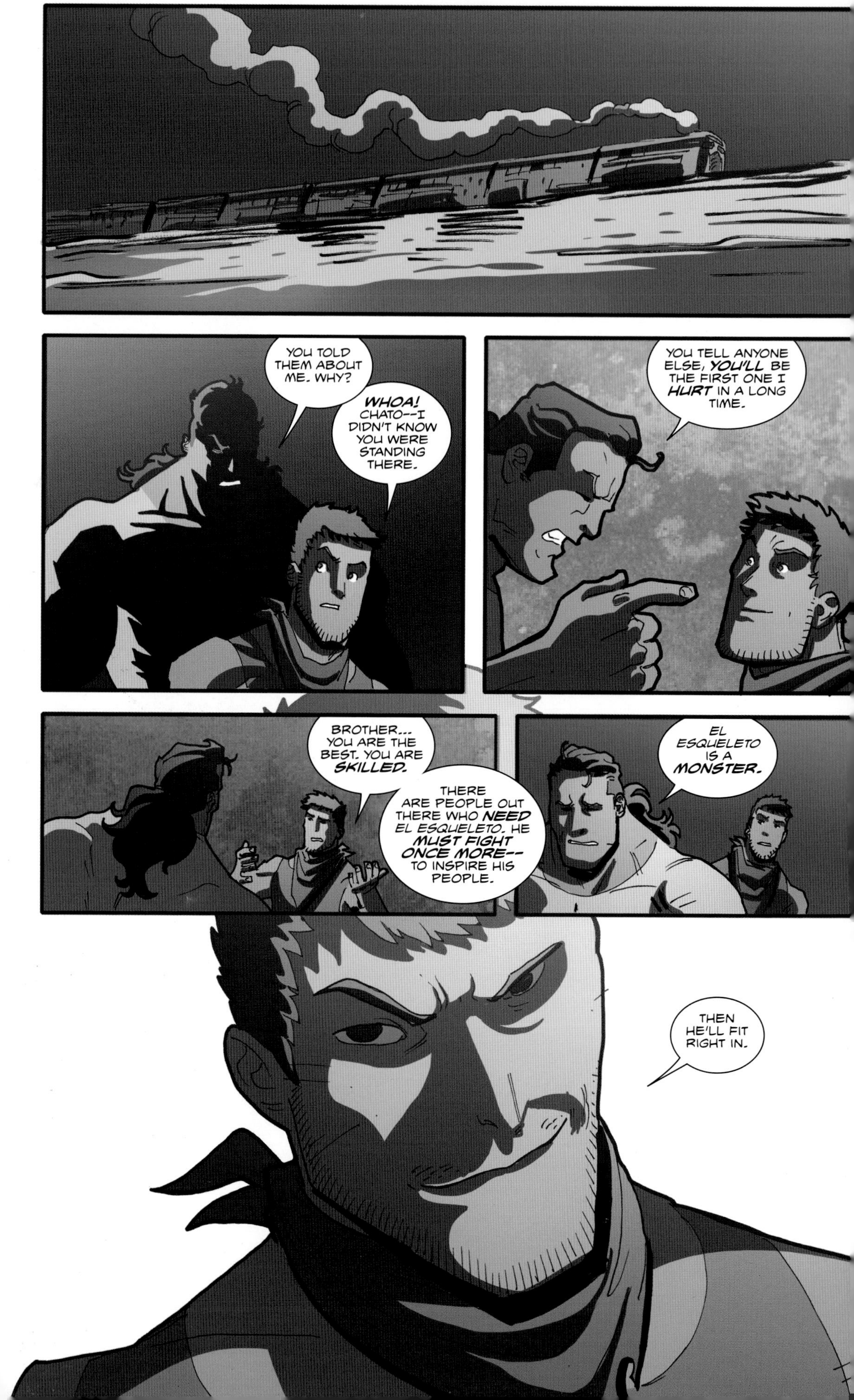
YOU TOLD THEM ABOUT ME. WHY?
WHOA! CHATO--I DIDN'T KNOW YOU WERE STANDING THERE.
YOU TELL ANYONE ELSE, YOU'LL BE THE FIRST ONE I HURT IN A LONG TIME.
BROTHER... YOU ARE THE BEST. YOU ARE SKILLED.
THERE ARE PEOPLE OUT THERE WHO NEED EL ESQUELETO. HE MUST FIGHT ONCE MORE-- TO INSPIRE HIS PEOPLE.
EL ESQUELETO IS A MONSTER.
THEN HE'LL FIT RIGHT IN.

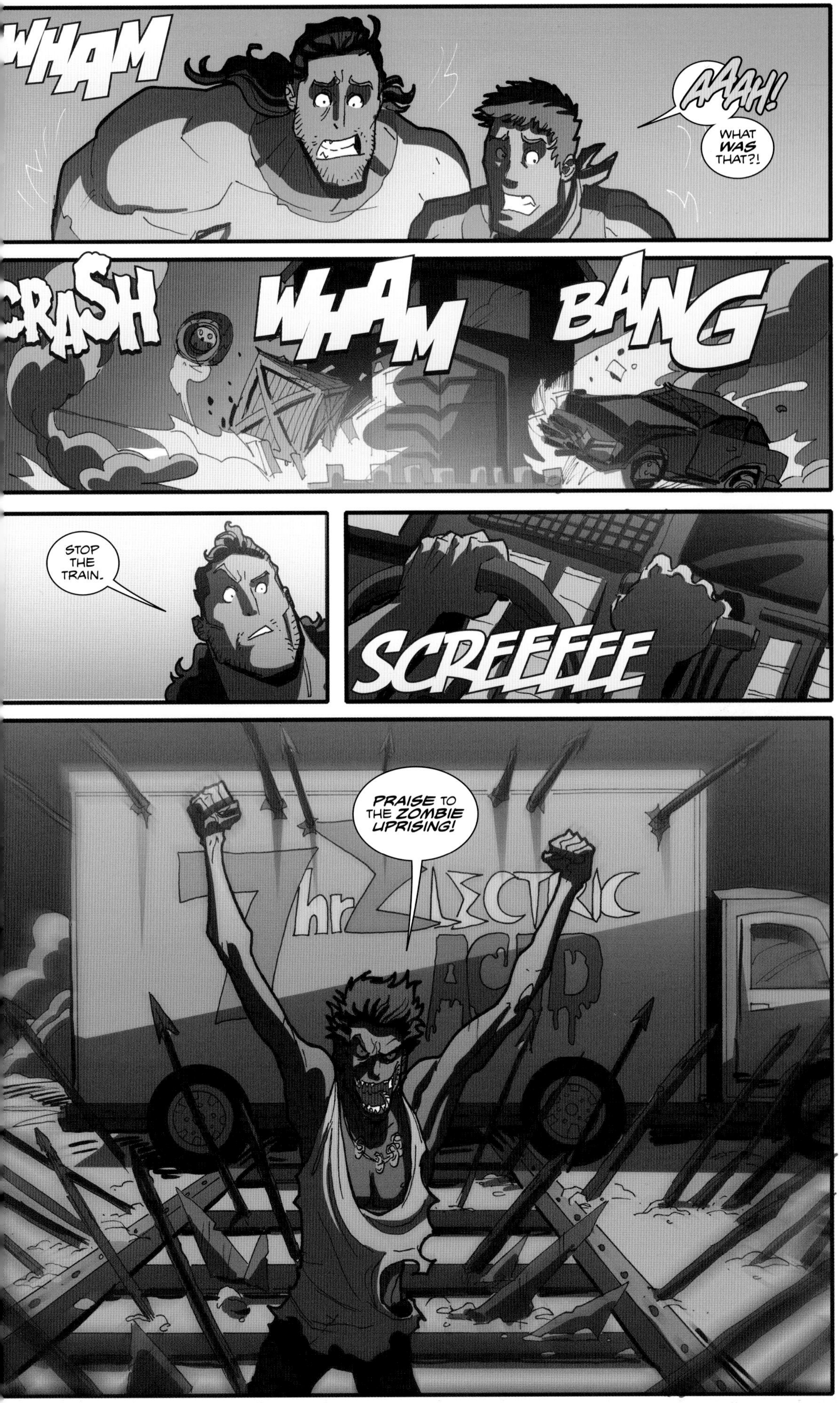
WHAM
AAAH!
WHAT WAS THAT?!
CRASH
WHAM
BANG
STOP THE TRAIN.
SCREEEEE
PRAISE TO THE ZOMBIE UPRISING!

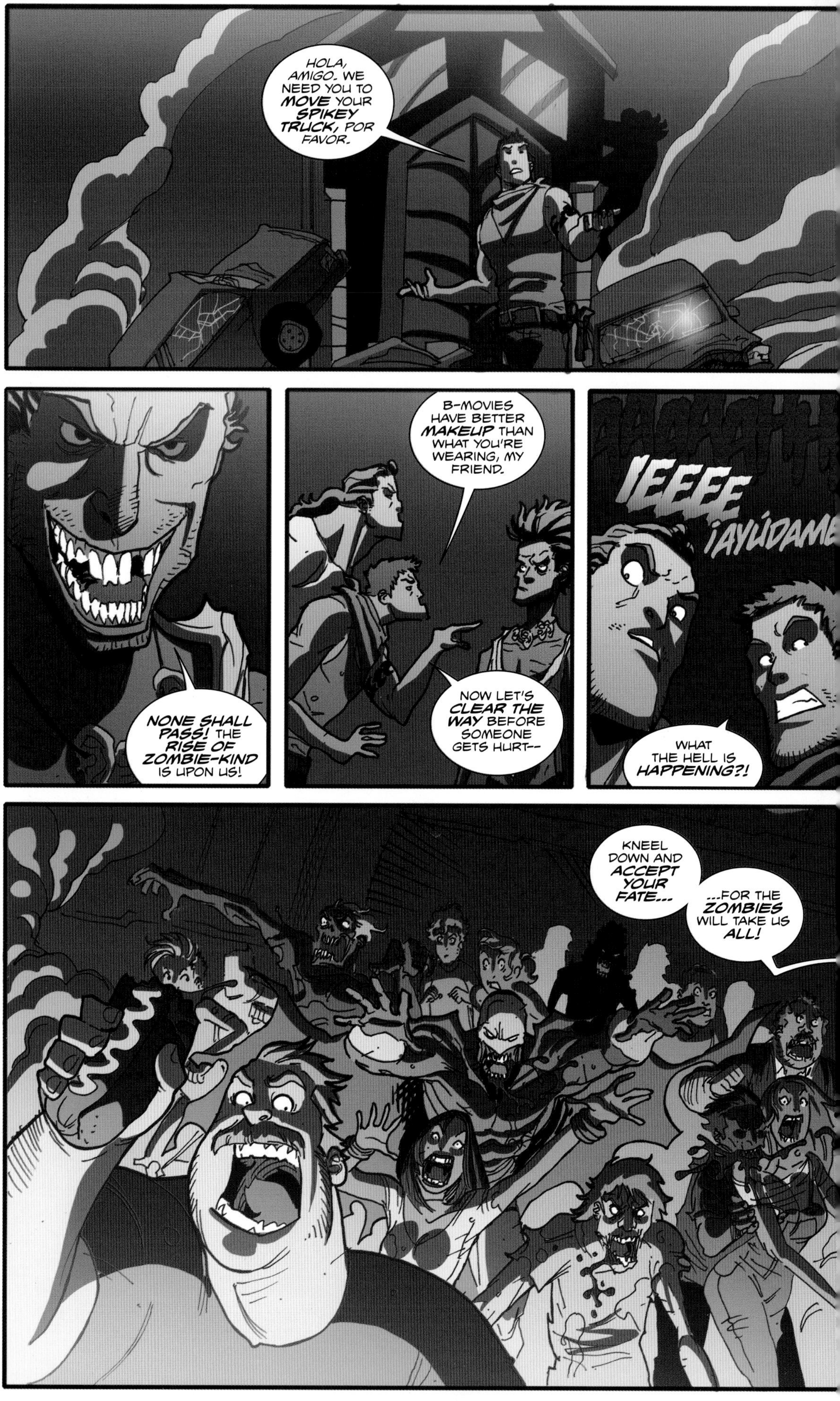
HOLA, AMIGO. WE NEED YOU TO MOVE YOUR SPIKEY TRUCK, POR FAVOR.
NONE SHALL PASS! THE RISE OF ZOMBIE-KIND IS UPON US!
B-MOVIES HAVE BETTER MAKEUP THAN WHAT YOU'RE WEARING, MY FRIEND.
NOW LET'S CLEAR THE WAY BEFORE SOMEONE GETS HURT--
IEEEE
¡AYÚDAME
WHAT THE HELL IS HAPPENING?!
KNEEL DOWN AND ACCEPT YOUR FATE...
...FOR THE ZOMBIES WILL TAKE US ALL!

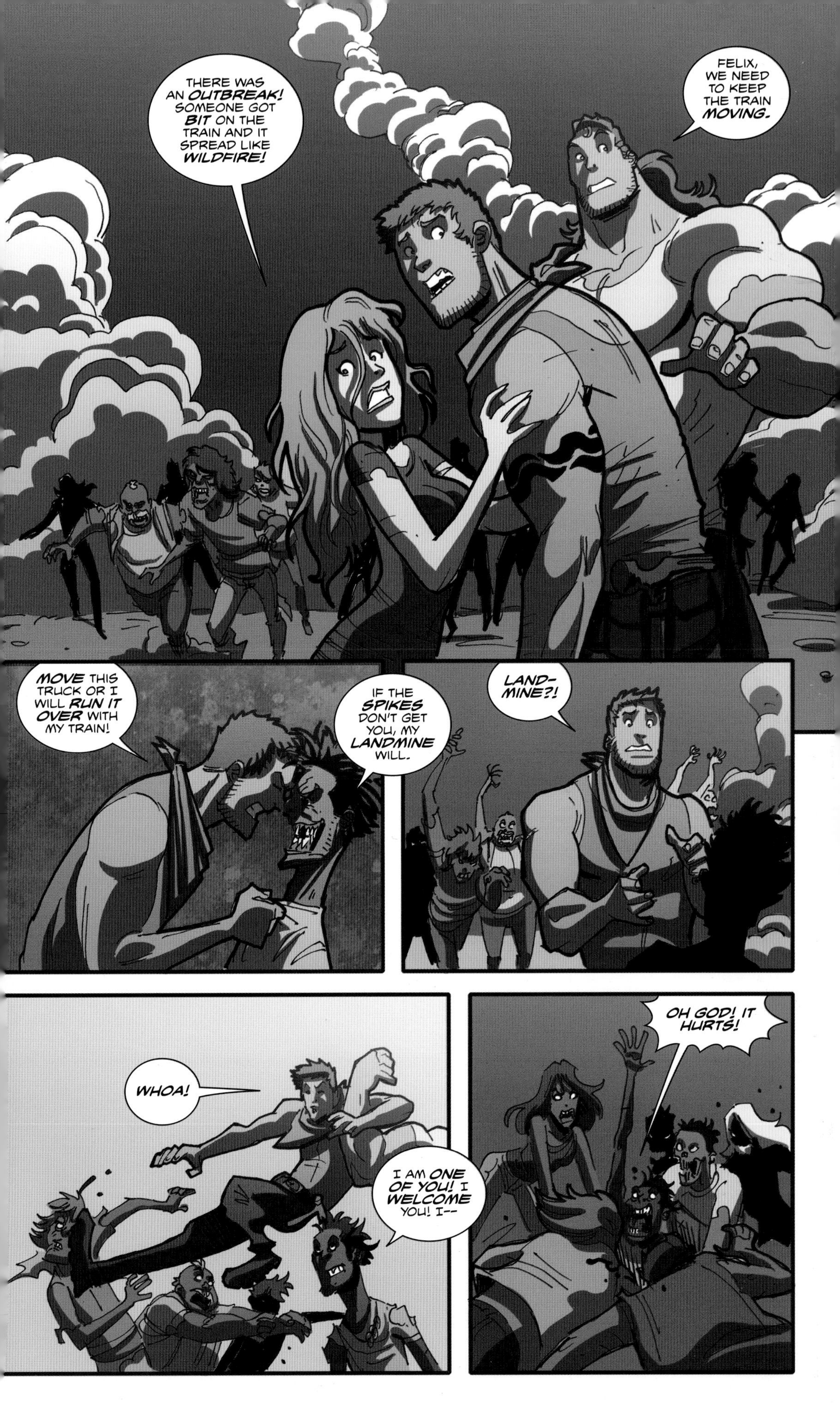
THERE WAS AN OUTBREAK! SOMEONE GOT BIT ON THE TRAIN AND IT SPREAD LIKE WILDFIRE!
FELIX, WE NEED TO KEEP THE TRAIN MOVING.
MOVE THIS TRUCK OR I WILL RUN IT OVER WITH MY TRAIN!
IF THE SPIKES DON'T GET YOU, MY LANDMINE WILL.
LAND-MINE?!
WHOA!
I AM ONE OF YOU! I WELCOME YOU! I--
OH GOD! IT HURTS!

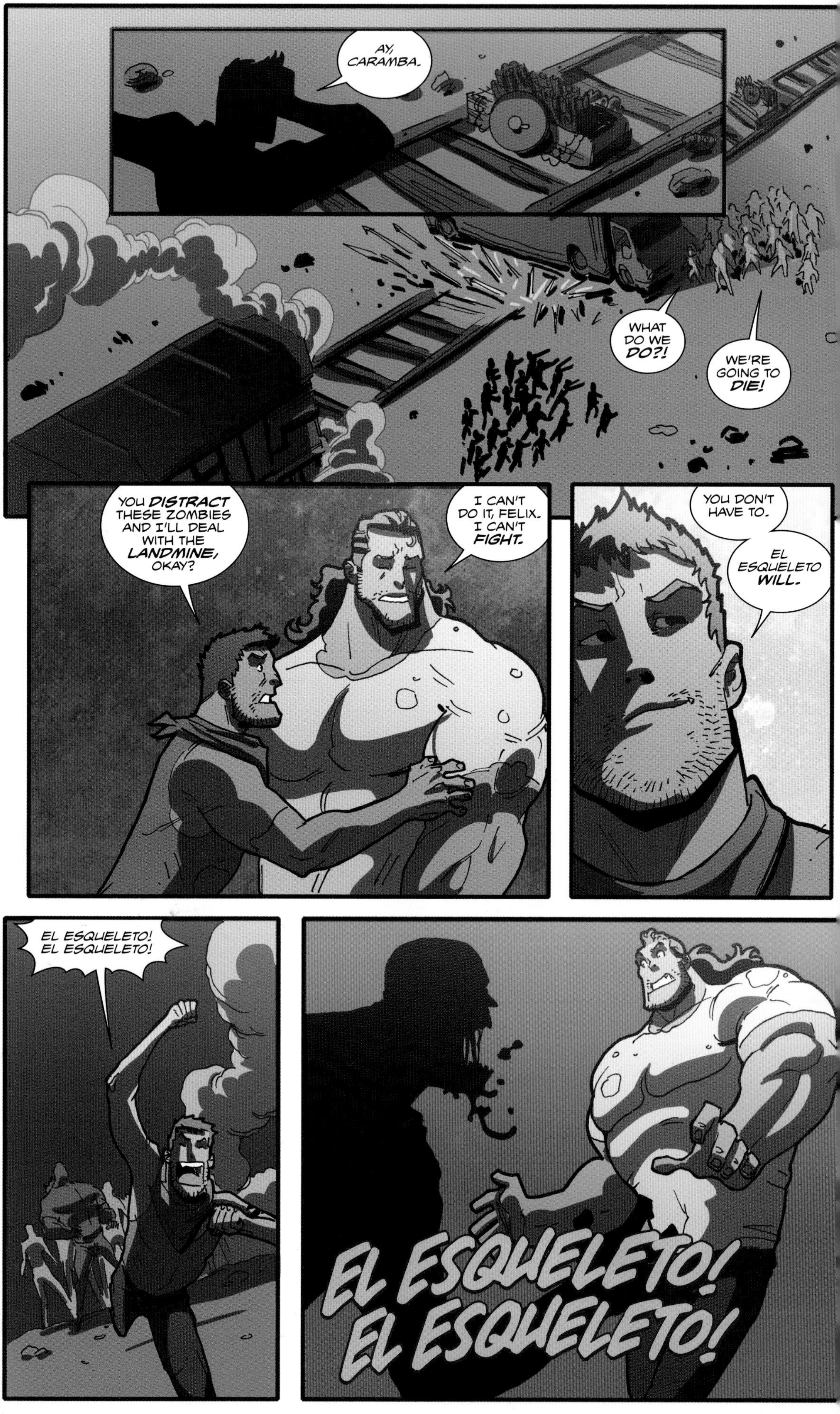

AY, CARAMBA.
WHAT DO WE DO?!
WE'RE GOING TO DIE!
YOU DISTRACT THESE ZOMBIES AND I'LL DEAL WITH THE LANDMINE, OKAY?
I CAN'T DO IT, FELIX. I CAN'T FIGHT.
YOU DON'T HAVE TO.
EL ESQUELETO WILL.
EL ESQUELETO! EL ESQUELETO!
EL ESQUELETO! EL ESQUELETO!

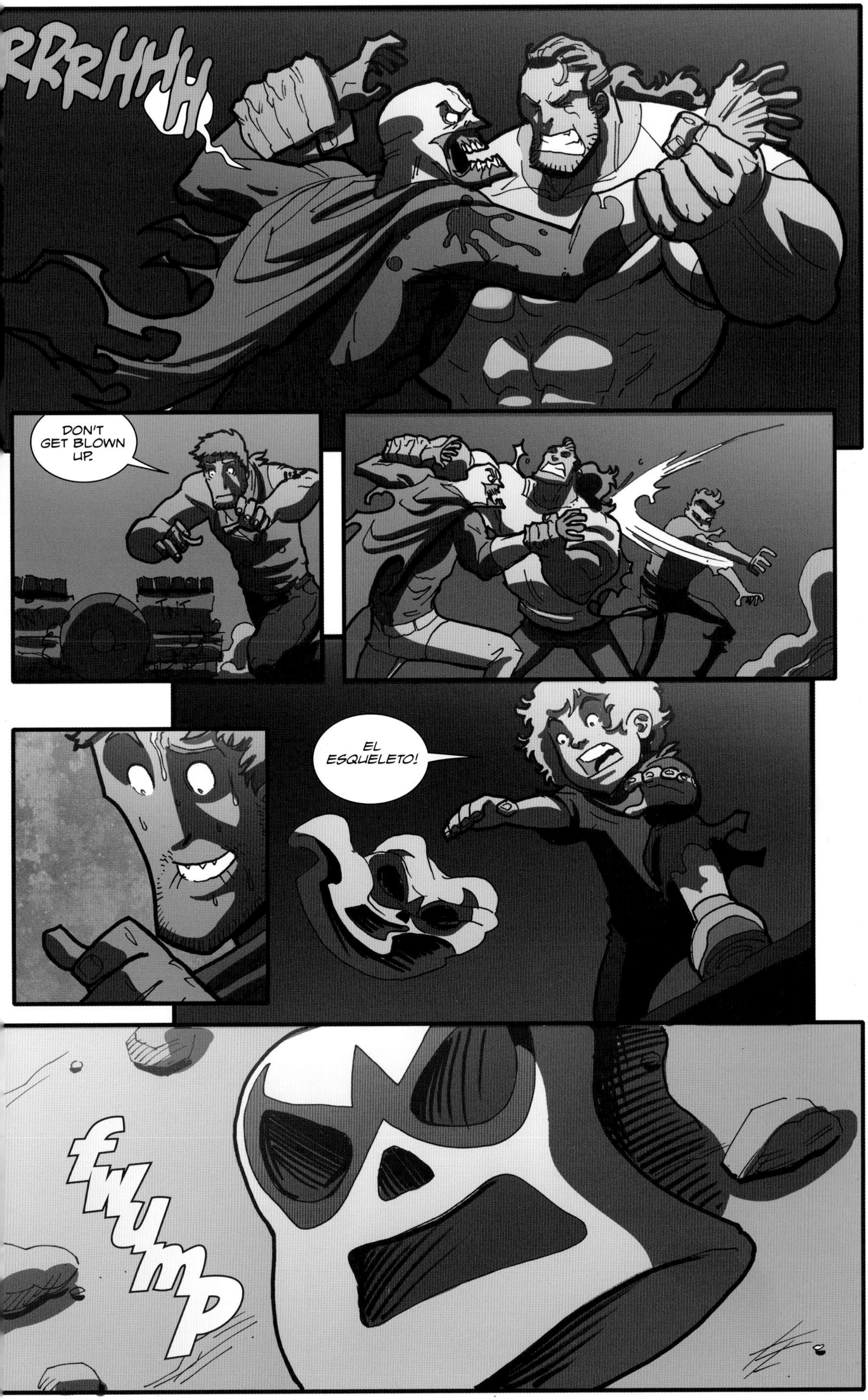
RRRHHH
DON'T GET BLOWN UP.
EL ESQUELETO!
FWUMP

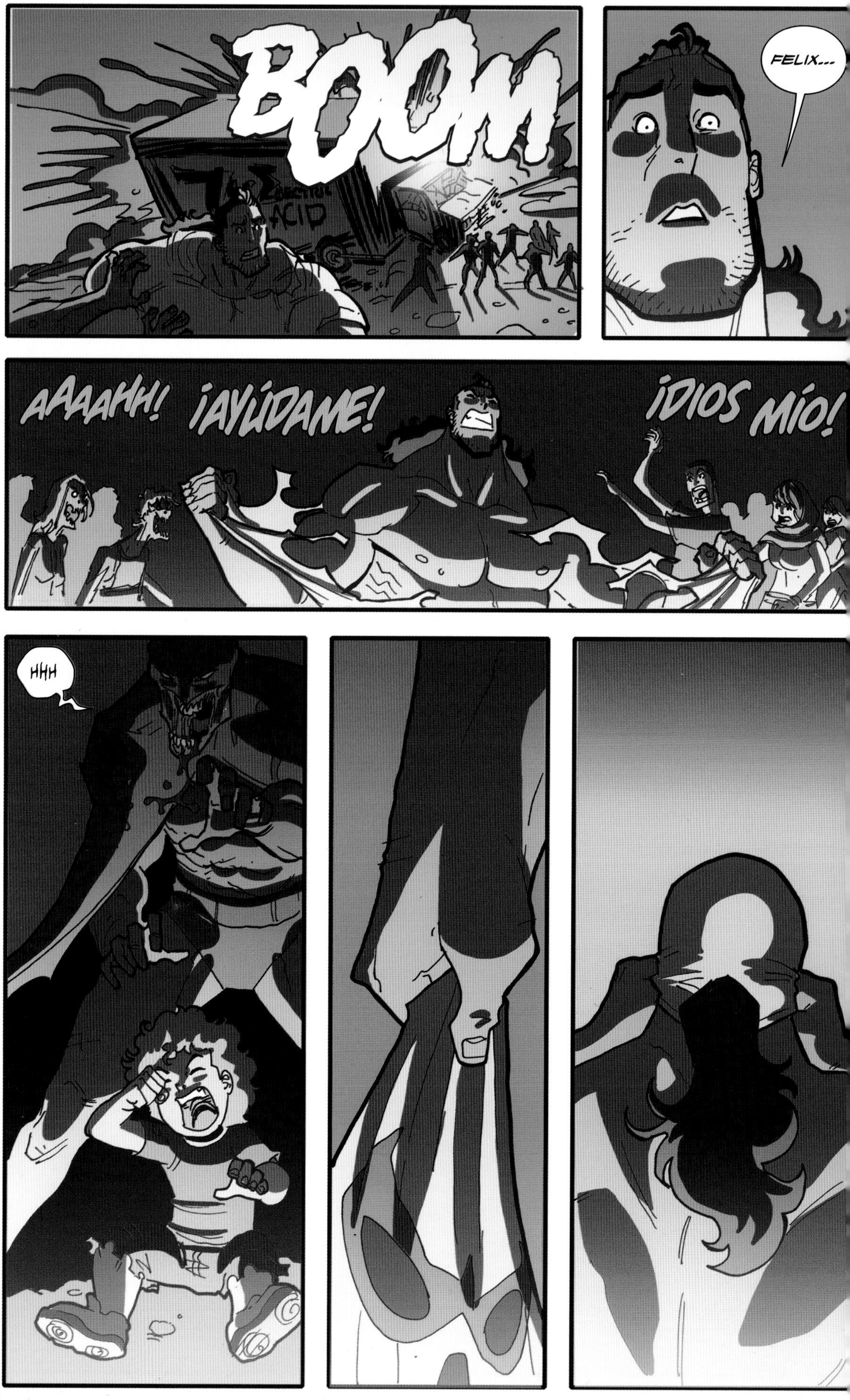
BOOM
FELIX...
AAAAHH!
¡AYÚDAME!
¡DIOS MÍO!
HHH

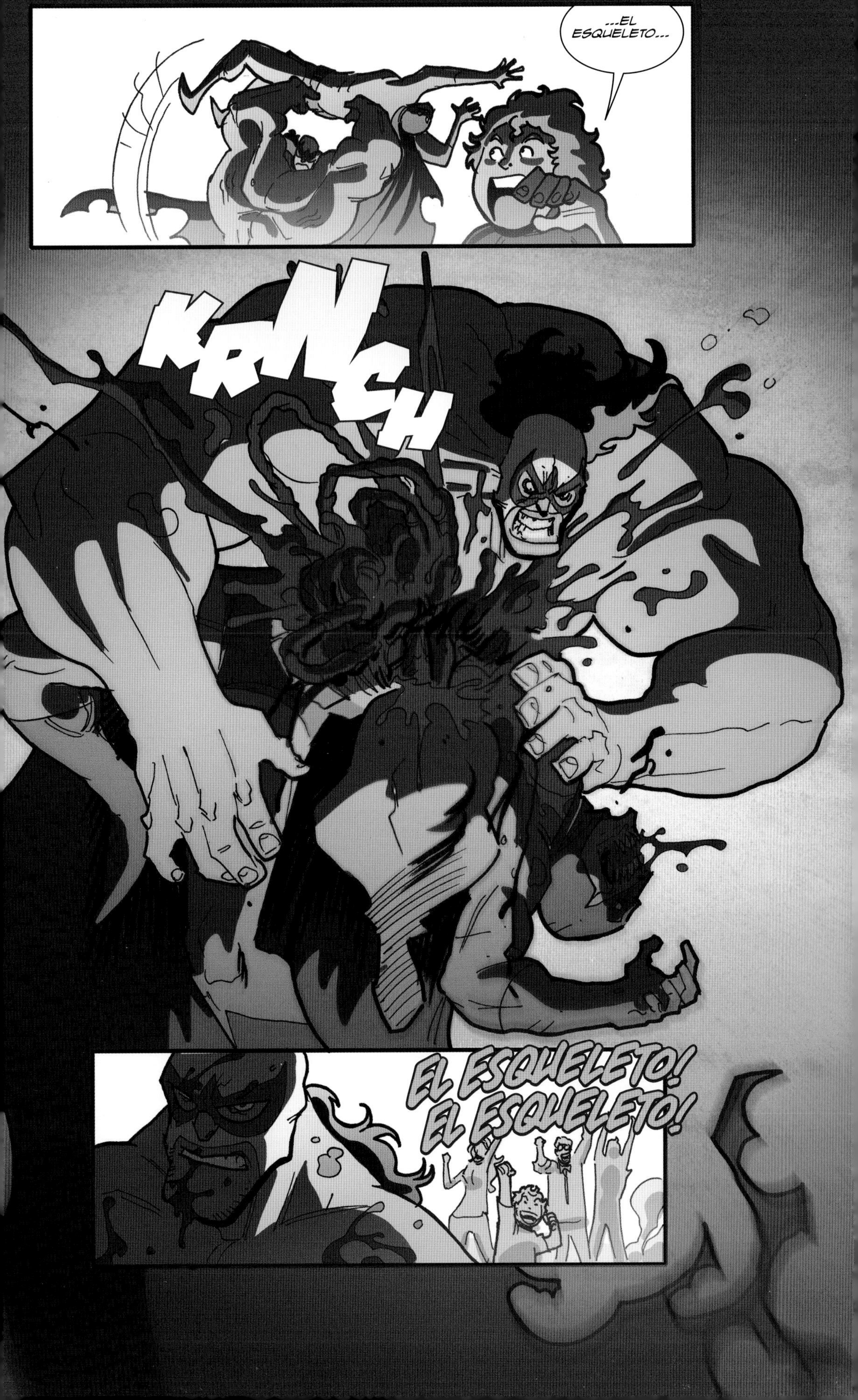
...EL ESQUELETO...
KRNCH
EL ESQUELETO!
EL ESQUELETO!

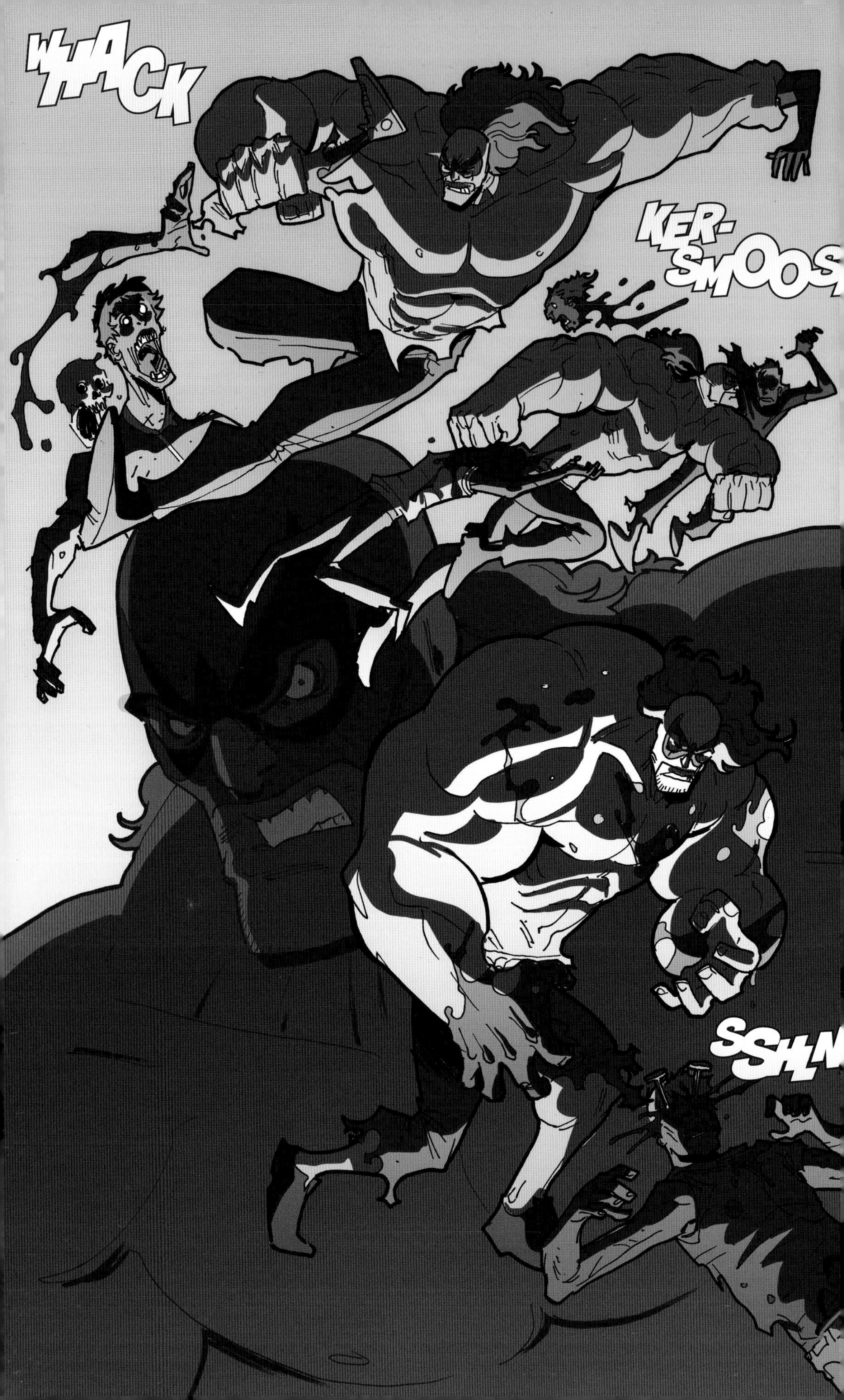
WHACK
KER-SMOOS
SSHN

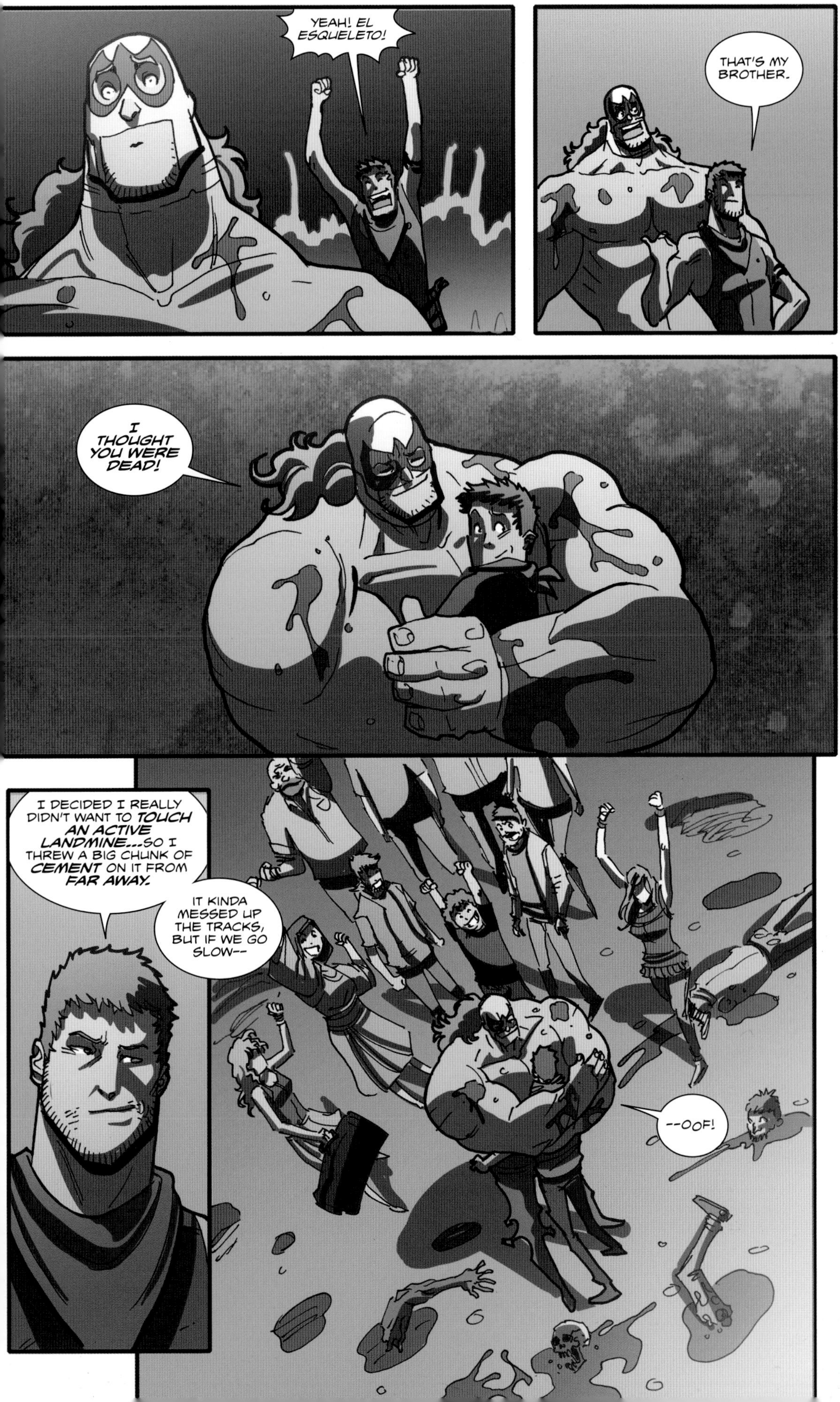
YEAH! EL ESQUELETO!
THAT'S MY BROTHER.
I THOUGHT YOU WERE DEAD!
I DECIDED I REALLY DIDN'T WANT TO TOUCH AN ACTIVE LANDMINE...SO I THREW A BIG CHUNK OF CEMENT ON IT FROM FAR AWAY.
IT KINDA MESSED UP THE TRACKS, BUT IF WE GO SLOW--
--OOF!

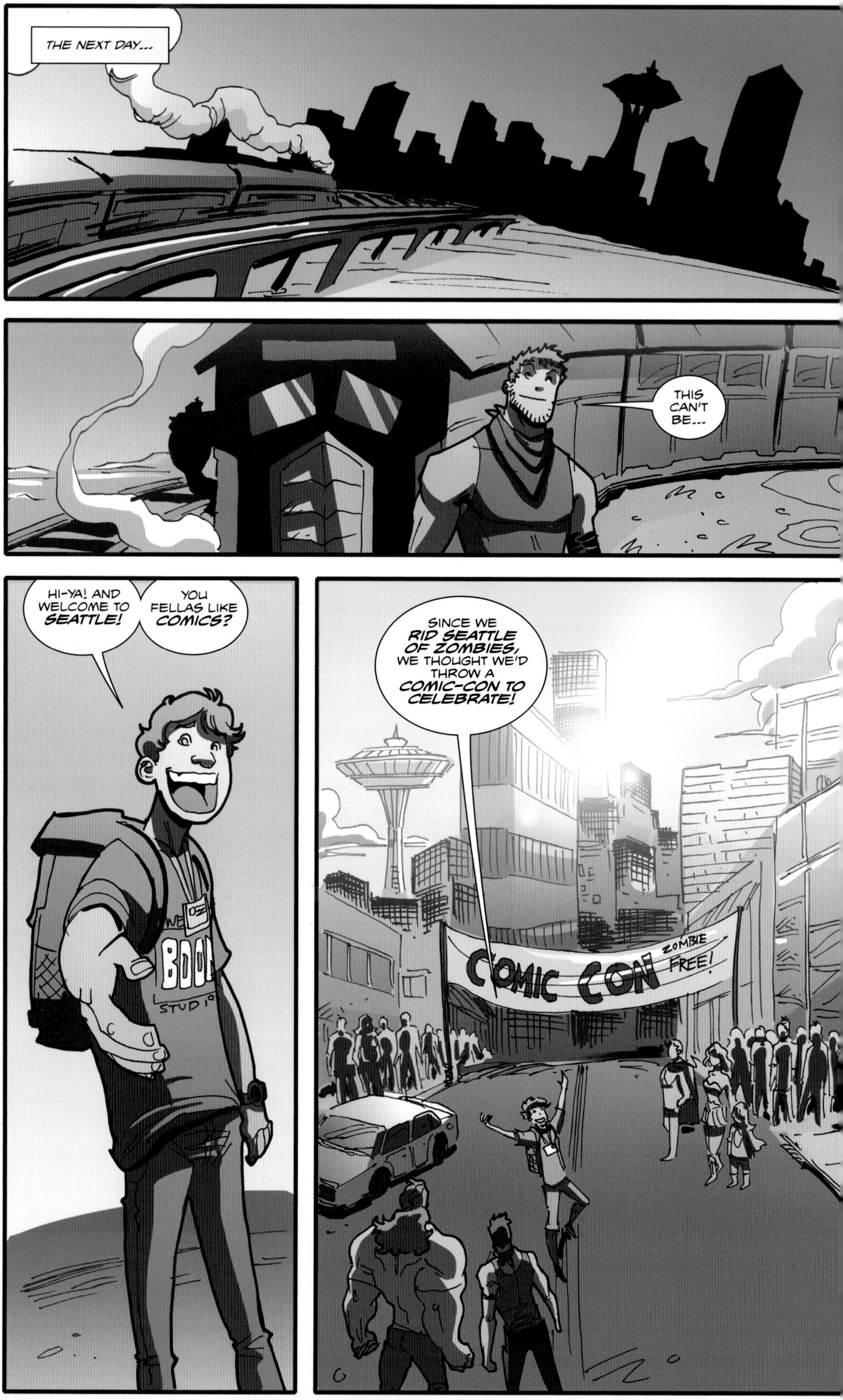

THE NEXT DAY...
THIS CAN'T BE...
HI-YA! AND WELCOME TO SEATTLE!
YOU FELLAS LIKE COMICS?
SINCE WE RID SEATTLE OF ZOMBIES, WE THOUGHT WE'D THROW A COMIC-CON TO CELEBRATE!
COMIC CON
ZOMBIE FREE!

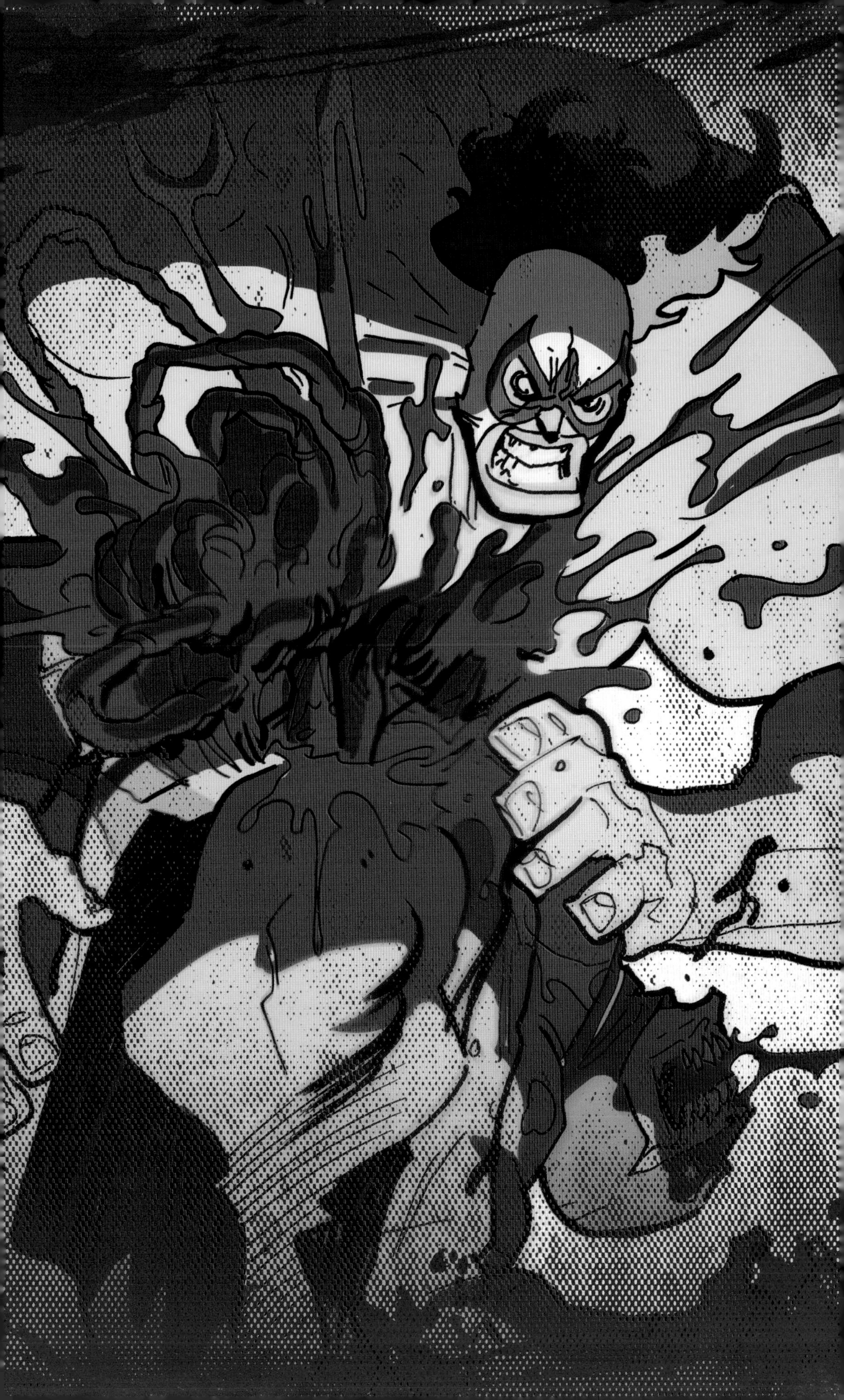

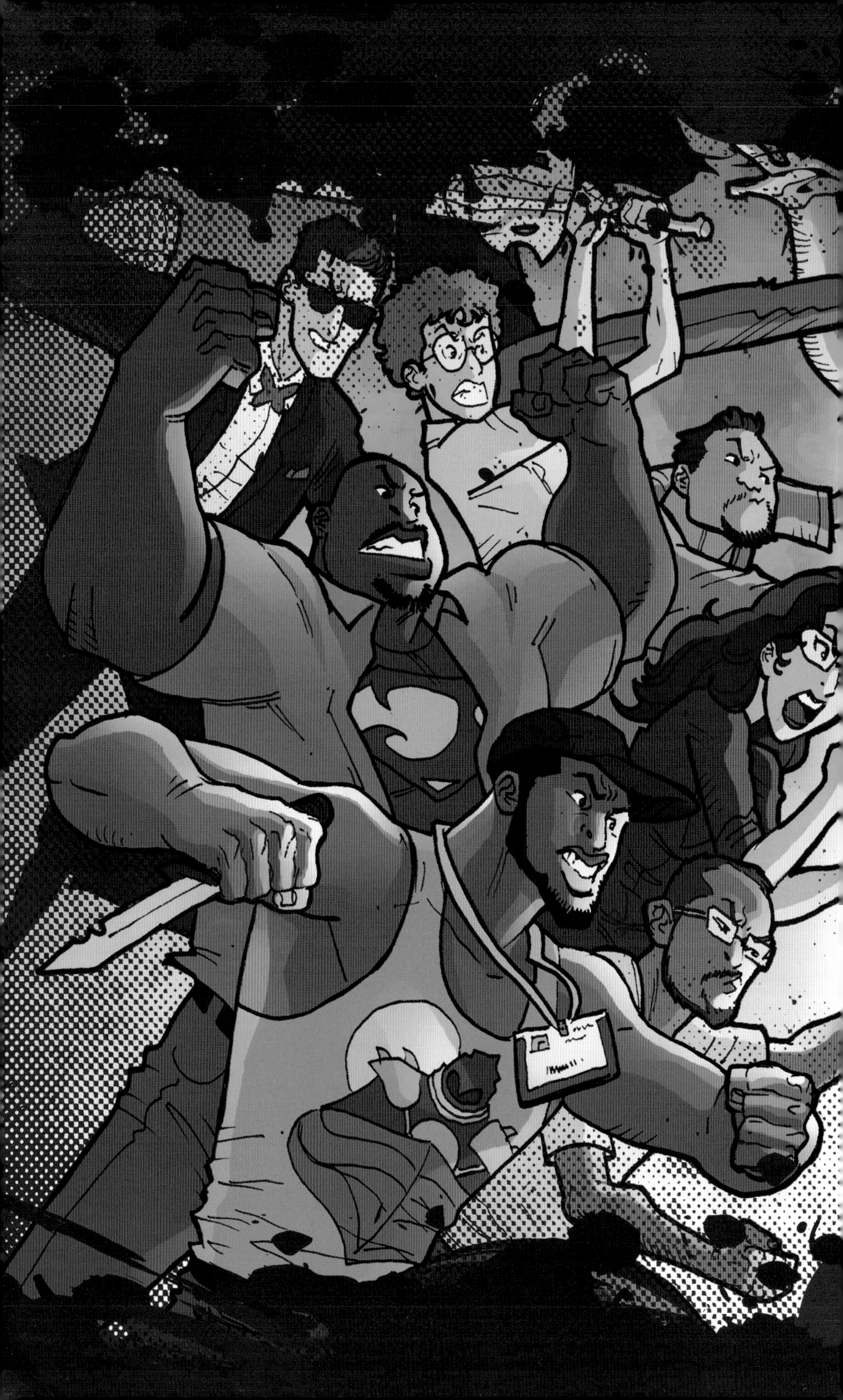

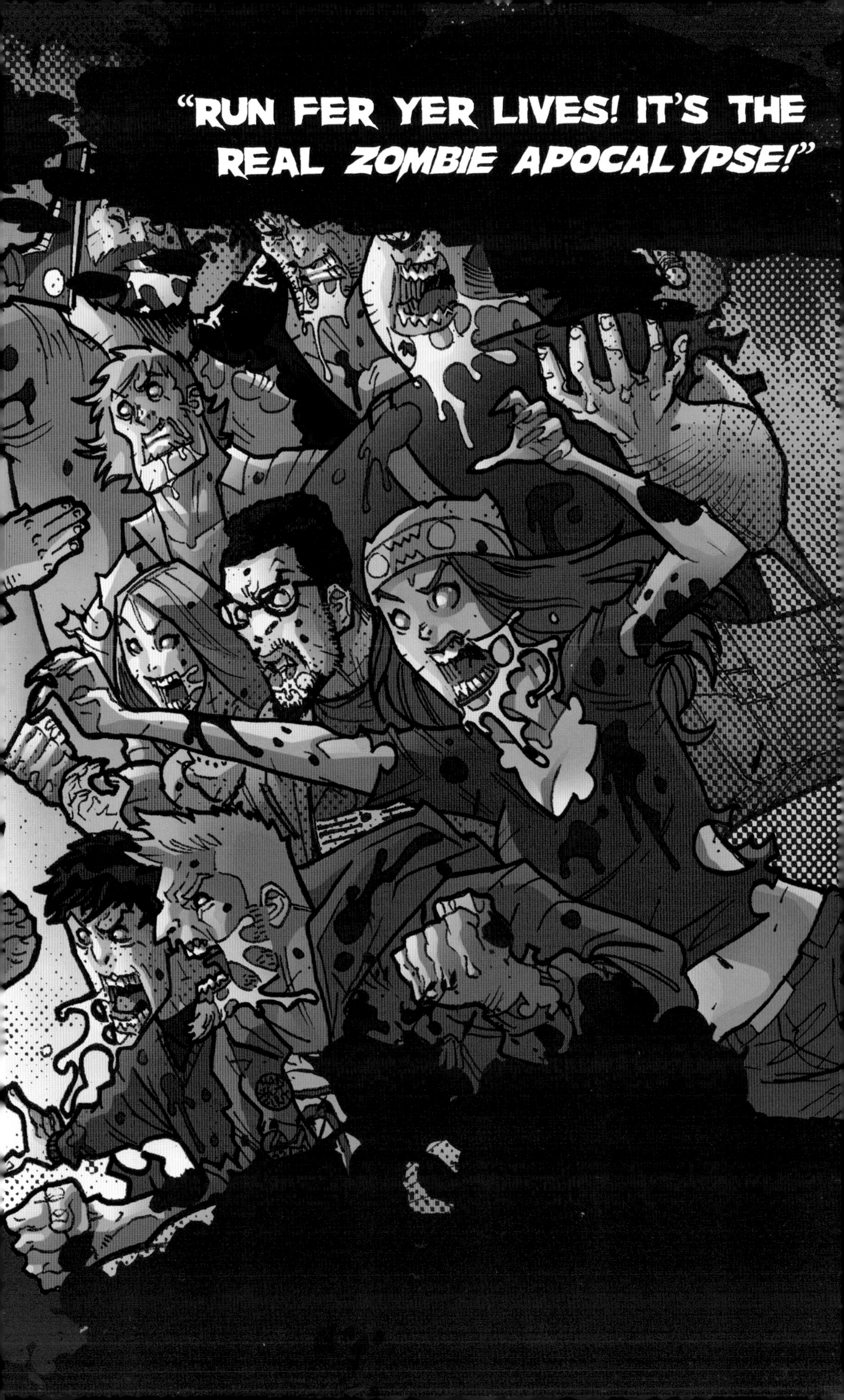
"RUN FER YER LIVES! IT'S THE REAL ZOMBIE APOCALYPSE!"

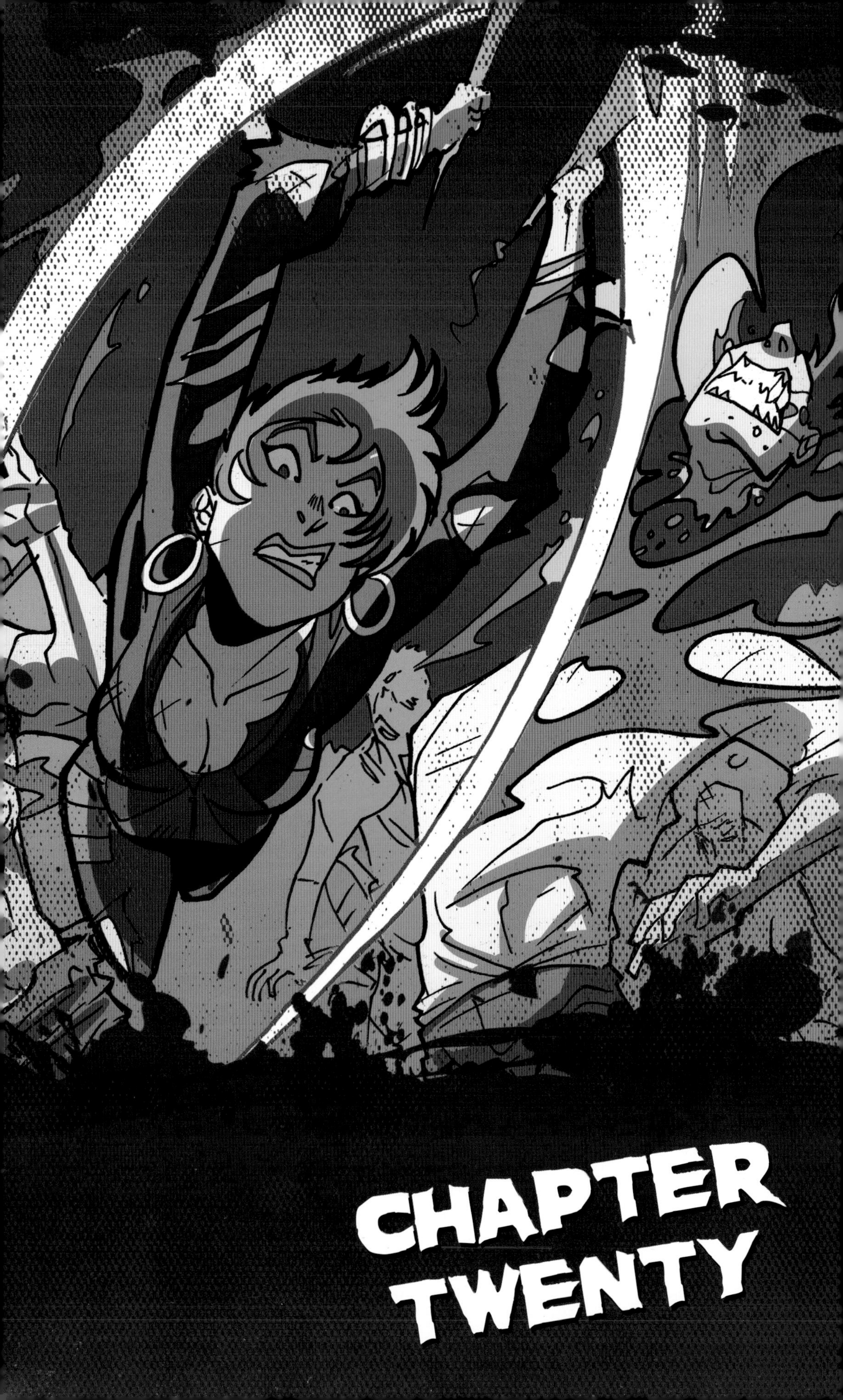

CHAPTER TWENTY

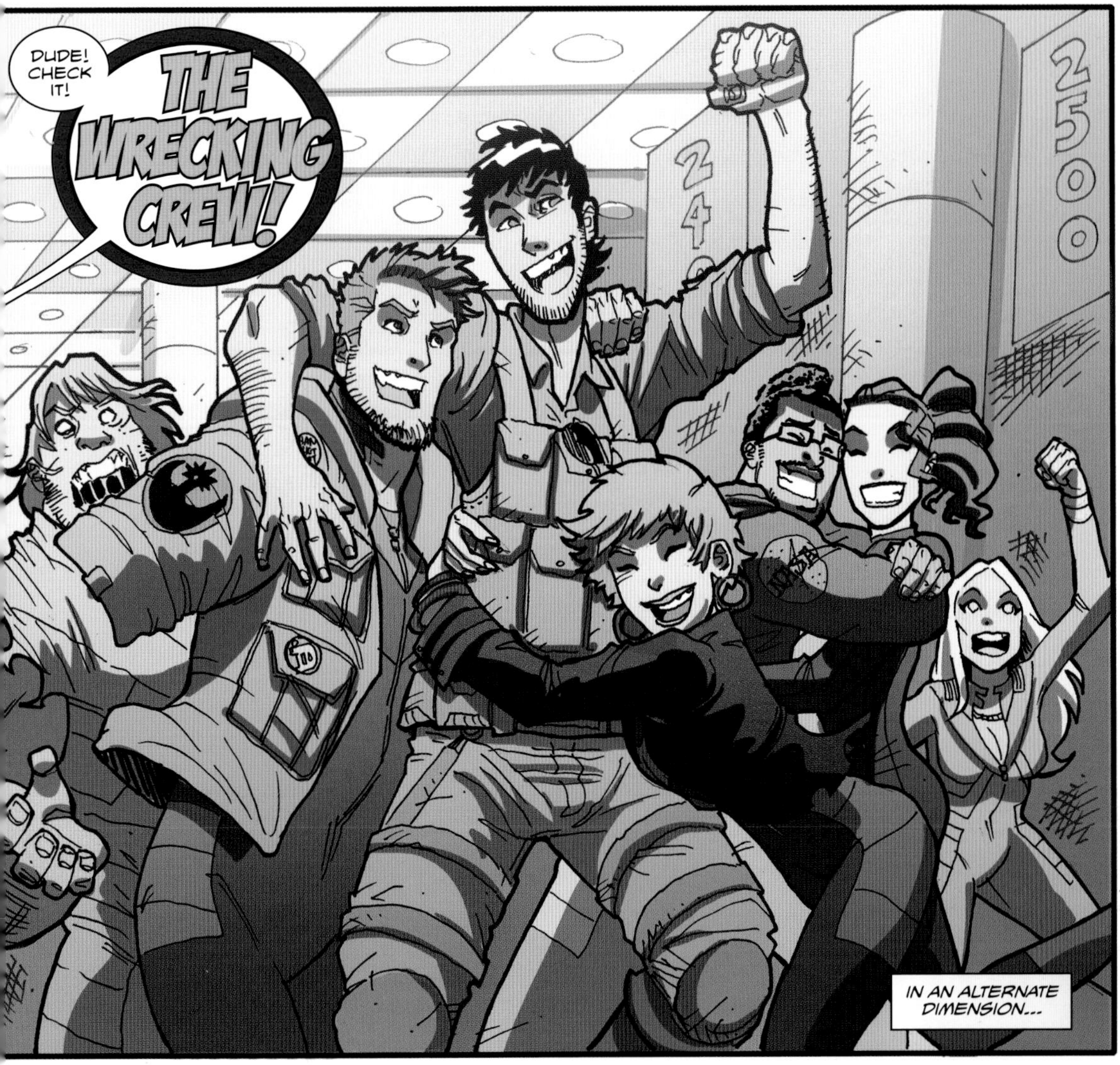
DUDE! CHECK IT!
THE WRECKING CREW!
2400
2500
IN AN ALTERNATE DIMENSION...

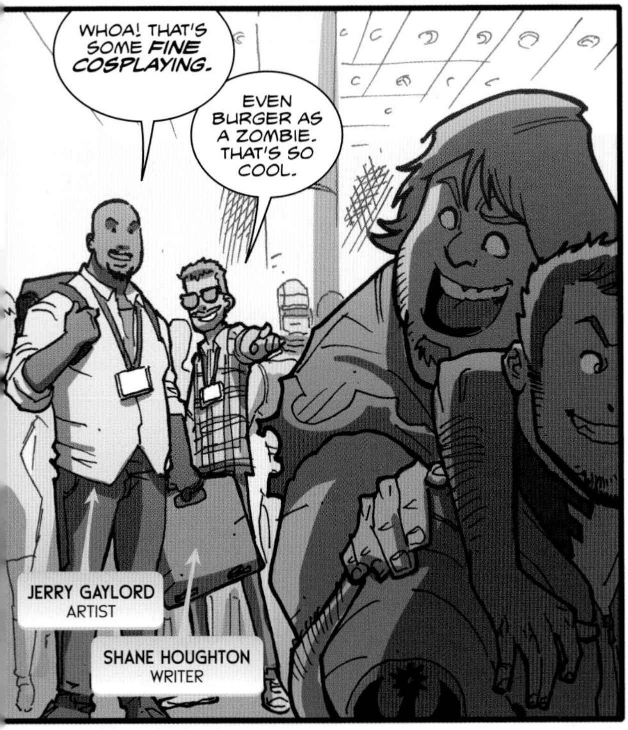
WHOA! THAT'S SOME *FINE COSPLAYING.*
EVEN BURGER AS A ZOMBIE. THAT'S SO COOL.
JERRY GAYLORD
ARTIST
SHANE HOUGHTON
WRITER

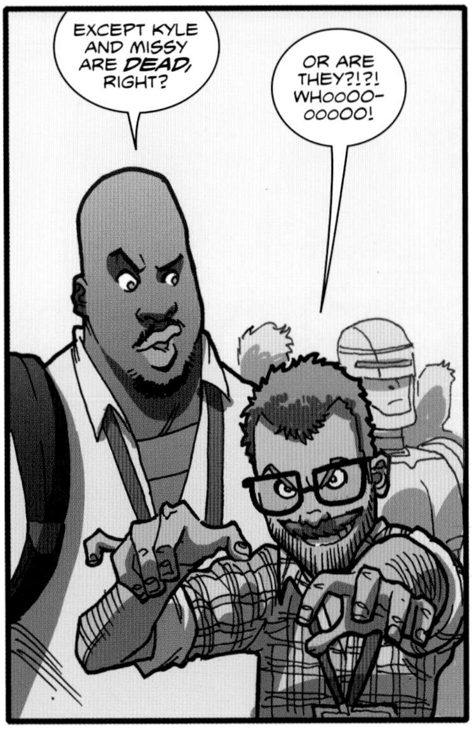
EXCEPT KYLE AND MISSY ARE *DEAD,* RIGHT?
OR ARE THEY?!?! WHOOOO-OOOOO!

YOU BRINGING KYLE BACK? HE WAS EVERYONE'S FAVORITE.

THAT'S *CLASSIFIED* INFORMATION! BESIDES, YOU SAID YOU DON'T LIKE KNOWING WHAT'S GOING TO HAPPEN IN *FANBOYS VS. ZOMBIES* UNTIL YOU READ THE *SCRIPT*.

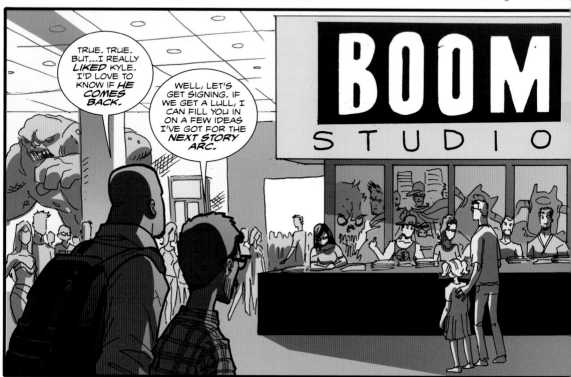

TRUE. TRUE. BUT...I REALLY *LIKED* KYLE. I'D LOVE TO KNOW IF *HE COMES BACK.*

WELL, LET'S GET SIGNING. IF WE GET A LULL, I CAN FILL YOU IN ON A FEW IDEAS I'VE GOT FOR THE *NEXT STORY ARC.*

BOOM STUDIO

HEY, GUYS!

PENELOPE "PENG" GAYLORD
INK ASSISTS

BRYAN TURNER
FILL-IN ARTIST

MIRKA ANDOLFO
COLORIST

ANDREA DOTTA
COLORIST

ED DUKESHIRE
LETTERER

JERRY... WOULD YOU GET ME A CUP OF COFFEE? I KNOW THEY'RE LIKE $15 AT THE CONVENTION CENTER, BUT I NEEEEED ONE!

OUR SIGNING STARTS IN FIVE MINUTES. I'LL SNAG YOU ONE WHEN WE WRAP UP, OKAY?

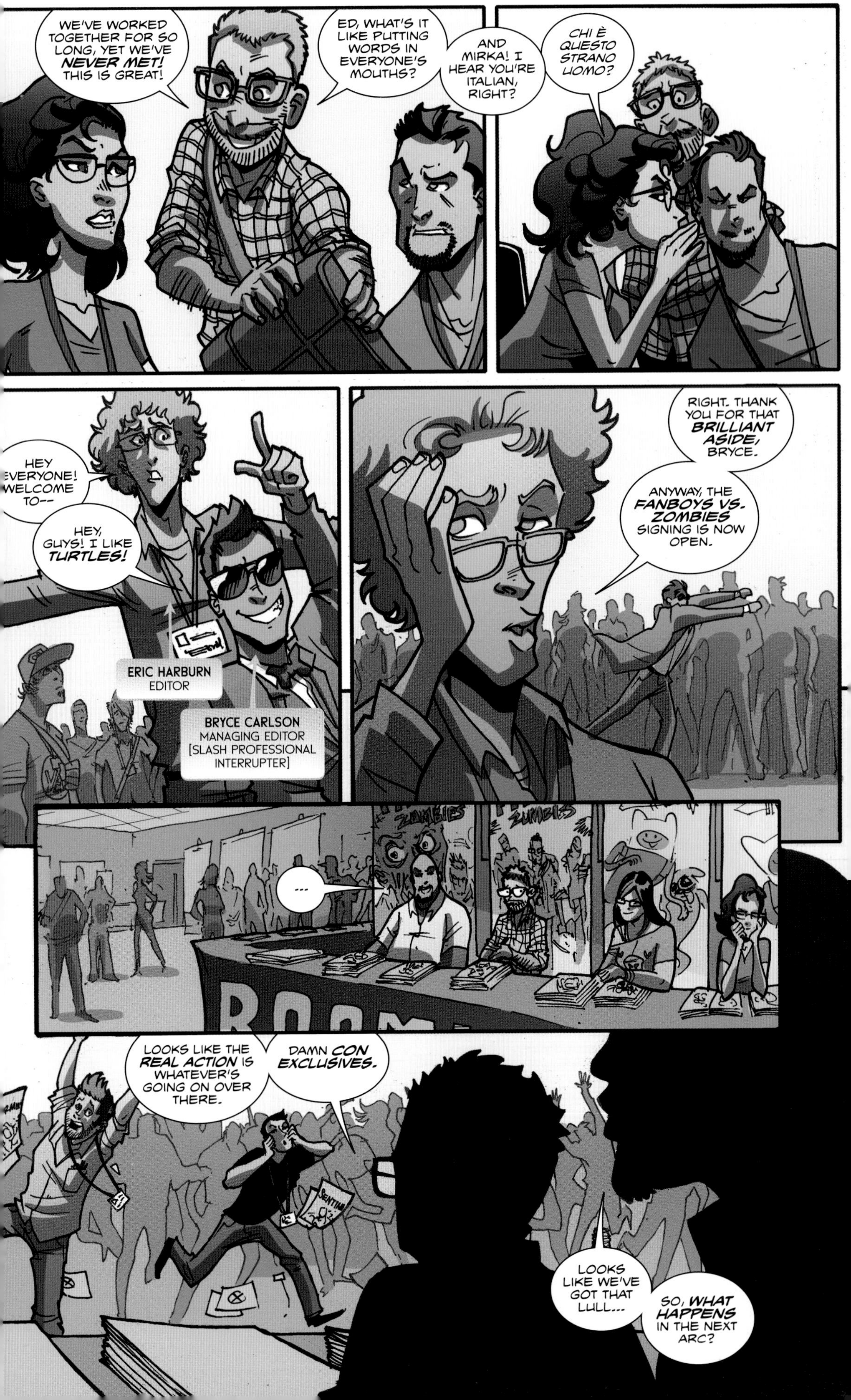
WE'VE WORKED TOGETHER FOR SO LONG, YET WE'VE NEVER MET! THIS IS GREAT!
ED, WHAT'S IT LIKE PUTTING WORDS IN EVERYONE'S MOUTHS?
AND MIRKA! I HEAR YOU'RE ITALIAN, RIGHT?
CHI È QUESTO STRANO UOMO?
HEY EVERYONE! WELCOME TO--
HEY, GUYS! I LIKE TURTLES!
ERIC HARBURN
EDITOR
BRYCE CARLSON
MANAGING EDITOR
[SLASH PROFESSIONAL INTERRUPTER]
RIGHT. THANK YOU FOR THAT BRILLIANT ASIDE, BRYCE.
ANYWAY, THE FANBOYS VS. ZOMBIES SIGNING IS NOW OPEN.
...
LOOKS LIKE THE REAL ACTION IS WHATEVER'S GOING ON OVER THERE.
DAMN CON EXCLUSIVES.
LOOKS LIKE WE'VE GOT THAT LULL...
SO, WHAT HAPPENS IN THE NEXT ARC?

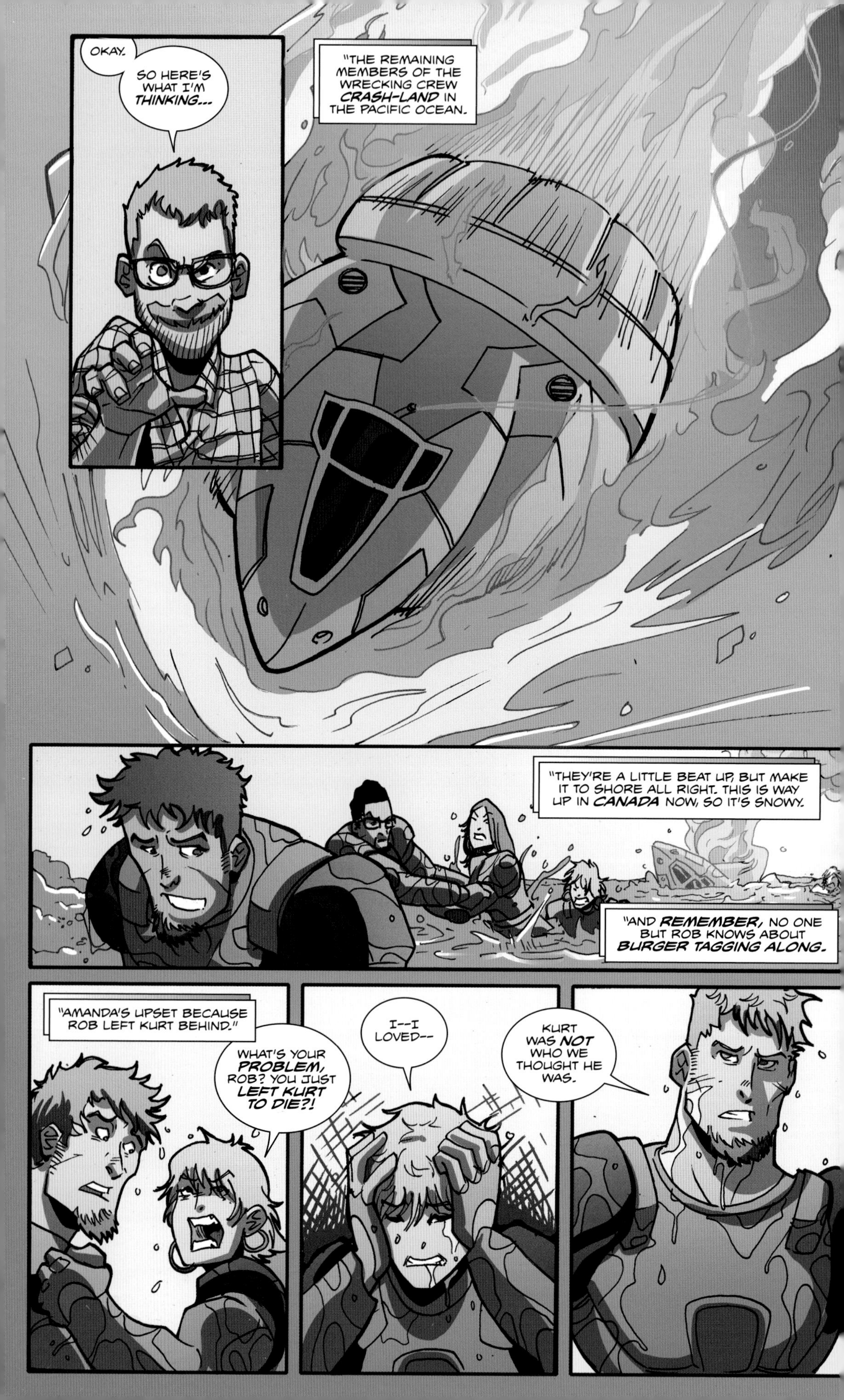
OKAY.
SO HERE'S WHAT I'M THINKING...
"THE REMAINING MEMBERS OF THE WRECKING CREW CRASH-LAND IN THE PACIFIC OCEAN.
"THEY'RE A LITTLE BEAT UP, BUT MAKE IT TO SHORE ALL RIGHT. THIS IS WAY UP IN CANADA NOW, SO IT'S SNOWY.
"AND REMEMBER, NO ONE BUT ROB KNOWS ABOUT BURGER TAGGING ALONG.
"AMANDA'S UPSET BECAUSE ROB LEFT KURT BEHIND."
WHAT'S YOUR PROBLEM, ROB? YOU JUST LEFT KURT TO DIE?!
I--I LOVED--
KURT WAS NOT WHO WE THOUGHT HE WAS.

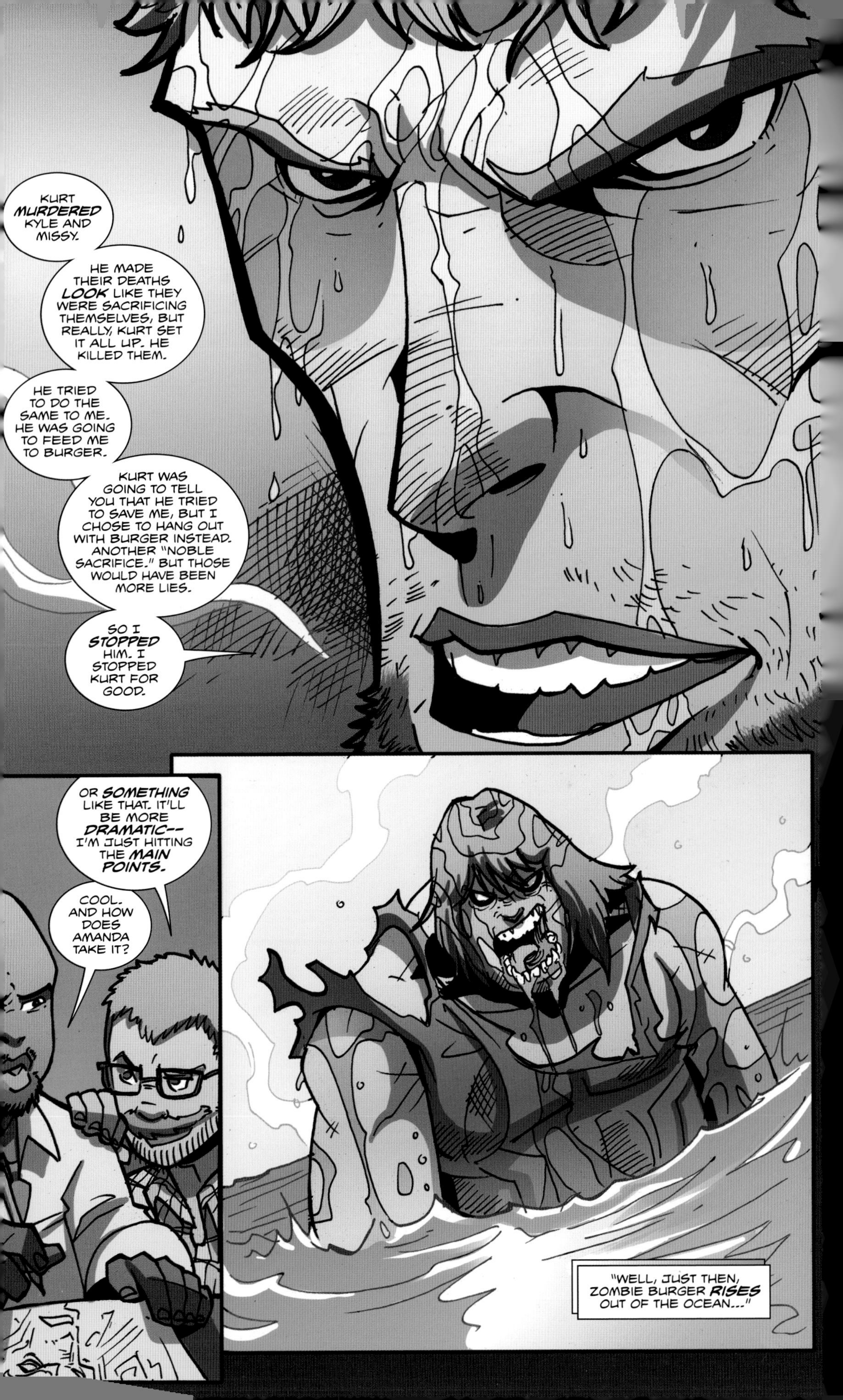
KURT MURDERED KYLE AND MISSY.
HE MADE THEIR DEATHS LOOK LIKE THEY WERE SACRIFICING THEMSELVES, BUT REALLY, KURT SET IT ALL UP. HE KILLED THEM.
HE TRIED TO DO THE SAME TO ME. HE WAS GOING TO FEED ME TO BURGER.
KURT WAS GOING TO TELL YOU THAT HE TRIED TO SAVE ME, BUT I CHOSE TO HANG OUT WITH BURGER INSTEAD. ANOTHER "NOBLE SACRIFICE." BUT THOSE WOULD HAVE BEEN MORE LIES.
SO I STOPPED HIM. I STOPPED KURT FOR GOOD.
OR SOMETHING LIKE THAT. IT'LL BE MORE DRAMATIC-- I'M JUST HITTING THE MAIN POINTS.
COOL. AND HOW DOES AMANDA TAKE IT?
"WELL, JUST THEN, ZOMBIE BURGER RISES OUT OF THE OCEAN..."

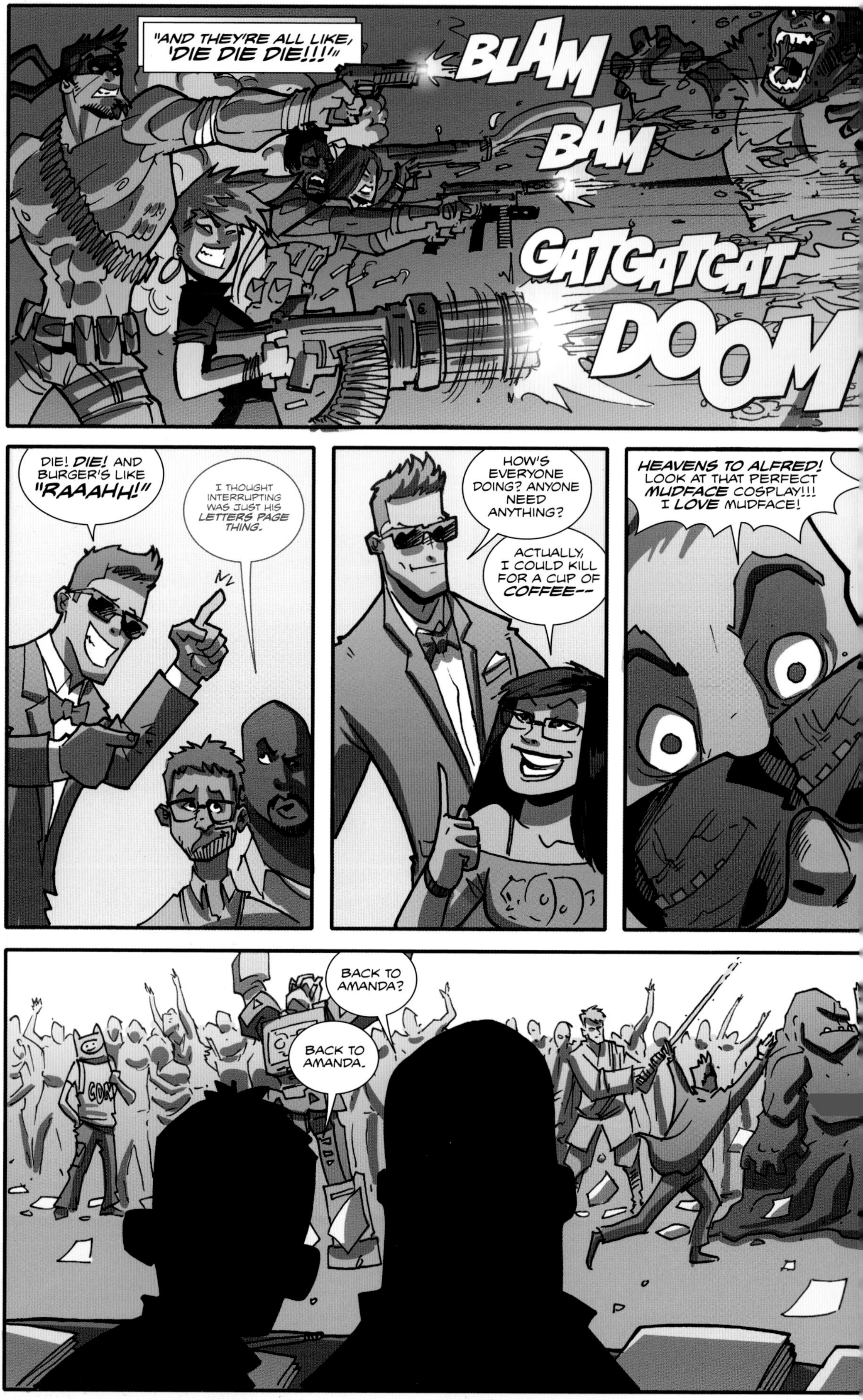
"AND THEY'RE ALL LIKE, 'DIE DIE DIE!!!'"
BLAM
BAM
GATGATGAT
DOOM
DIE! DIE! AND BURGER'S LIKE "RAAAHH!"
I THOUGHT INTERRUPTING WAS JUST HIS LETTERS PAGE THING.
HOW'S EVERYONE DOING? ANYONE NEED ANYTHING?
ACTUALLY, I COULD KILL FOR A CUP OF COFFEE--
HEAVENS TO ALFRED! LOOK AT THAT PERFECT MUDFACE COSPLAY!!! I LOVE MUDFACE!
BACK TO AMANDA?
BACK TO AMANDA.

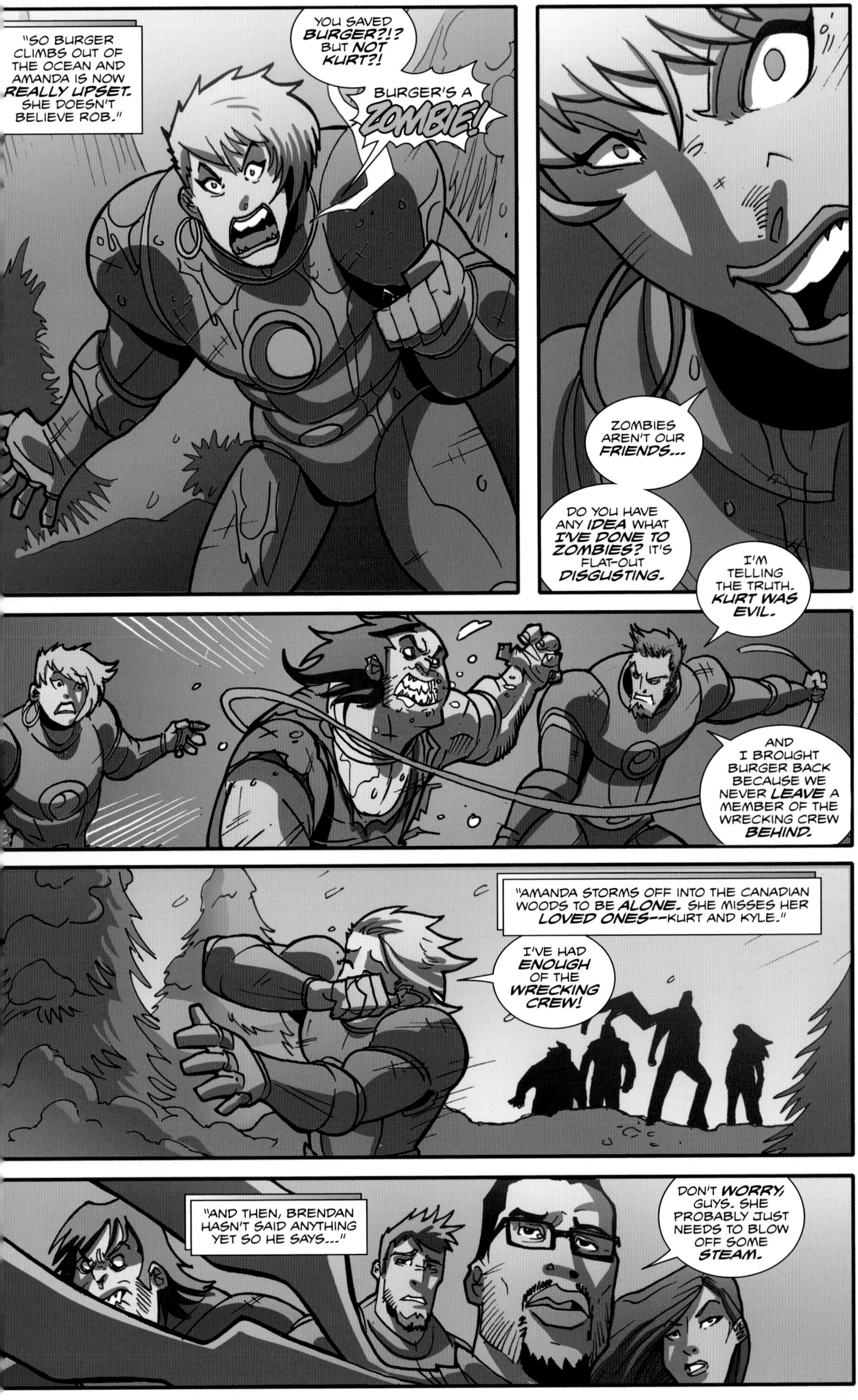
"SO BURGER CLIMBS OUT OF THE OCEAN AND AMANDA IS NOW REALLY UPSET. SHE DOESN'T BELIEVE ROB."
YOU SAVED BURGER?!? BUT NOT KURT?!
BURGER'S A ZOMBIE!
ZOMBIES AREN'T OUR FRIENDS...
DO YOU HAVE ANY IDEA WHAT I'VE DONE TO ZOMBIES? IT'S FLAT-OUT DISGUSTING.
I'M TELLING THE TRUTH. KURT WAS EVIL.
AND I BROUGHT BURGER BACK BECAUSE WE NEVER LEAVE A MEMBER OF THE WRECKING CREW BEHIND.
"AMANDA STORMS OFF INTO THE CANADIAN WOODS TO BE ALONE. SHE MISSES HER LOVED ONES--KURT AND KYLE."
I'VE HAD ENOUGH OF THE WRECKING CREW!
"AND THEN, BRENDAN HASN'T SAID ANYTHING YET SO HE SAYS..."
DON'T WORRY, GUYS. SHE PROBABLY JUST NEEDS TO BLOW OFF SOME STEAM.

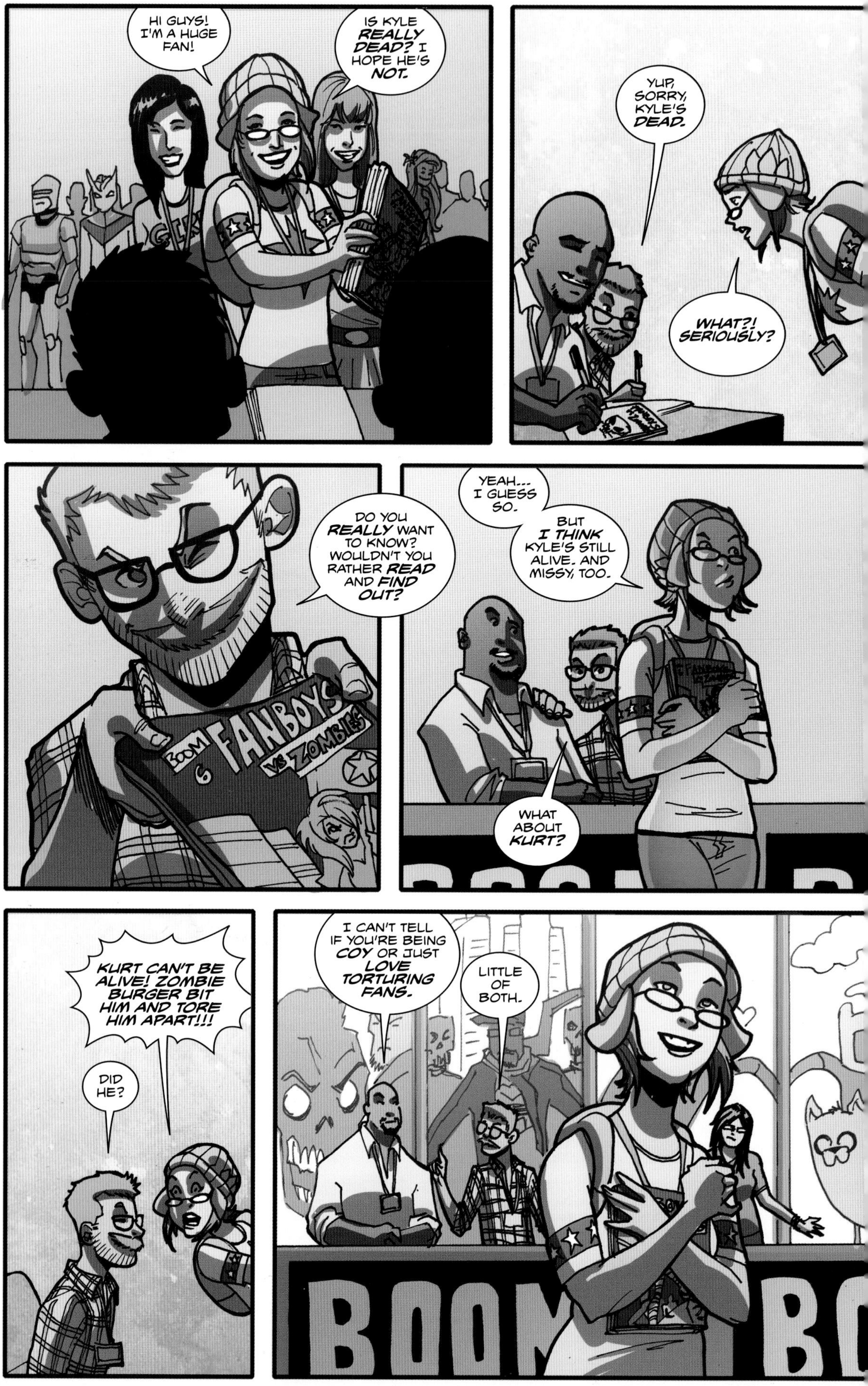

HI GUYS! I'M A HUGE FAN!
IS KYLE REALLY DEAD? I HOPE HE'S NOT.
YUP, SORRY, KYLE'S DEAD.
WHAT?! SERIOUSLY?
DO YOU REALLY WANT TO KNOW? WOULDN'T YOU RATHER READ AND FIND OUT?
BOOM
FANBOYS VS ZOMBIES
YEAH... I GUESS SO.
BUT I THINK KYLE'S STILL ALIVE. AND MISSY, TOO.
WHAT ABOUT KURT?
KURT CAN'T BE ALIVE! ZOMBIE BURGER BIT HIM AND TORE HIM APART!!!
DID HE?
I CAN'T TELL IF YOU'RE BEING COY OR JUST LOVE TORTURING FANS.
LITTLE OF BOTH.
BOOM

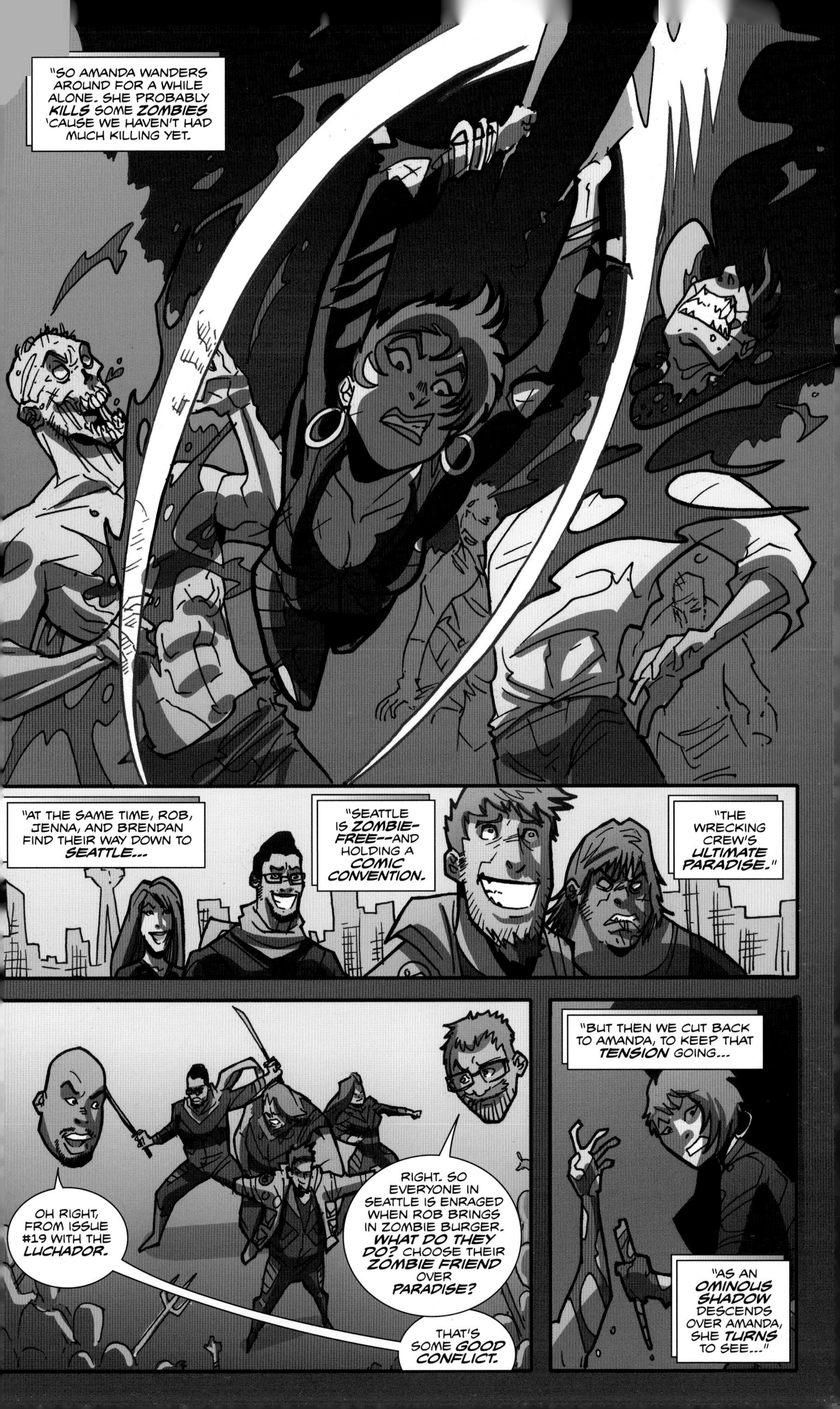
"SO AMANDA WANDERS AROUND FOR A WHILE ALONE. SHE PROBABLY KILLS SOME ZOMBIES 'CAUSE WE HAVEN'T HAD MUCH KILLING YET.
"AT THE SAME TIME, ROB, JENNA, AND BRENDAN FIND THEIR WAY DOWN TO SEATTLE...
"SEATTLE IS ZOMBIE-FREE--AND HOLDING A COMIC CONVENTION.
"THE WRECKING CREW'S ULTIMATE PARADISE."
OH RIGHT, FROM ISSUE #19 WITH THE LUCHADOR.
RIGHT. SO EVERYONE IN SEATTLE IS ENRAGED WHEN ROB BRINGS IN ZOMBIE BURGER. WHAT DO THEY DO? CHOOSE THEIR ZOMBIE FRIEND OVER PARADISE?
THAT'S SOME GOOD CONFLICT.
"BUT THEN WE CUT BACK TO AMANDA, TO KEEP THAT TENSION GOING...
"AS AN OMINOUS SHADOW DESCENDS OVER AMANDA, SHE TURNS TO SEE..."

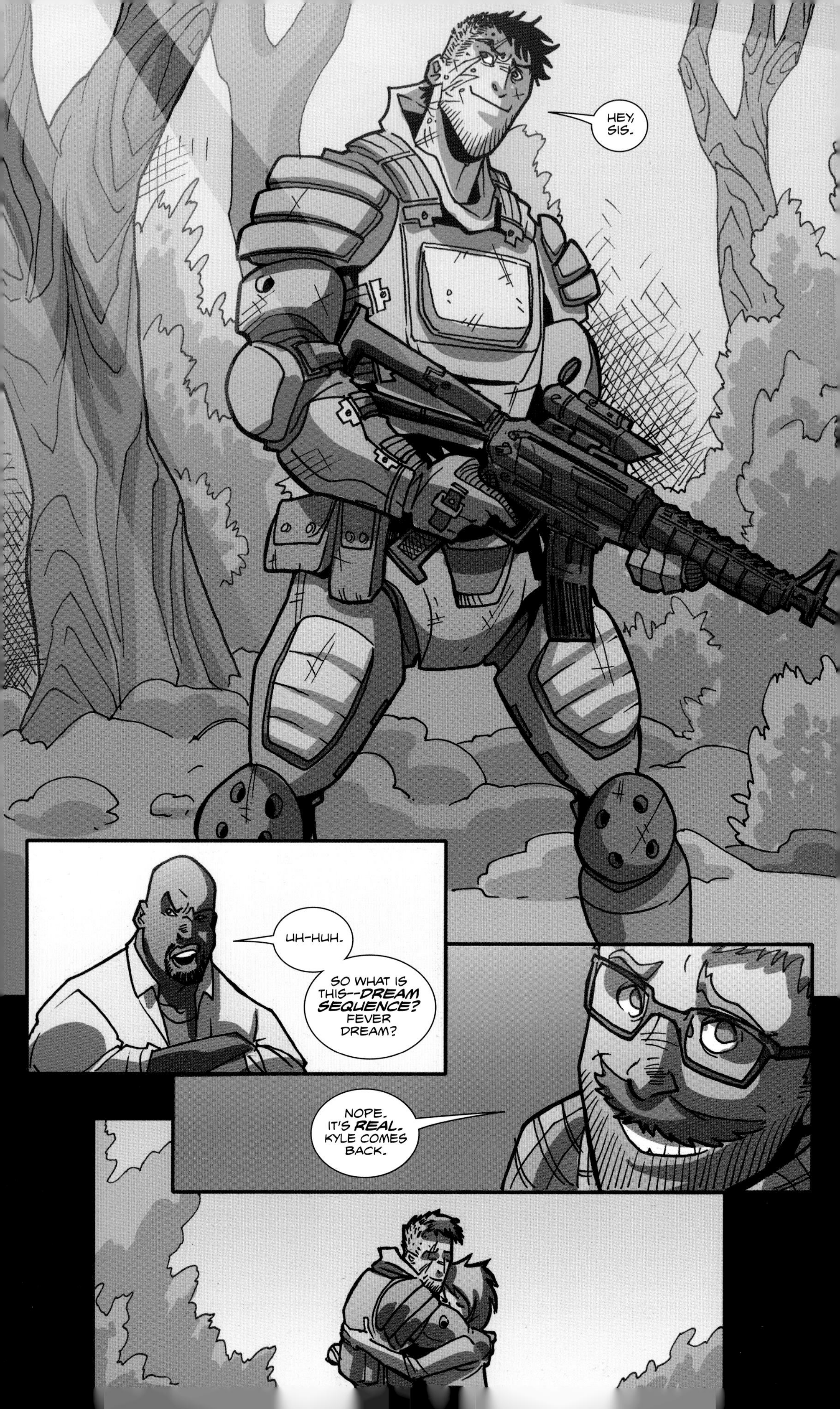
HEY, SIS.
UH-HUH.
SO WHAT IS THIS--DREAM SEQUENCE? FEVER DREAM?
NOPE. IT'S REAL. KYLE COMES BACK.

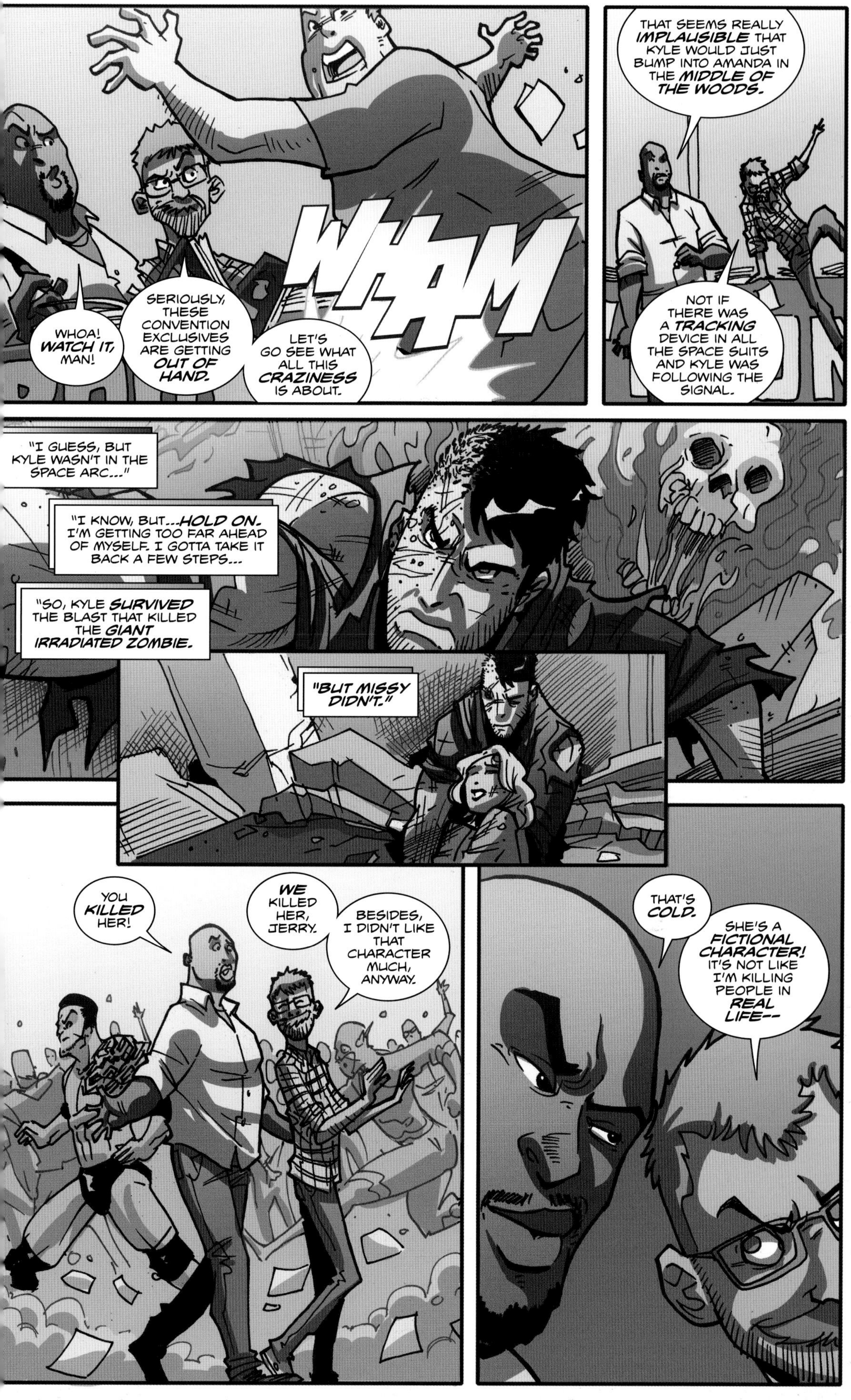
WHOA! WATCH IT, MAN!
SERIOUSLY, THESE CONVENTION EXCLUSIVES ARE GETTING OUT OF HAND.
LET'S GO SEE WHAT ALL THIS CRAZINESS IS ABOUT.
WHAM
THAT SEEMS REALLY IMPLAUSIBLE THAT KYLE WOULD JUST BUMP INTO AMANDA IN THE MIDDLE OF THE WOODS.
NOT IF THERE WAS A TRACKING DEVICE IN ALL THE SPACE SUITS AND KYLE WAS FOLLOWING THE SIGNAL.
"I GUESS, BUT KYLE WASN'T IN THE SPACE ARC..."
"I KNOW, BUT...HOLD ON. I'M GETTING TOO FAR AHEAD OF MYSELF. I GOTTA TAKE IT BACK A FEW STEPS...
"SO, KYLE SURVIVED THE BLAST THAT KILLED THE GIANT IRRADIATED ZOMBIE.
"BUT MISSY DIDN'T."
YOU KILLED HER!
WE KILLED HER, JERRY.
BESIDES, I DIDN'T LIKE THAT CHARACTER MUCH, ANYWAY.
THAT'S COLD.
SHE'S A FICTIONAL CHARACTER! IT'S NOT LIKE I'M KILLING PEOPLE IN REAL LIFE--

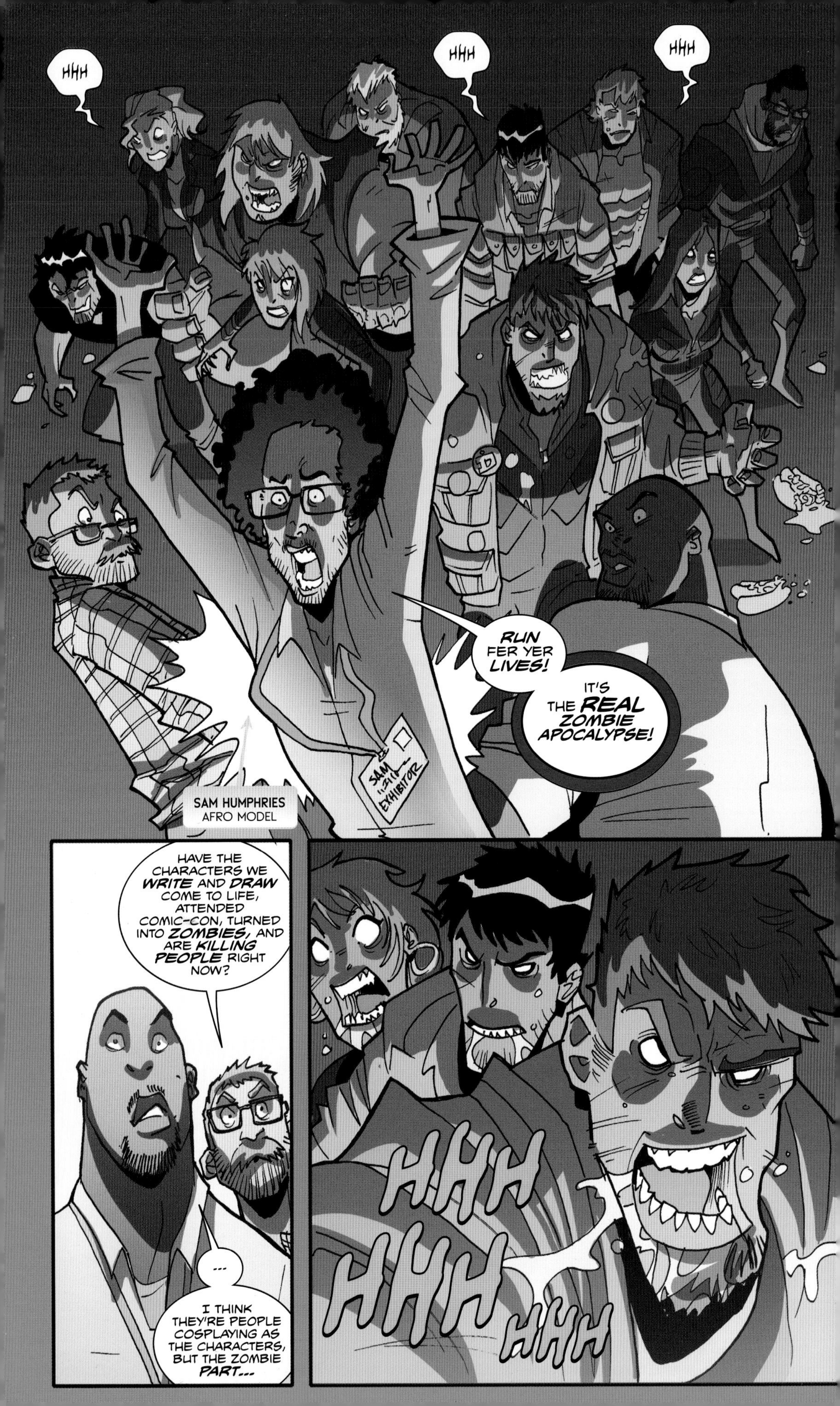
HHH
HHH
HHH
RUN FER YER LIVES!
IT'S THE REAL ZOMBIE APOCALYPSE!
SAM EXHIBITOR
SAM HUMPHRIES
AFRO MODEL
HAVE THE CHARACTERS WE WRITE AND DRAW COME TO LIFE, ATTENDED COMIC-CON, TURNED INTO ZOMBIES, AND ARE KILLING PEOPLE RIGHT NOW?
...
I THINK THEY'RE PEOPLE COSPLAYING AS THE CHARACTERS, BUT THE ZOMBIE PART...
HHH HHH HHH

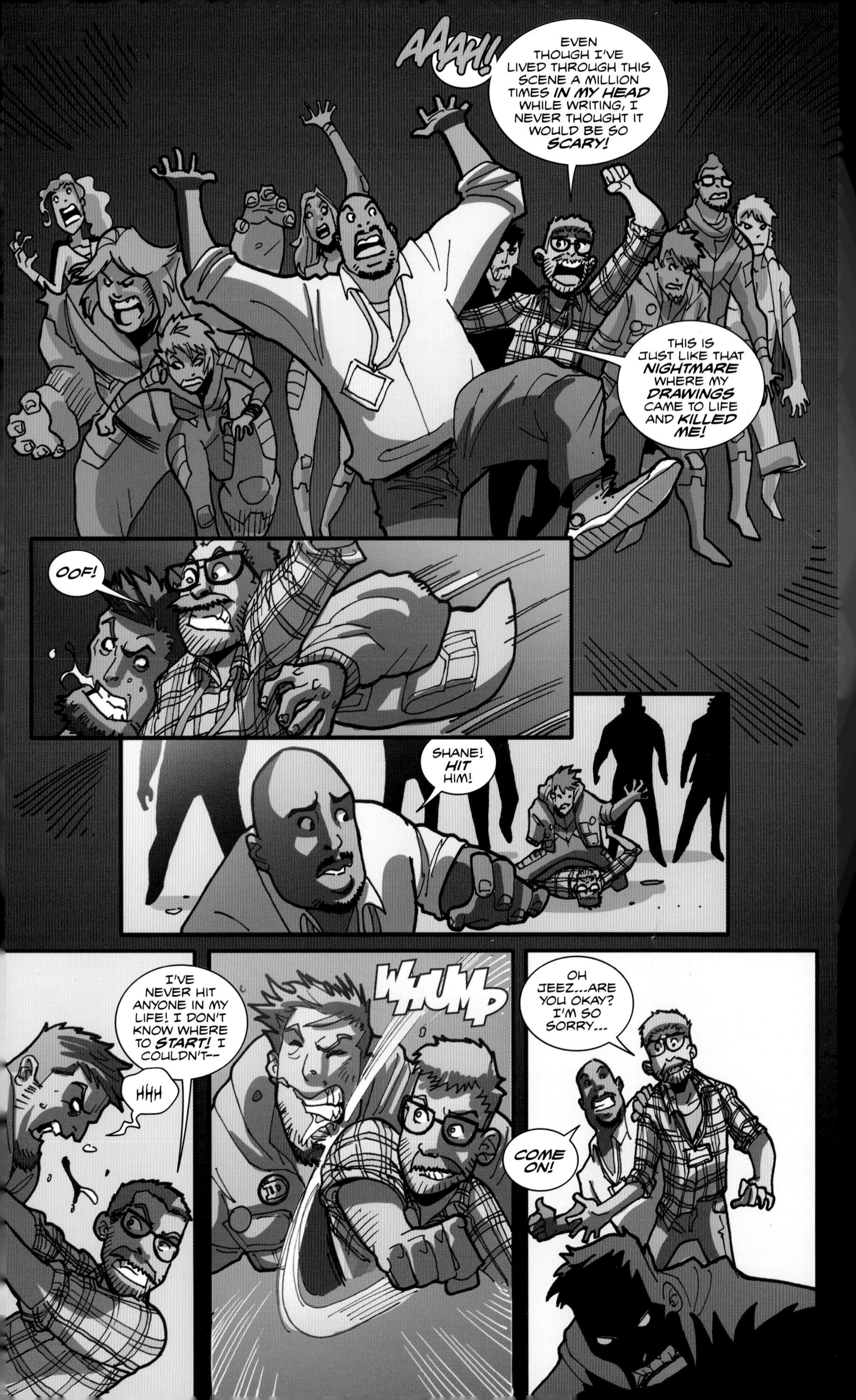
AAAAH!!
EVEN THOUGH I'VE LIVED THROUGH THIS SCENE A MILLION TIMES IN MY HEAD WHILE WRITING, I NEVER THOUGHT IT WOULD BE SO SCARY!
THIS IS JUST LIKE THAT NIGHTMARE WHERE MY DRAWINGS CAME TO LIFE AND KILLED ME!
OOF!
SHANE! HIT HIM!
I'VE NEVER HIT ANYONE IN MY LIFE! I DON'T KNOW WHERE TO START! I COULDN'T--
HHH
WHUMP
OH JEEZ...ARE YOU OKAY? I'M SO SORRY...
COME ON!

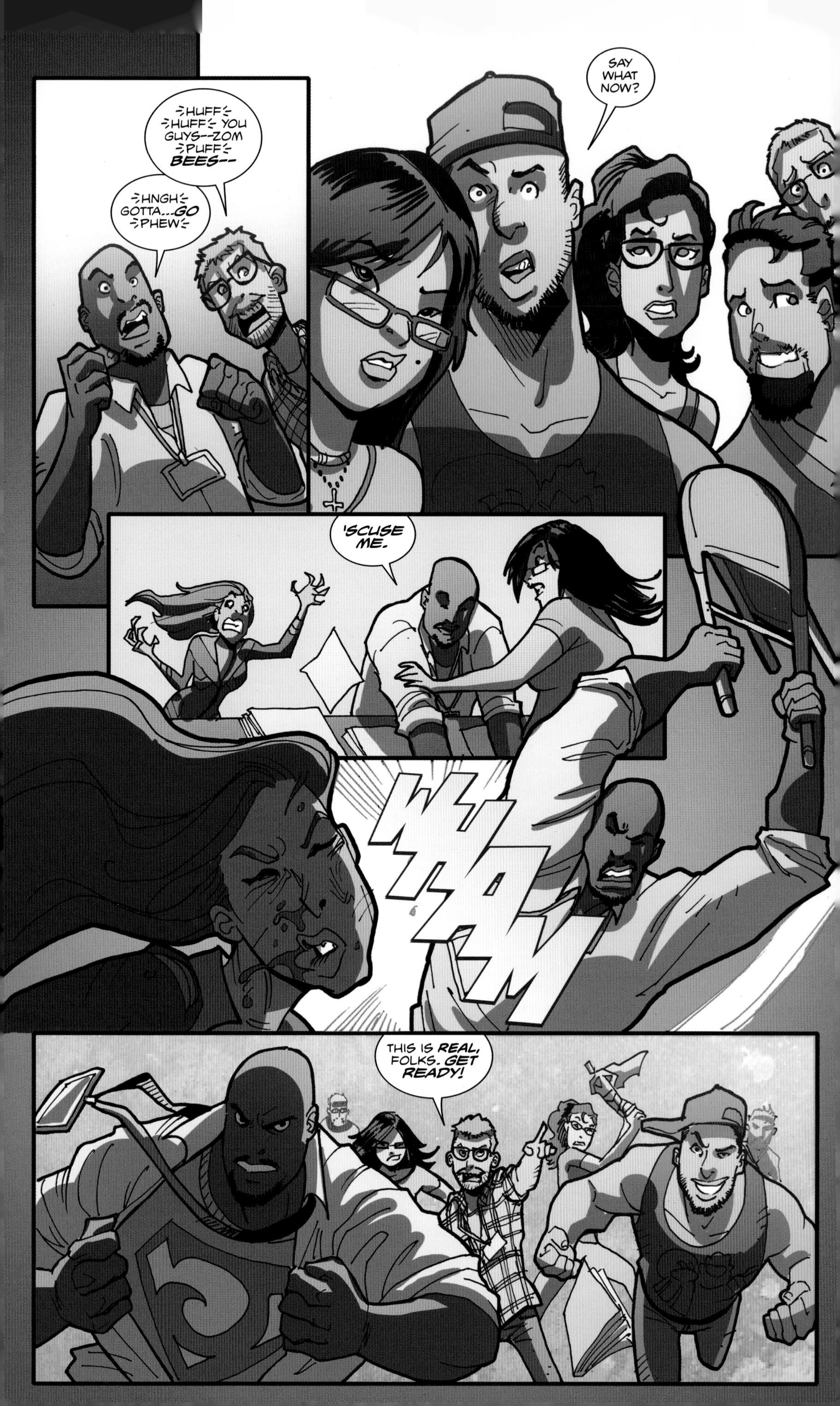
HUFF HUFF YOU GUYS--ZOM PUFF BEES--
HNGH GOTTA...GO PHEW
SAY WHAT NOW?
'SCUSE ME.
WHAM
THIS IS REAL, FOLKS. GET READY!

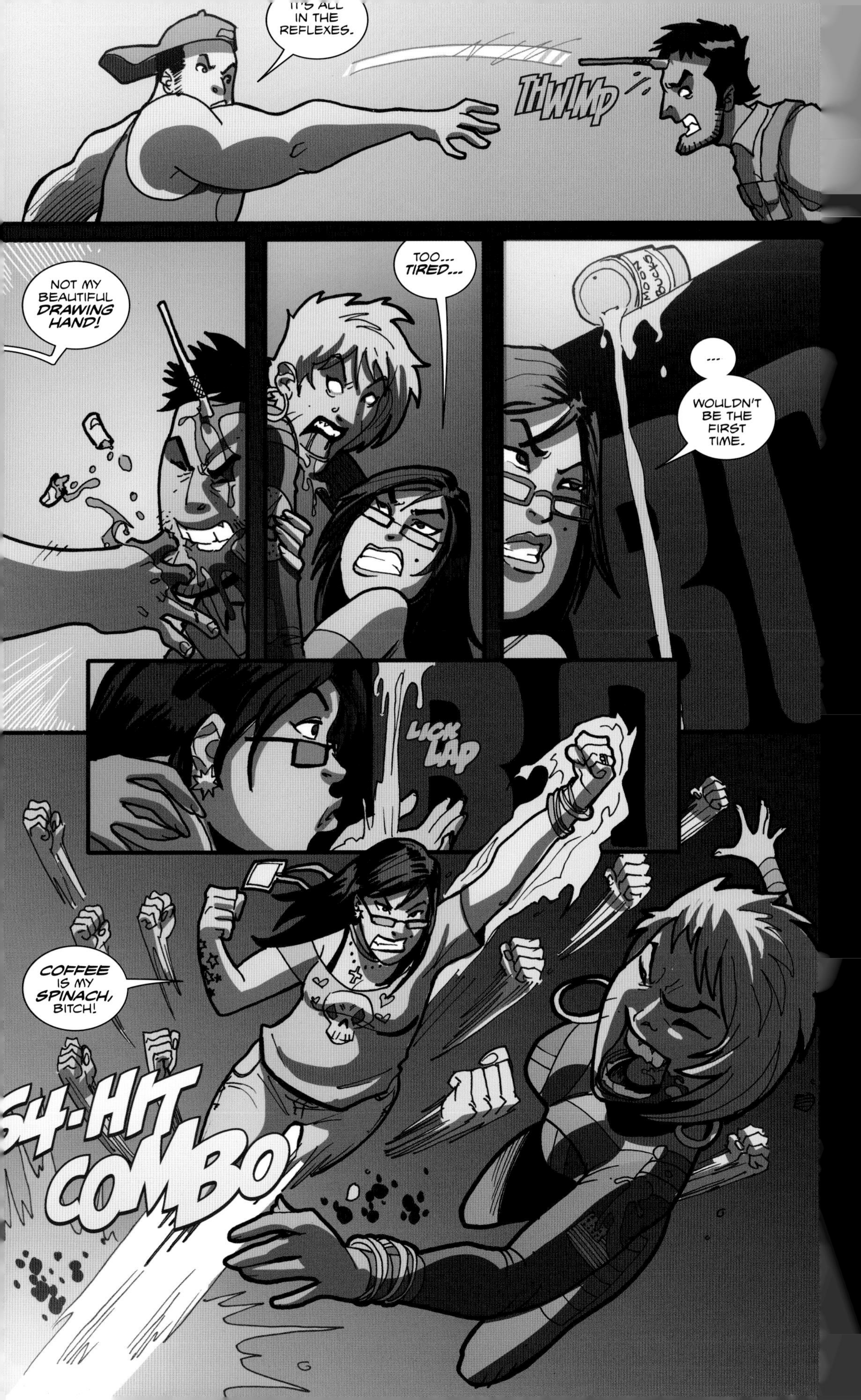

IT'S ALL IN THE REFLEXES.
THWIMP
NOT MY BEAUTIFUL DRAWING HAND!
TOO... TIRED...
MOON BUCKS
...
WOULDN'T BE THE FIRST TIME.
LICK LAP
COFFEE IS MY SPINACH, BITCH!
54-HIT COMBO!

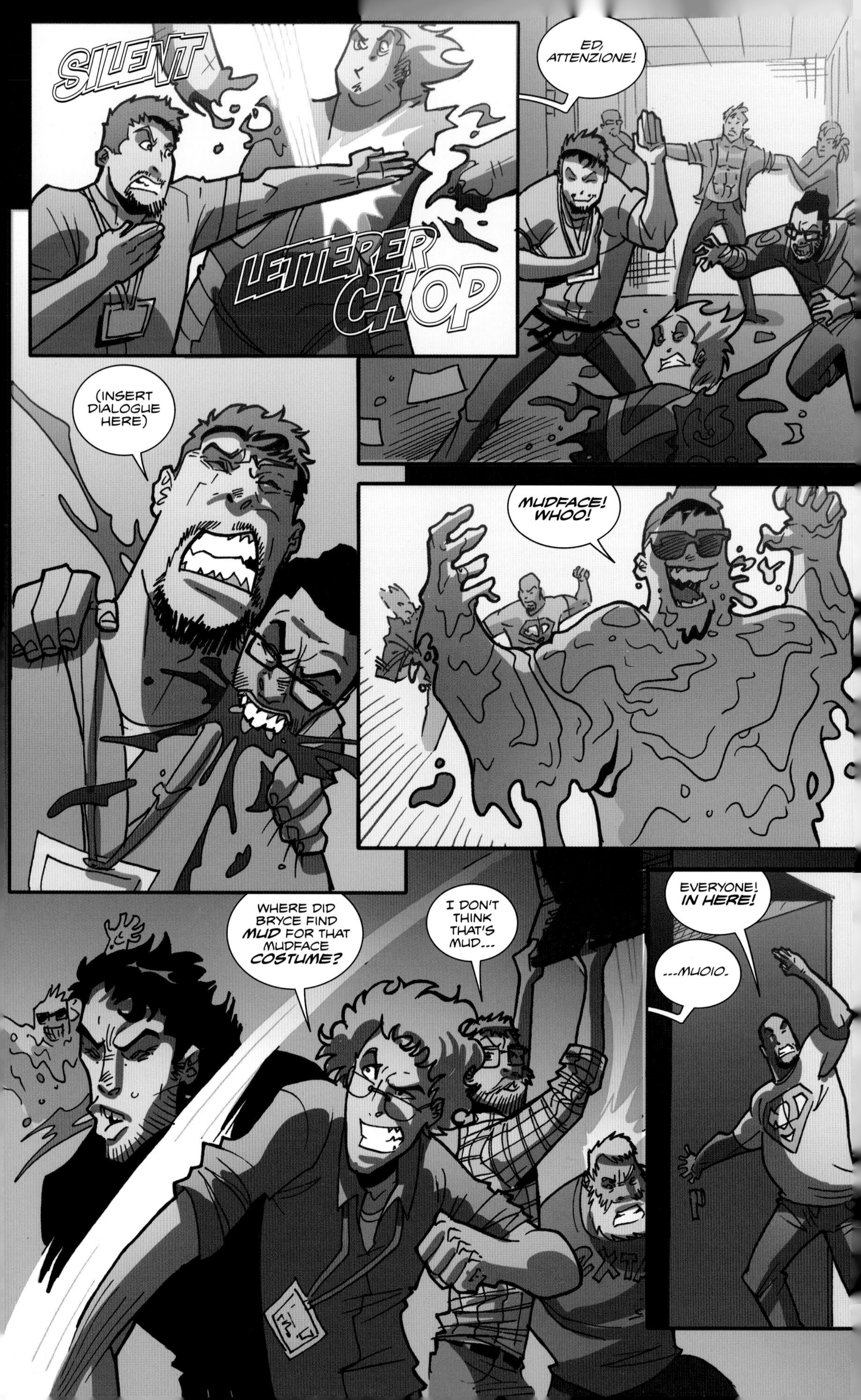
SILENT
LETTERER CHOP
ED, ATTENZIONE!
(INSERT DIALOGUE HERE)
MUDFACE! WHOO!
WHERE DID BRYCE FIND MUD FOR THAT MUDFACE COSTUME?
I DON'T THINK THAT'S MUD...
EVERYONE! IN HERE!
...MUOIO.

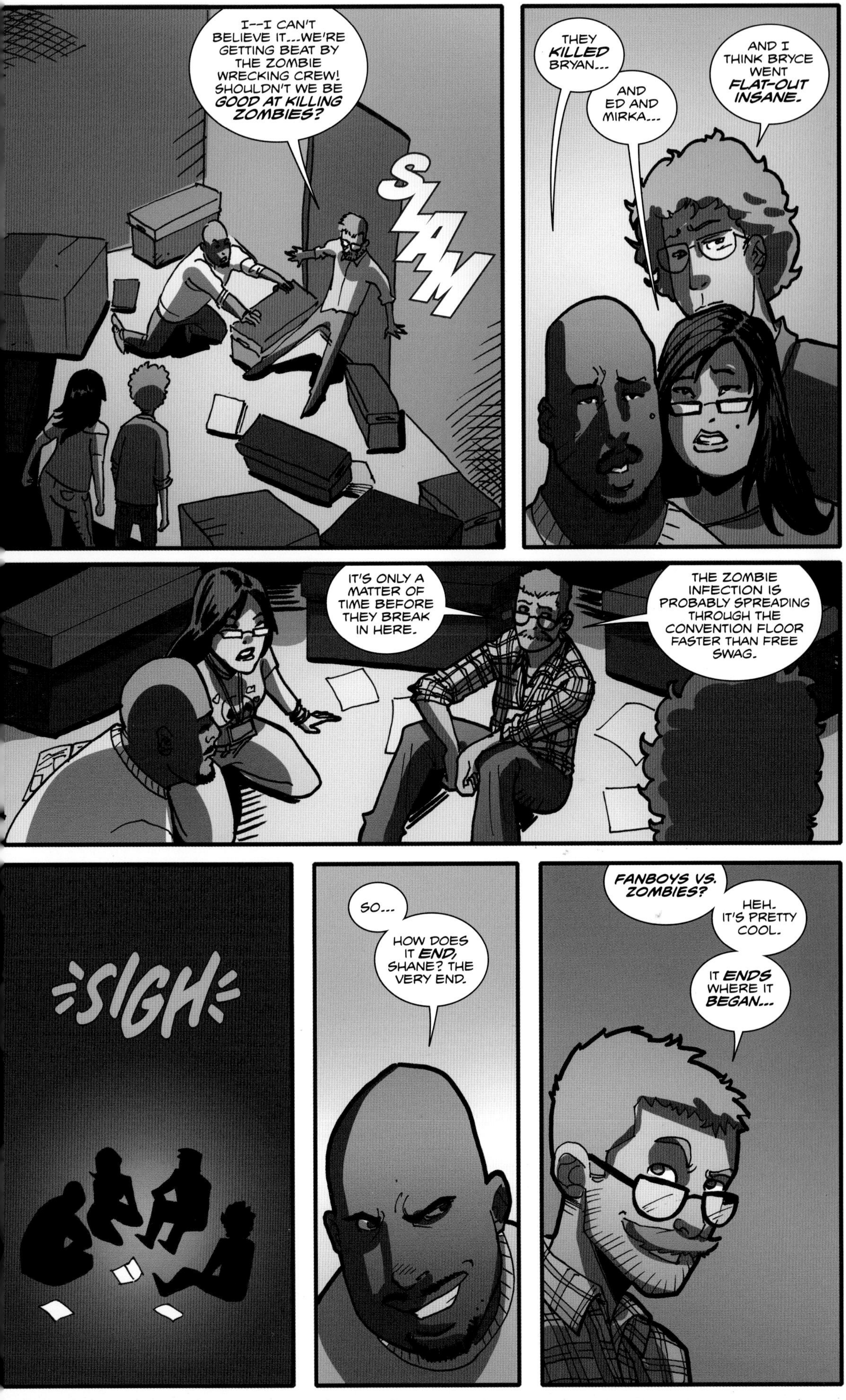
I--I CAN'T BELIEVE IT...WE'RE GETTING BEAT BY THE ZOMBIE WRECKING CREW! SHOULDN'T WE BE GOOD AT KILLING ZOMBIES?
SLAM
THEY KILLED BRYAN...
AND ED AND MIRKA...
AND I THINK BRYCE WENT FLAT-OUT INSANE.
IT'S ONLY A MATTER OF TIME BEFORE THEY BREAK IN HERE.
THE ZOMBIE INFECTION IS PROBABLY SPREADING THROUGH THE CONVENTION FLOOR FASTER THAN FREE SWAG.
SIGH
SO...
HOW DOES IT END, SHANE? THE VERY END.
FANBOYS VS. ZOMBIES?
HEH. IT'S PRETTY COOL.
IT ENDS WHERE IT BEGAN...

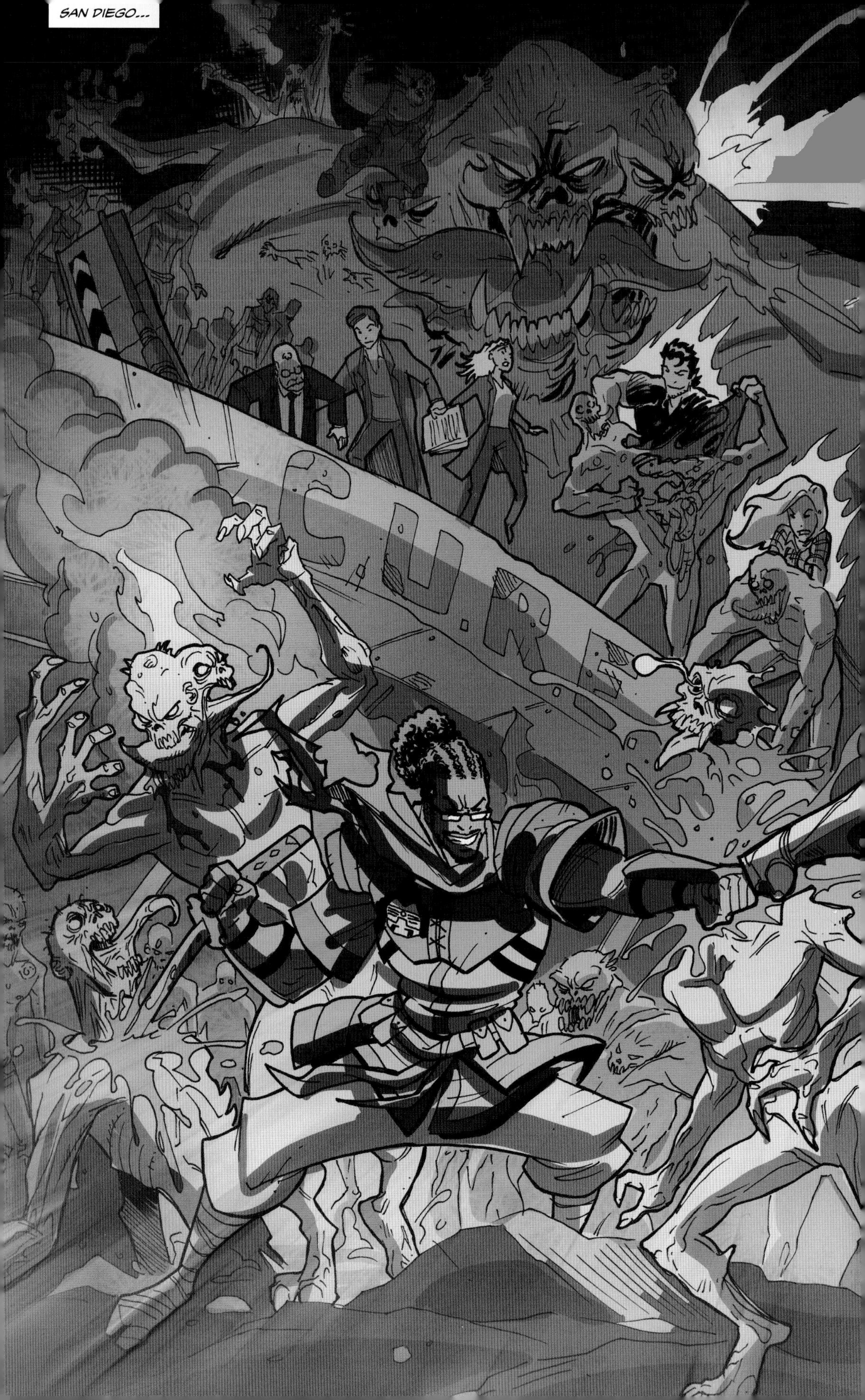
SAN DIEGO...

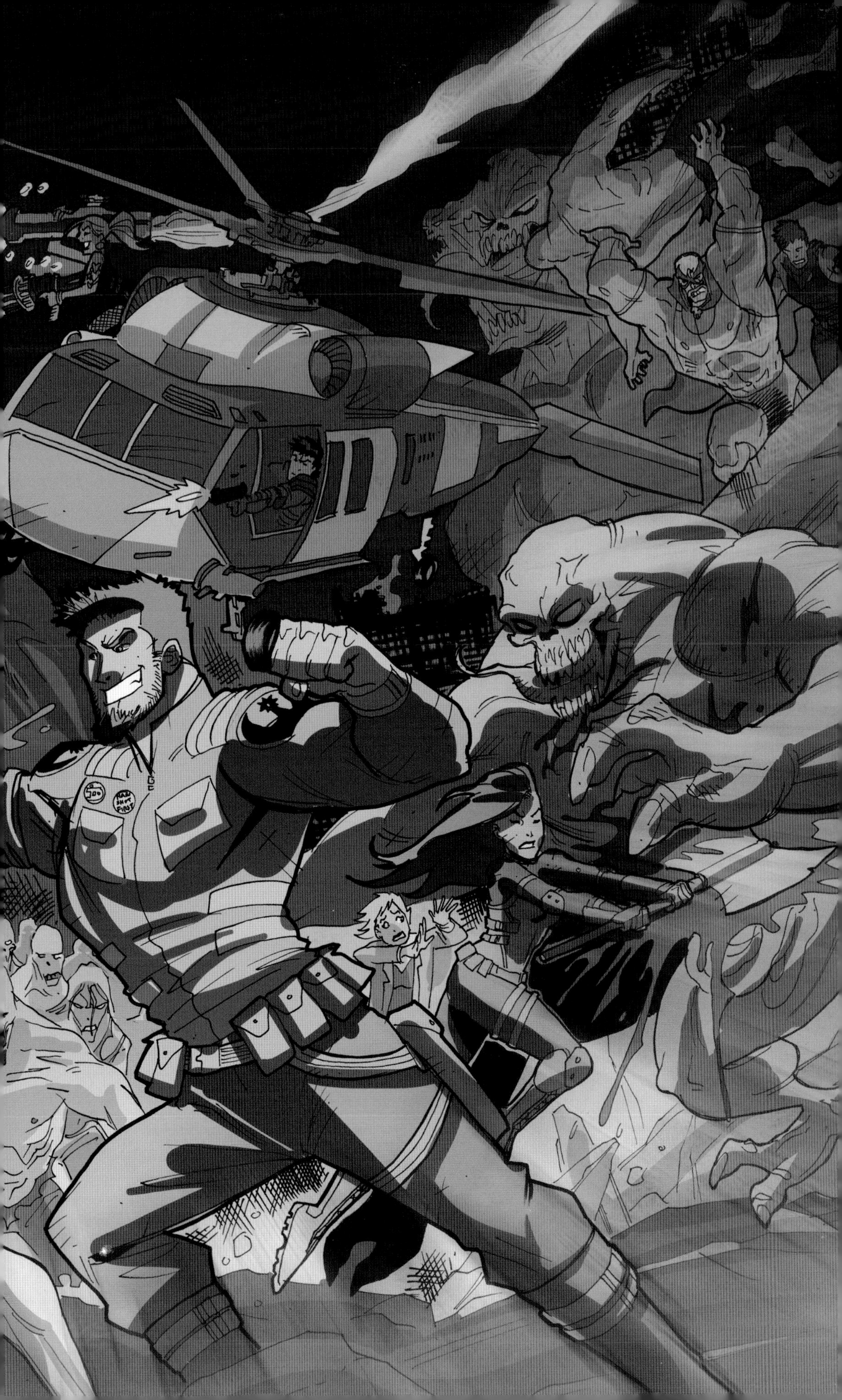
500
HAN SHOT FIRST

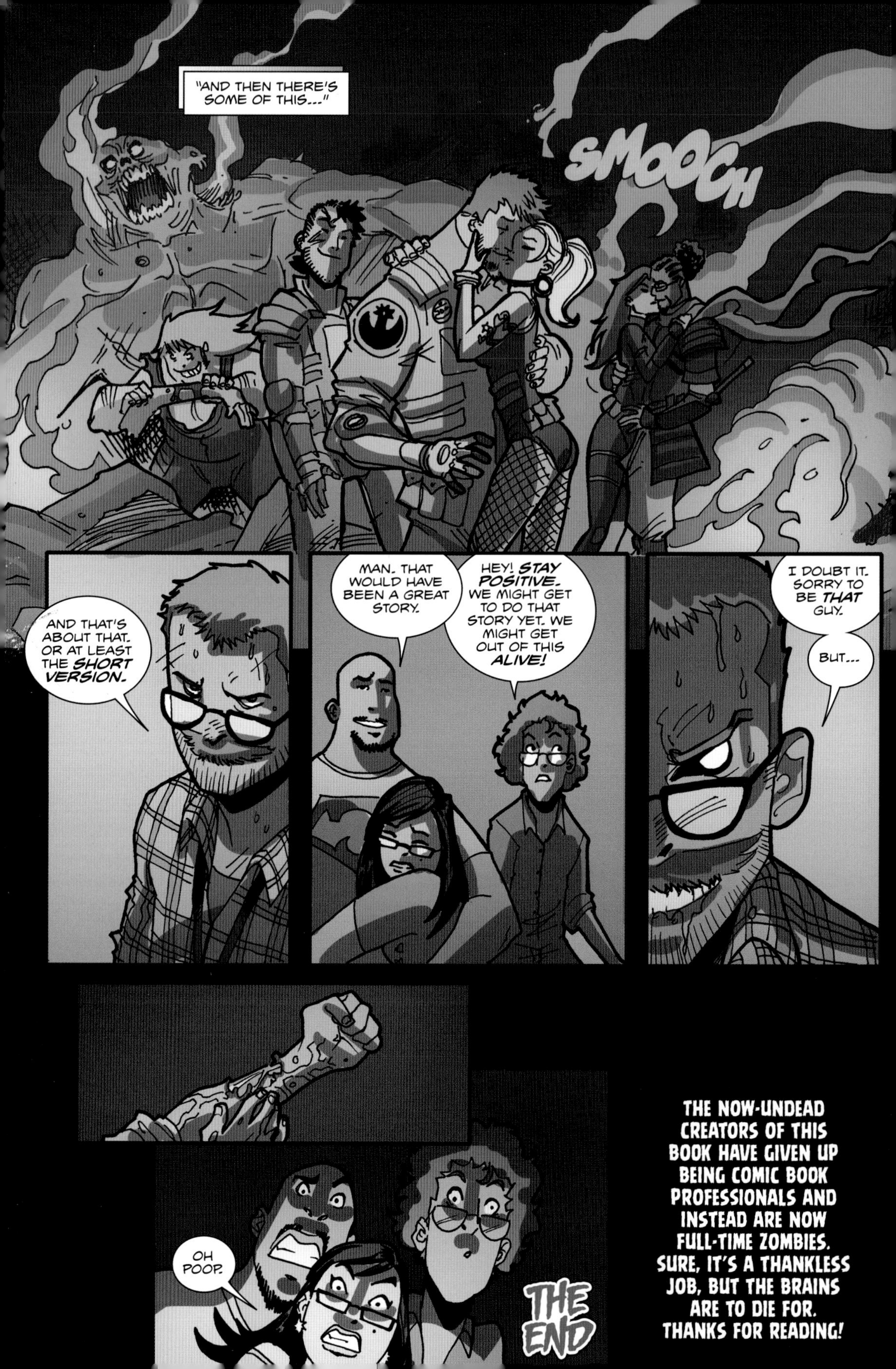

"AND THEN THERE'S SOME OF THIS..."
SMOOCH
AND THAT'S ABOUT THAT. OR AT LEAST THE SHORT VERSION.
MAN. THAT WOULD HAVE BEEN A GREAT STORY.
HEY! STAY POSITIVE. WE MIGHT GET TO DO THAT STORY YET. WE MIGHT GET OUT OF THIS ALIVE!
I DOUBT IT. SORRY TO BE THAT GUY.
BUT...
OH POOP.
THE END
THE NOW-UNDEAD CREATORS OF THIS BOOK HAVE GIVEN UP BEING COMIC BOOK PROFESSIONALS AND INSTEAD ARE NOW FULL-TIME ZOMBIES. SURE, IT'S A THANKLESS JOB, BUT THE BRAINS ARE TO DIE FOR. THANKS FOR READING!

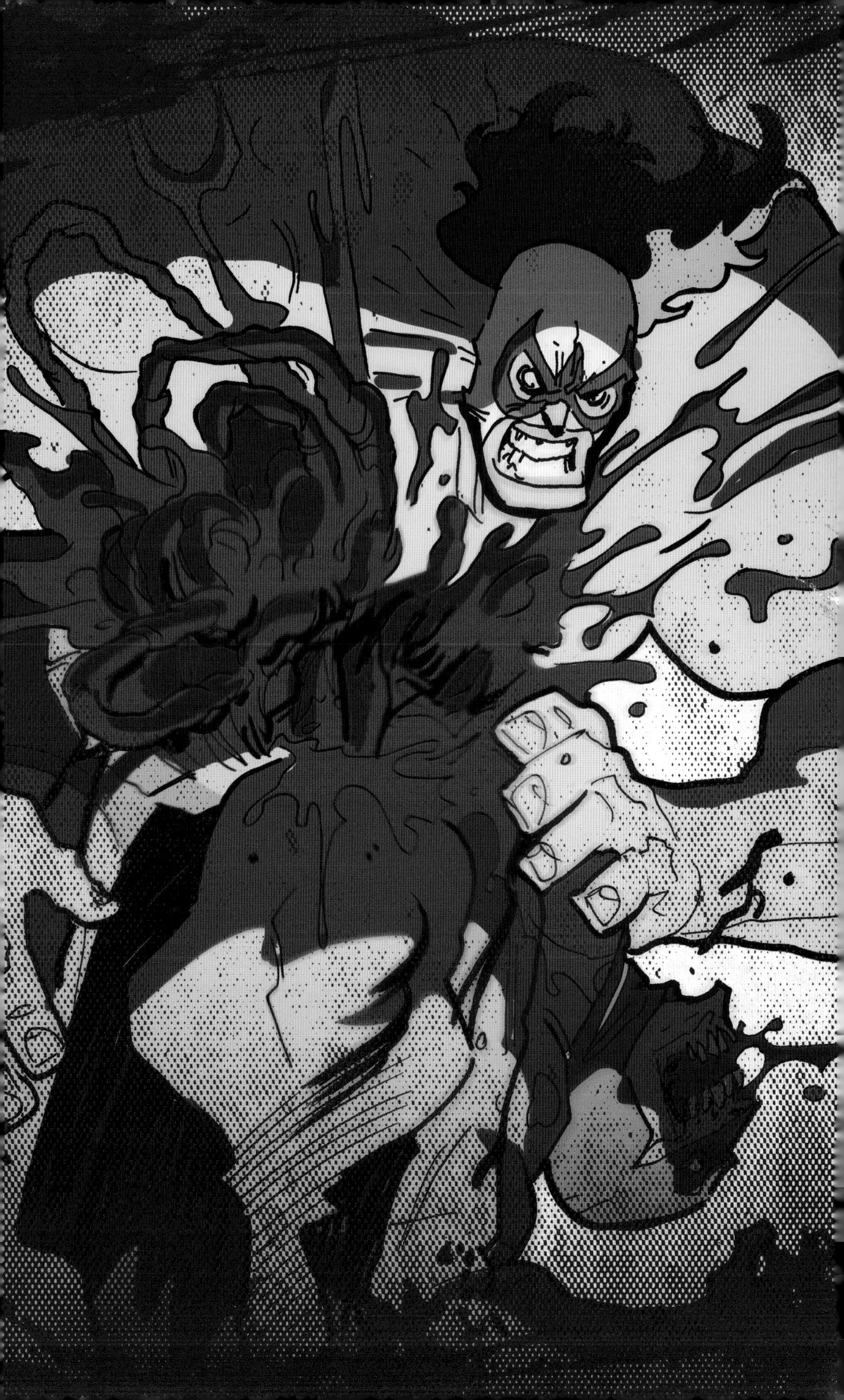

COVER GALLERY

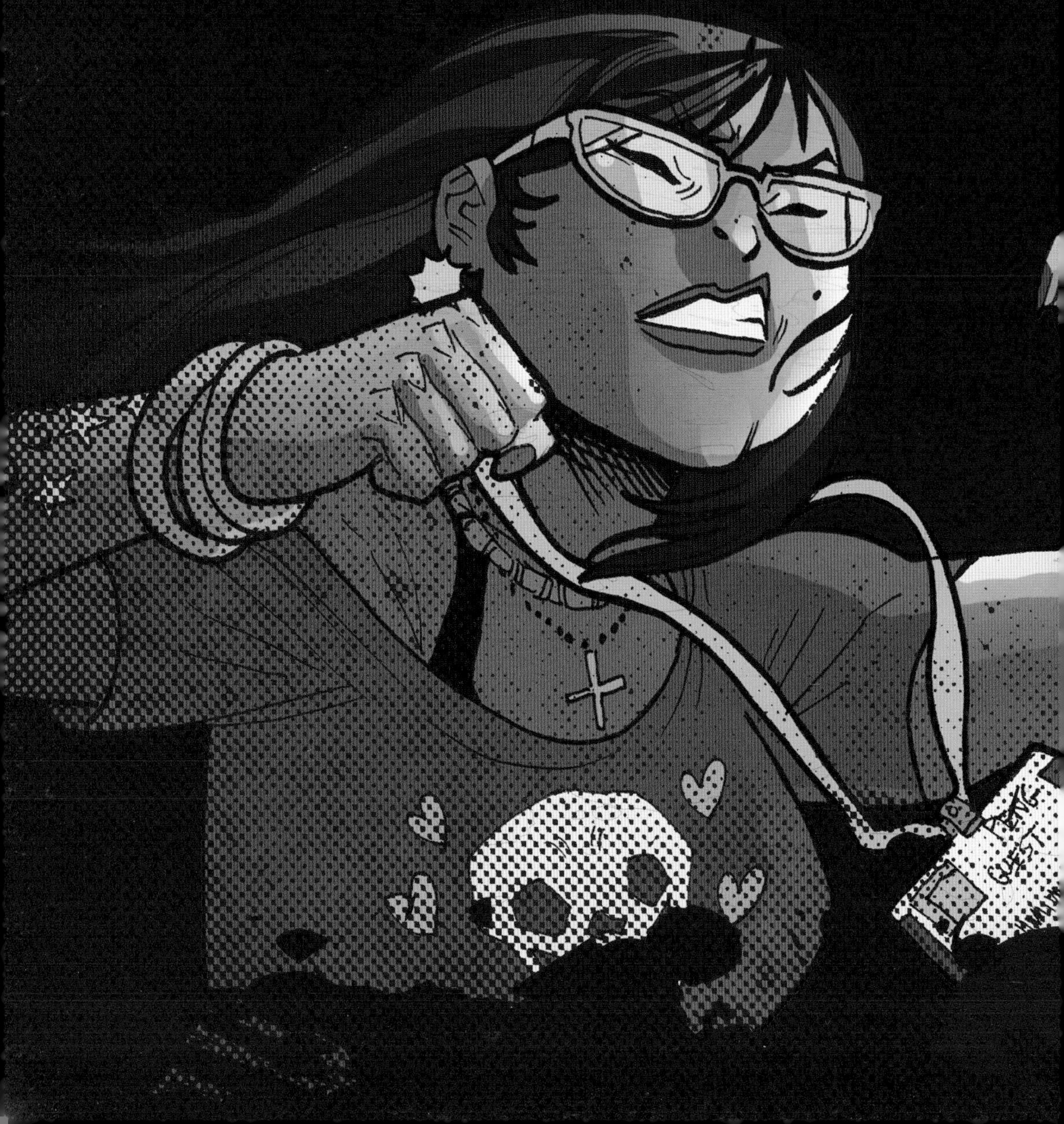

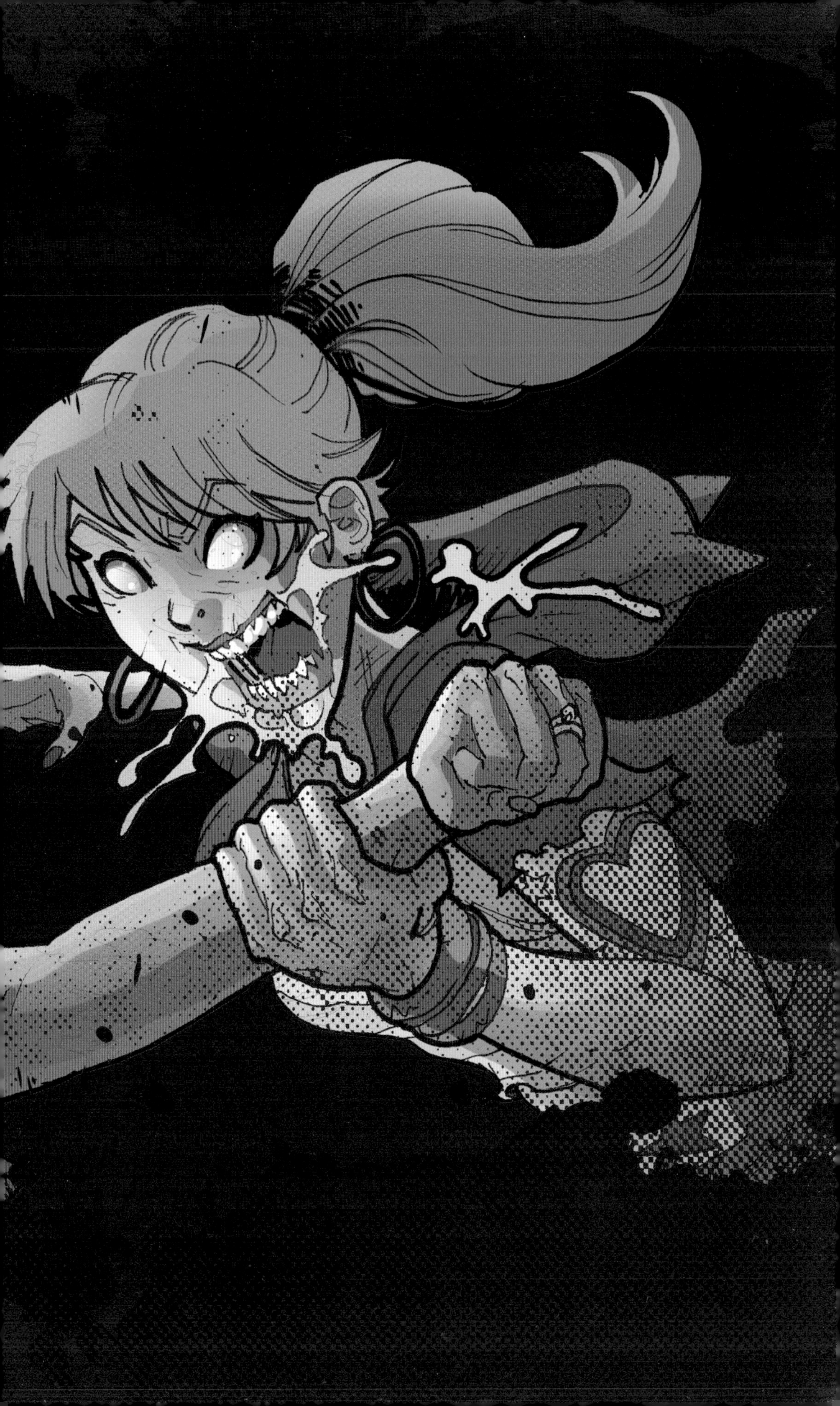

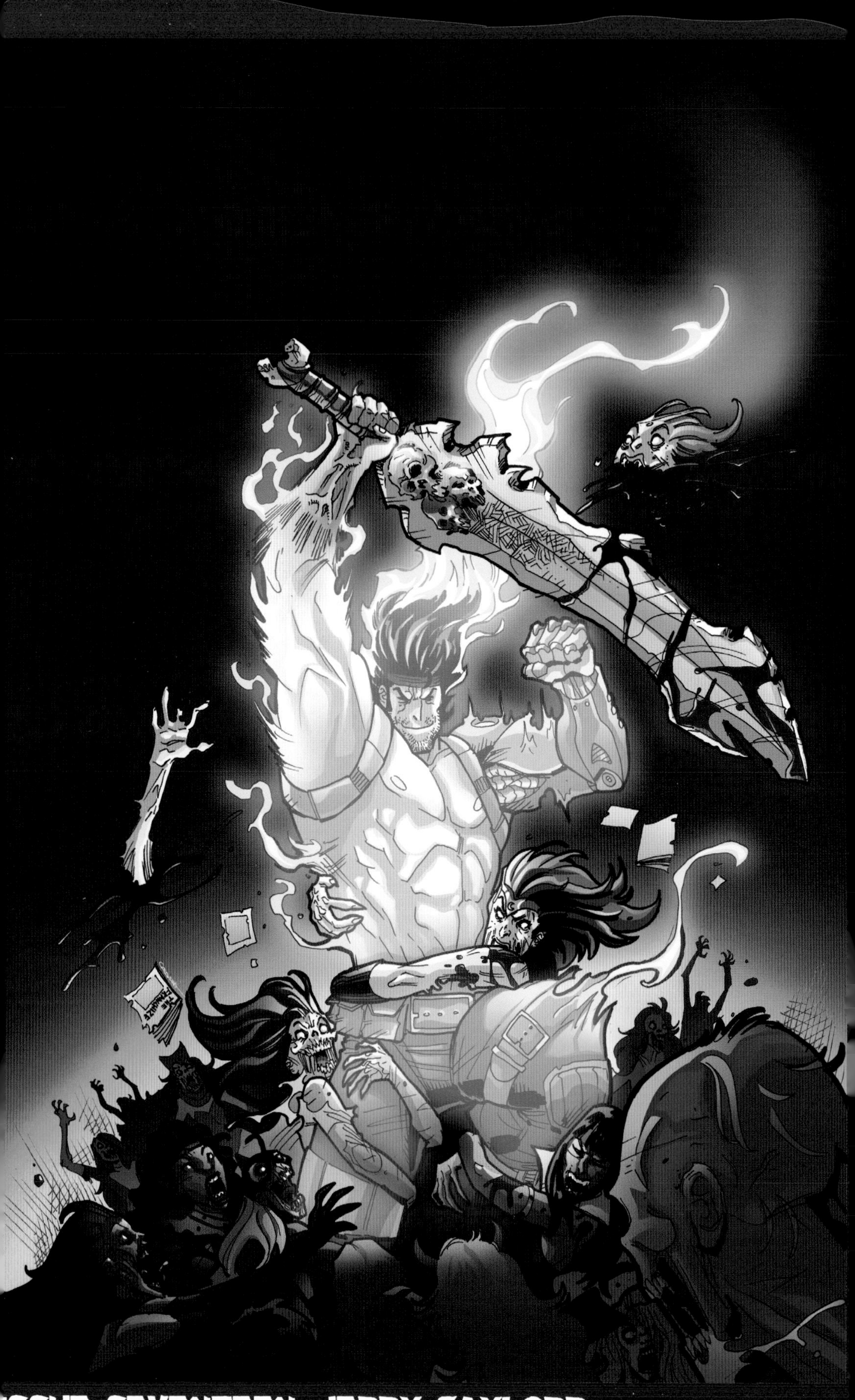

ISSUE SEVENTEEN: JERRY GAYLORD
WITH COLORS BY GABRIEL CASSATA

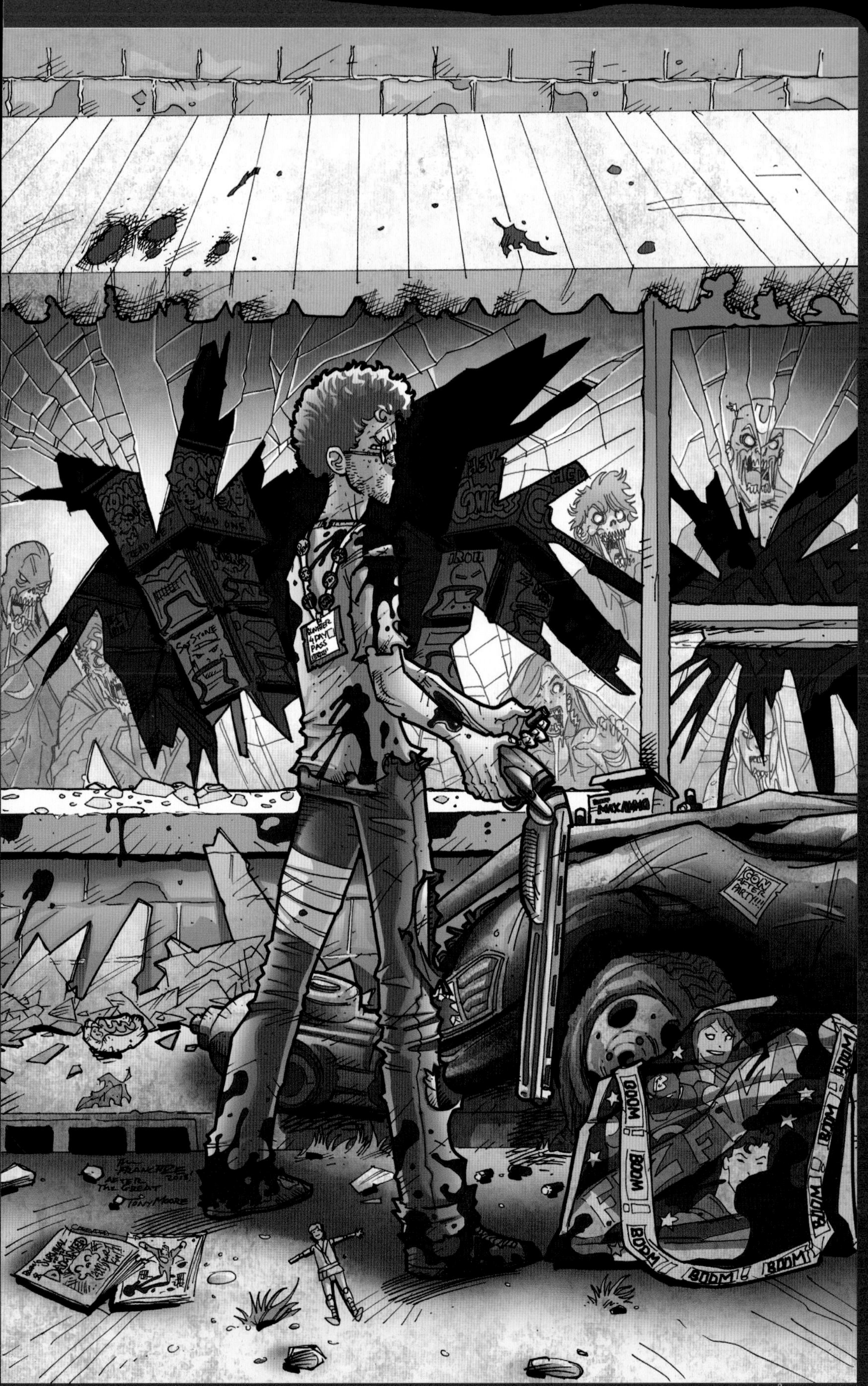
4 DAY PASS
MAX AMMO
CON AFTER PARTY!!!
BOOM

ISSUE EIGHTEEN: JERRY GAYLORD
WITH COLORS BY GABRIEL CASSATA

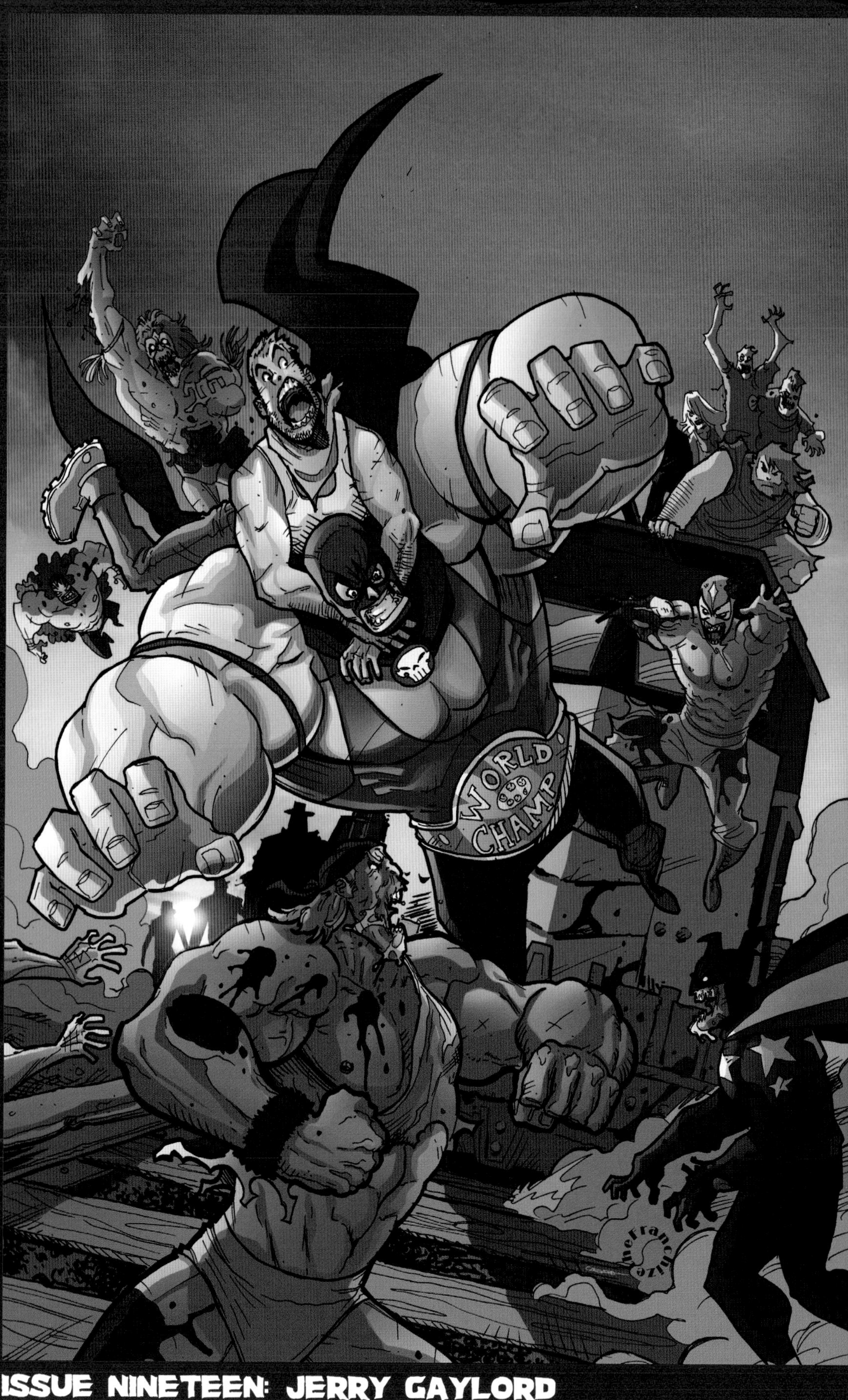
WORLD CHAMP

ISSUE NINETEEN: JERRY GAYLORD
WITH COLORS BY GABRIEL CASSATA

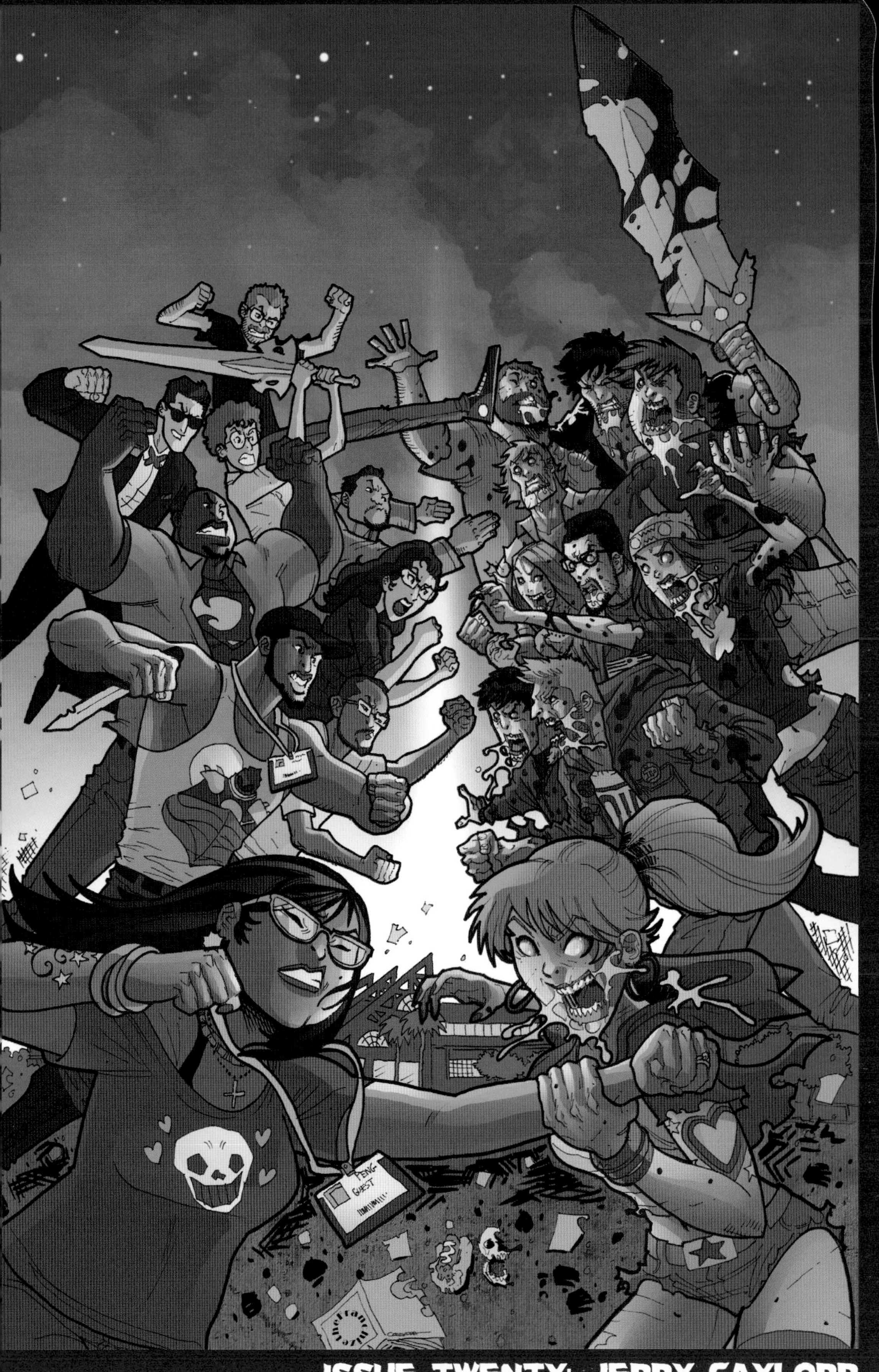

ISSUE TWENTY: JERRY GAYLORD
WITH COLORS BY GABRIEL CASSATA

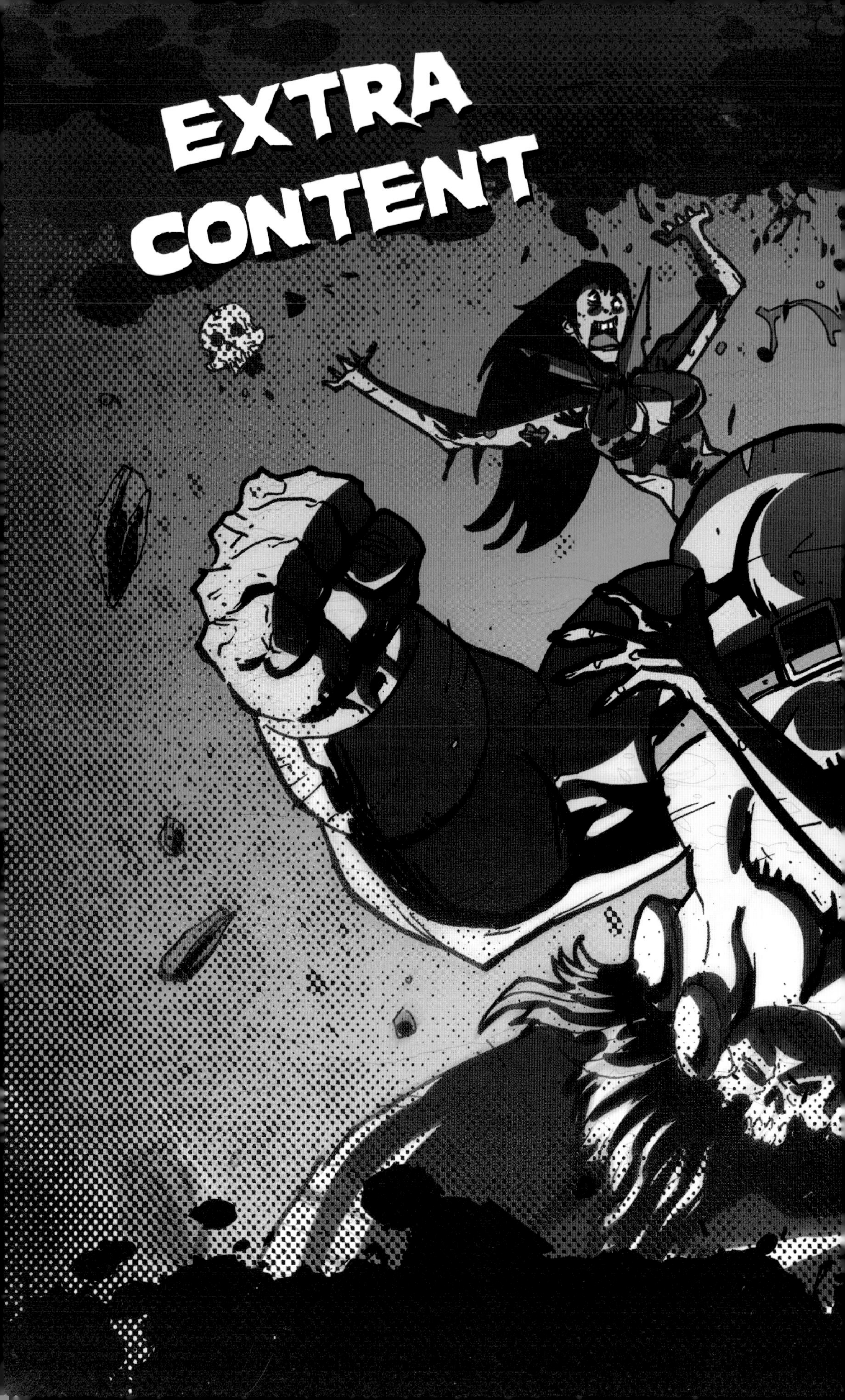
EXTRA CONTENT

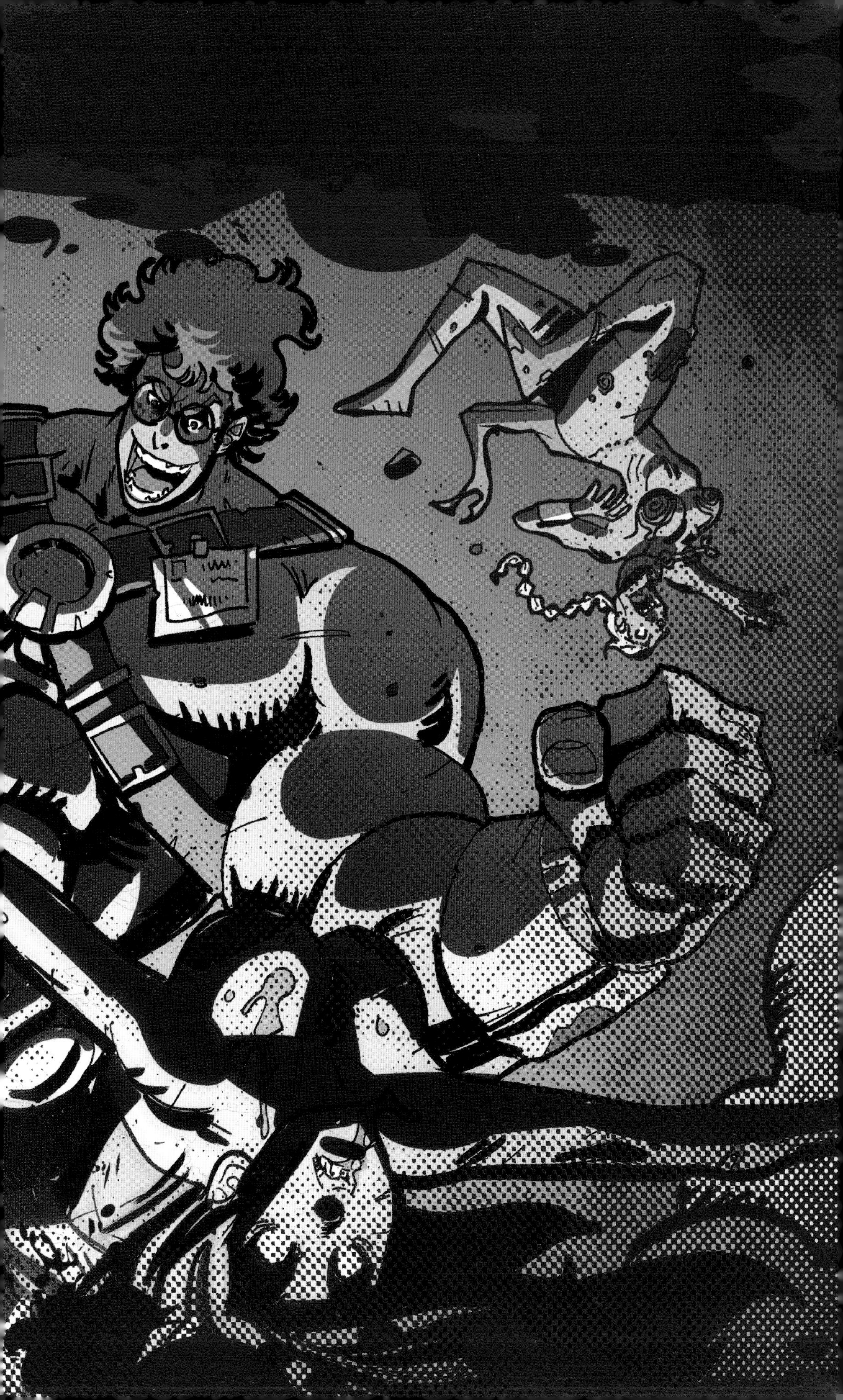

HOW TO SURVIVE A
ZOMBIE APOCALYPSE COMIC BOOK
(WITH ONLY MINIMAL BITES AND FLESH WOUNDS)

Working in comics can be a dangerous place: There are rabid fans*, probably a few stairs to climb at the local convention, and the threat of constant paper cuts looms over you like a halo on an angel. That's a terrible analogy, but you get what I'm saying. I can deal with that stuff. I'm a leather-jacket-wearing cool guy dude when it comes to that stuff. What I wasn't prepared for were the coworkers.

I started writing FANBOYS VS. ZOMBIES on Issue #9 after Sam Humphries left the book for unknown reasons. Sam passed the writing torch off to me and said, "Watch out for Jerry. He's a biter." I laughed and nodded politely like I actually understood what he was saying.

When I showed up to the BOOM! Studios offices the next Monday morning for work I was greeted by a shifty-eyed editor named Eric Harburn. He tightly grasped my hand in his moist palms and said, "Follow me or run. It's your choice." Wanting to make a good first impression, I said, "Your hands are really sweaty."

Eric led me up to the offices where I met the rest of the BOOM! crew. The overall vibe was...uneasy. Everyone was sweating or bleeding or oozing in some odd manner. But they had free soda in the fridge so who was I to complain?

While sucking down a Diet 7-Up, Eric kicked me into a window-less office and locked the door. I thought it was strange at first, but then I found out that was where they kept my coworker and artist on the book. In the corner sat Jerry Gaylord, hunched over a small trash can, chewing on what looked like one of those rubber human hands you see around Halloween time. I knew right away: My office buddy was a practical joker!

Jerry snarled a greeting at me. I'm not a good snarler, but I attempted a similar salutation right back. It must have come out more like a grunt because Jerry was clearly offended. He leaped at me, pinning me against a bloodstained wall.

Jerry's jaws snapped at me as he tried to claw out my eyeballs. Luckily, he only got one of them. Even more luckily, I still had my can of Diet 7-Up. I don't normally like to do this to new coworkers, but I rammed the aluminum can down Jerry's windpipe. This seemed to quiet him down for a moment. Jerry looked confused, pawed at his neck a bit, then shrugged and began drawing decapitated Ninja Turtles over at his drawing table.

Over the next year, Jerry and I worked on twelve issues of FANBOYS VS. ZOMBIES in that tiny, dark office, each taking turns at using the trash can as a toilet. We'd turn in scripts written with hair and fingernail scraps and final sequential pages inked in spit and mucus through a tiny slot under the door. Years later I saw what a final issue of FvZ looked like, all lettered and colored and everything, and I gotta say… Photoshop is magic.

Anyway, after one full year of working on FvZ, Eric the editor unlocked and opened the office door and confirmed my initial suspicions: Jerry was, in fact, a zombie the whole time.

"I never thought the series would go on for this long," Eric said. "I expected Jerry to literally eat you alive in there."

"Well, you don't know Jack…and I'm Jack," I said, trying to sound cool.

I walked out of the BOOM! Studios offices like a gladiator. I had survived. Oh, wait… wasn't this supposed to be some sort of How-To thing? Whatever. If you want to survive zombie comics, I guess the best thing to do is to write them. That way you can make up what ever you want and they have to print it. Kinda like this afterword.

Your pal,
SHANE HOUGHTON

* I have yet to actually meet a fan with rabies.

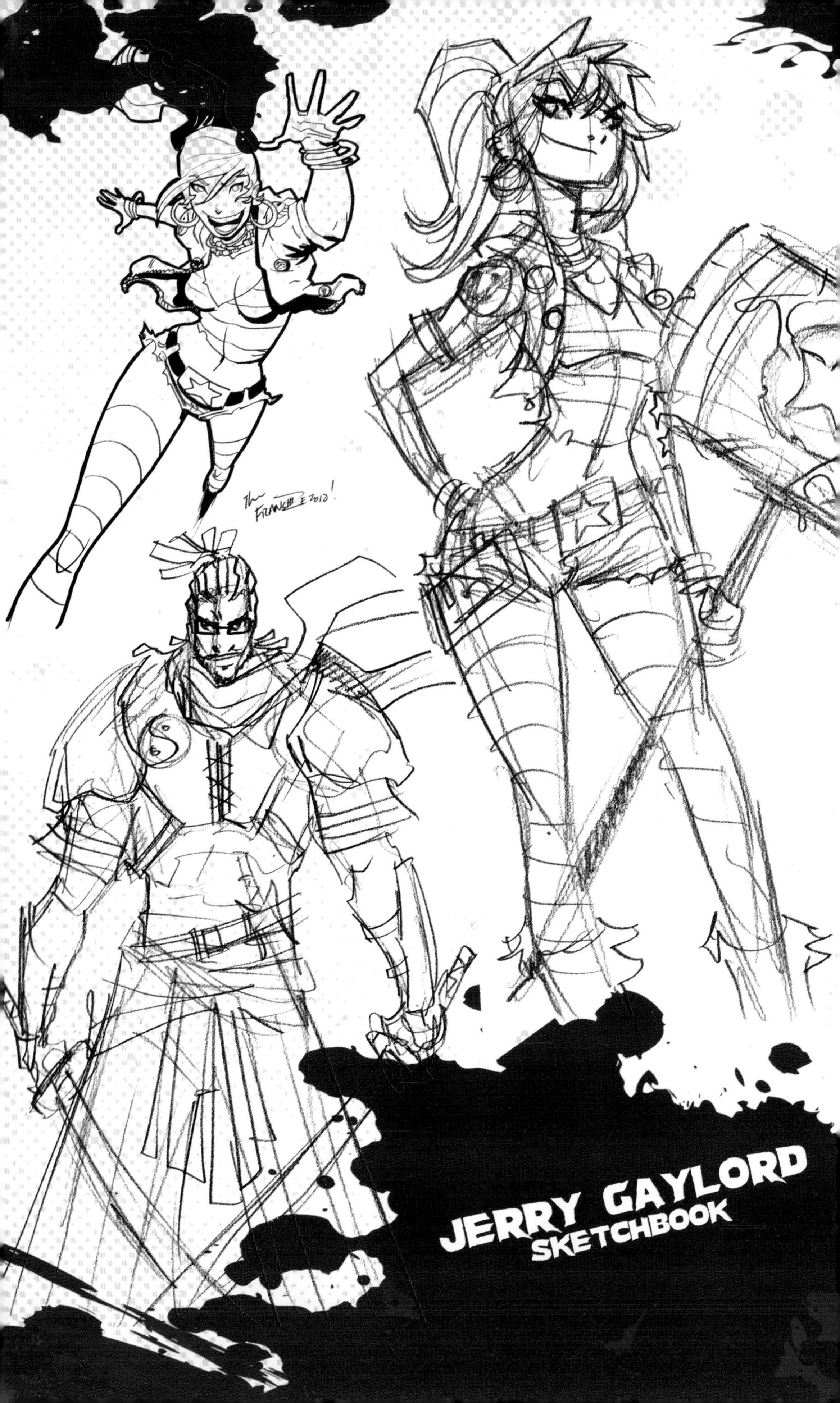
JERRY GAYLORD
SKETCHBOOK

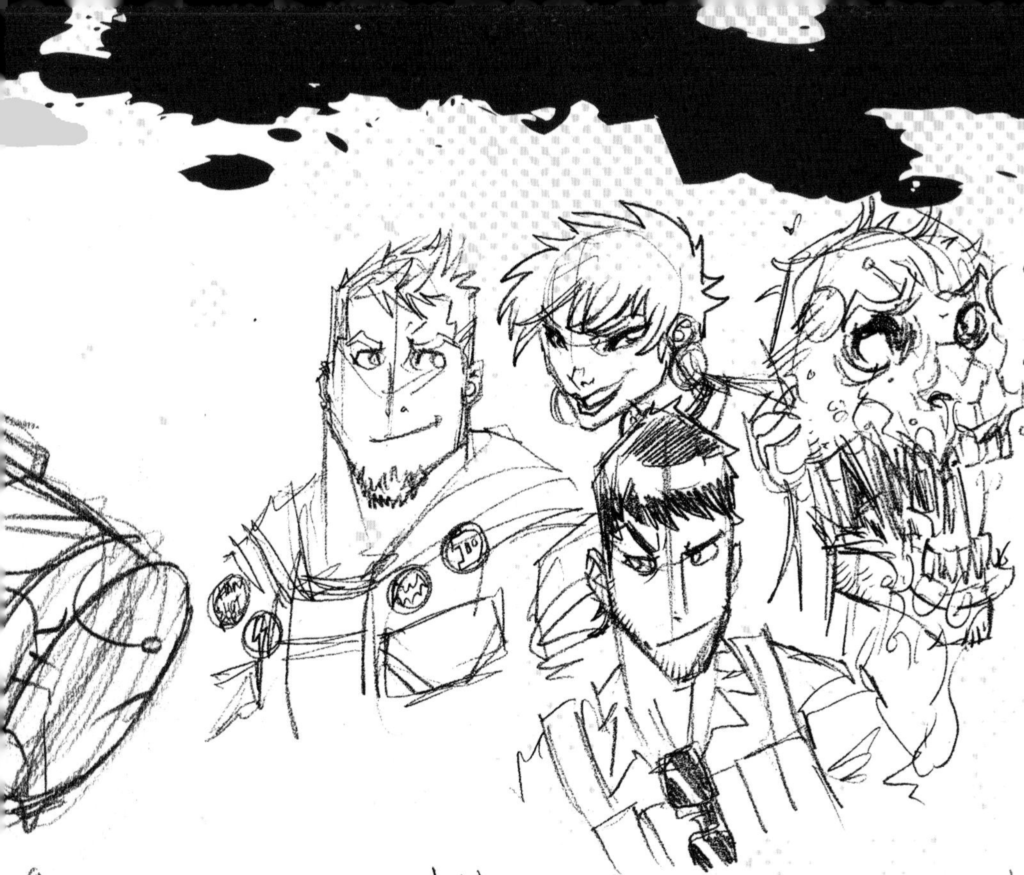

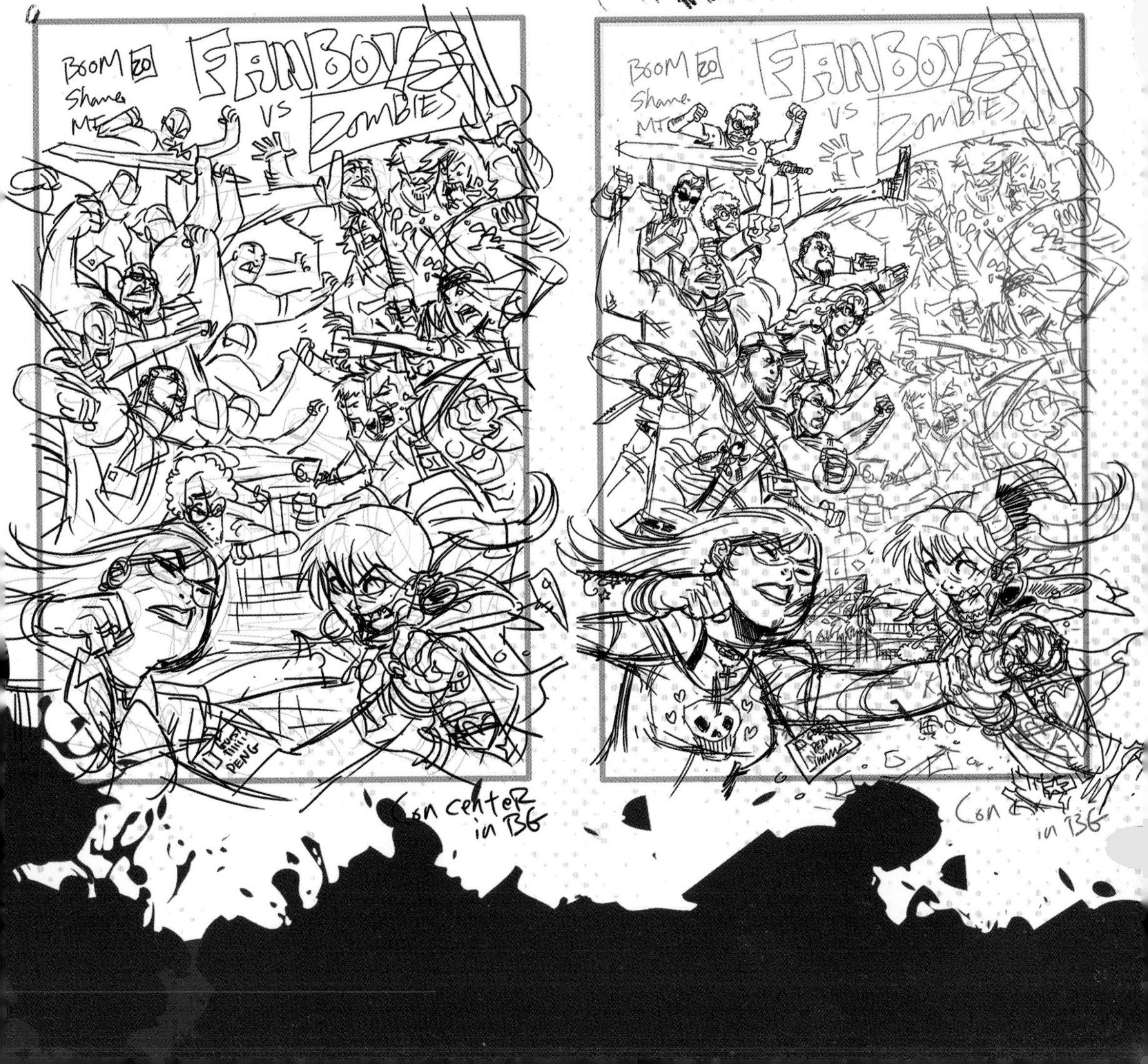
BOOM 20
Shane
MF
FANBOYS
VS
ZOMBIES
Con center in BG
BOOM 20
Shane
MF
FANBOYS
VS
ZOMBIES

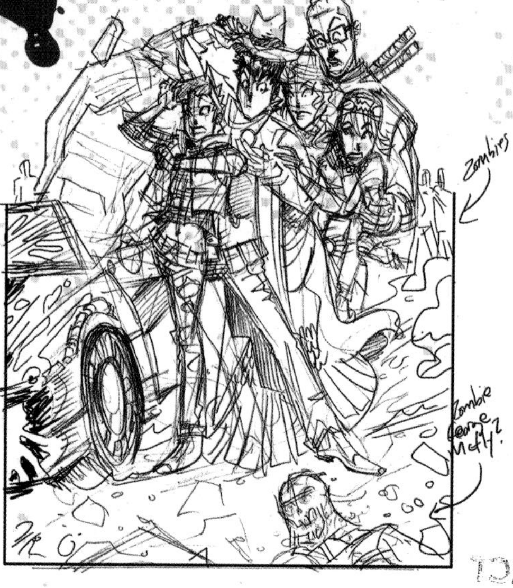
Zombies
Zombie George McFly?

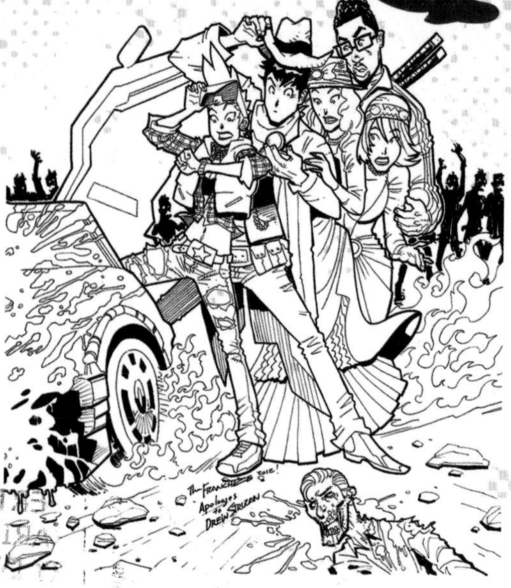
2012!
Apologies to DREW STRUZAN

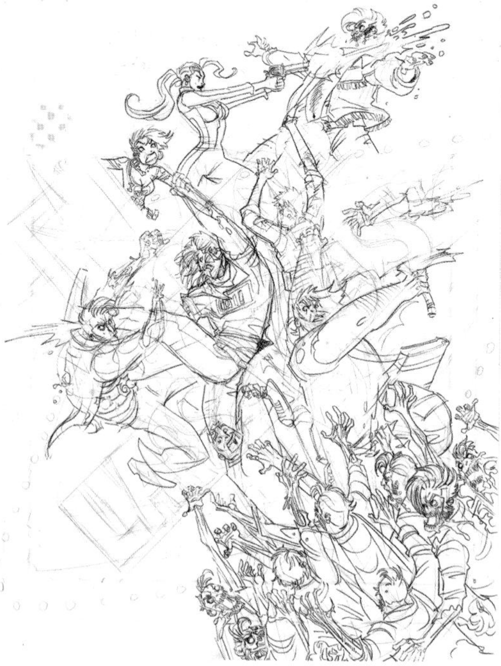

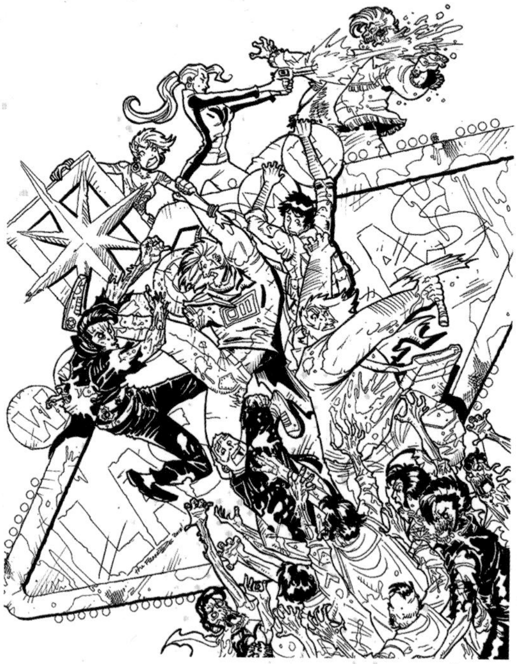

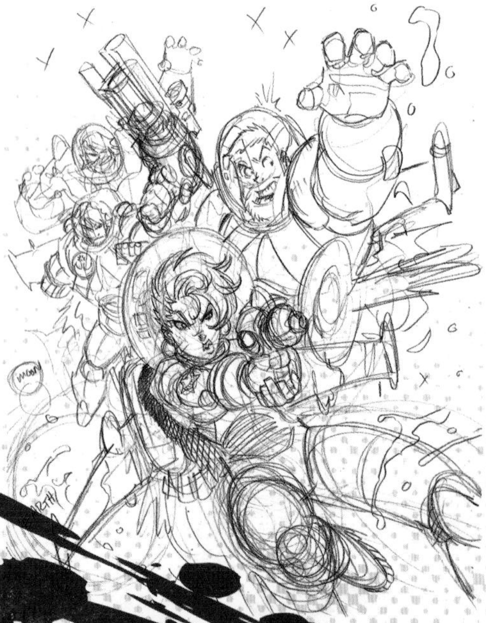

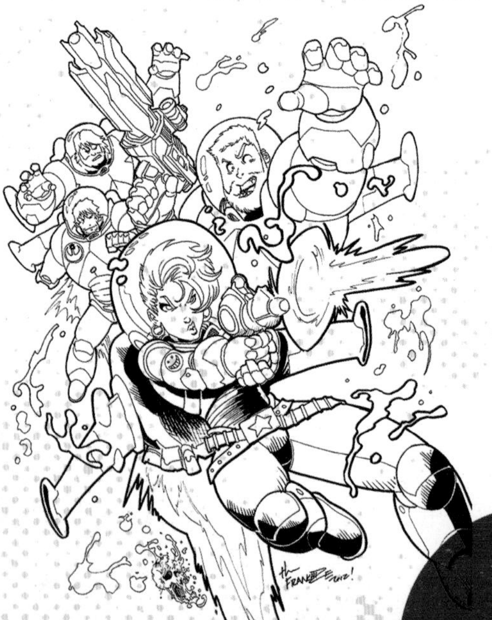
2012!